Varieties of Economic Nationalism in Cold War Europe

Varieties of Economic Nationalism in Cold War Europe

Small State Responses to Economic Changes, 1960s–1980s

Edited by
Adrian Brisku, Martin Gumiela
and Lars Fredrik Stöcker

BLOOMSBURY ACADEMIC
LONDON • NEW YORK • OXFORD • NEW DELHI • SYDNEY

BLOOMSBURY ACADEMIC
Bloomsbury Publishing Plc, 50 Bedford Square, London, WC1B 3DP, UK
Bloomsbury Publishing Inc, 1359 Broadway, New York, NY 10018, USA
Bloomsbury Publishing Ireland, 29 Earlsfort Terrace, Dublin 2, D02 AY28, Ireland

BLOOMSBURY, BLOOMSBURY ACADEMIC and the Diana logo are trademarks of Bloomsbury Publishing Plc

First published in Great Britain 2025
Paperback edition published 2026

Cover image: Sculpture by Josef Škoda (1901-1949) located on the Komercní on Bank Branch, Hradec Králové, Czechia © Adrian Brisku.

A catalogue record for this book is available from the British Library.

A catalog record for this book is available from the Library of Congress.

ISBN: HB: 978-1-3504-2864-5
ePDF: 978-1-3504-2865-2
eBook: 978-1-3504-2866-9

Typeset by Newgen KnowledgeWorks Pvt. Ltd., Chennai, India

For product safety related questions contact productsafety@bloomsbury.com.

To find out more about our authors and books visit www.bloomsbury.com and sign up for our newsletters.

FWF Austrian Science Fund

Published with the support of the Austrian Science Fund (FWF): 10.55776/PUB1140

Contents

Contributors

Kevin Axe is a PhD candidate at the Free University of Berlin and researcher at Berlin's 'Contestations of the Liberal Script – SCRIPTS' Cluster of Excellence. His research is focused on the spread of neoliberal economic thought within the (post)socialist world, especially Estonia.

Ioannis Brigkos is a PhD candidate in the Department of Byzantine and Modern Greek Studies at the University of Vienna. His academic and research interests focus on Modern Greek and European diplomatic history of the twentieth century and the implementation of the Cold War's foreign policy.

Adrian Brisku is the head of Small (Nation-)States Research Centre and associate professor in modern history at Charles University as well as associate professor in comparative history at Ilia State University. He is the author of several peer-reviewed, impact-factor articles, several edited volumes and two monographs: *Bittersweet Europe* (2013) and *Political Reform in the Ottoman and Russian Empires* ([2017] 2019).

Maximilian Graf is a historian working at the Austrian State Archives in Vienna who specializes in Cold War history and the history of communism. He earned his PhD from the University of Vienna and held postdoctoral positions at the Austrian Academy of Sciences, the European University Institute, and the Masaryk Institute and Archives of the Czech Academy of Sciences.

Martin Gumiela is a PhD candidate at the Research Centre for the History of Transformations at the University of Vienna and a research associate in the Polish-Austrian joint project 'A Breach in the System: The "Polonia Firms" 1976–1994'. His research interests are the contemporary history of East Central Europe and state socialism, with a focus on economic history.

Thomas Kolnberger holds a PhD in History and coordinates research projects at the University of Luxembourg; most recently, he co-edited *Agency, Security and Governance of Small States: A Global Perspective*. His fields of interest are the history of Luxembourg; small-state studies; military history; historical and urban geography.

Barbora Menclová is an assistant professor at the Institute of International Relations, Faculty of Social Studies, Charles University. She deals with the interaction between Czechoslovakia and Lusophone African countries during the Cold War. She has lectured and published studies on these issues in peer-reviewed journals. Her PhD thesis focused on Czechoslovakia's engagement in Angola and Mozambique after 1975.

Lars Fredrik Stöcker is a research associate at the Research Centre for the History of Transformations and coordinator for Baltic Sea Region Studies at the University of Vienna. He has published extensively on the Cold War, anti-communist opposition and socialist economic reforms. Among his recent publications is the monograph *Bridging the Baltic Sea: Networks of Resistance and Opposition during the Cold War Era* (2018).

Benedetto Zaccaria is an assistant professor in the Department of Political Science, Law and International Studies at the University of Padova. He specializes in the history of European integration and the Cold War in Europe. He is the author of *The EEC's Yugoslav Policy in Cold War Europe, 1968–1980* (2016) and *La strada per Osimo. Italia e Jugoslavia allo specchio (1965–1975)* (2018).

Abbreviations

ABS ČR	Archiv bezpečnostních složek (Archive of Security Services)
ACDH	Austrian Centre for Digital Humanities
AJ	Arhiv Jugoslavije (Archives of Yugoslavia)
AMZV	Archiv ministerstva zahraničních věcí (Archive of Ministry of Foreign Affairs)
ATS	Austrian Schillings
Benelux	Economic Union of Belgium, the Netherlands, and Luxembourg
BLEU	Belgium Luxembourg Economic Union
CCP	Common Commercial Policy
CCPA	Companhia de Celulose e Papel de Angola (Cellulose and Paper Company of Angola)
CME	coordinated market economy
CMEA	Council for Mutual Economic Assistance
CoCom	Coordinating Committee for Multilateral Export Controls
COMECON	Council for Mutual Economic Assistance
ČR	Czech Republic
CSCE	Conference on Security and Co-operation
ČSSR	Czech Socialist Republic
CSV	Chrëschtlech-Sozial Vollekspartei (The Christian Social Party)
CVCE	Centre Virtuel de la Connaissance sur l'Europe (Virtual Centre for Knowledge on Europe)
DAC	Development Assistance Committee
DFG	Deutsche Forschungsgemeinschaft (German Research Foundation)
DIAL	digital access to libraries
DME	dependent market economy
DP	Demokratesch Partei (Democratic Party)
EC	European Community
EEC	European Economic Community
Eesti NSV	Eesti Nõukogude Sotsialistlik Vabariik (Estonian Soviet Socialist Republic)

EFTA	European Free Trade Association
ELSTAT	Hellenic Statistical Authority
ERA	Eesti Rahvusarhiiv (Estonian National Archives)
ERC	European Research Council
Estonian SSR	Estonian Soviet Socialist Republic
EU	European Union
FAO	Food and Agriculture Organization
FDI	foreign direct investment
FEC	Federal Executive Council
FRELIMO	Frente de Libertação de Moçambique (Liberation Front of Mozambique)
FRG	Federal Republic of Germany
FWF	Austrian Science Fund
GDP	gross domestic product
GDR	German Democratic Republic
HME	hierarchical market economy
HQ	headquarters
IFC	International Financial Centre
IFLOMA	Indùstrias Florestais de Manica (Forest Industries of Manica)
IME	Isemajandav Eesti (Self-Managing Estonia)
IMF	International Monetary Fund
IPE	international political economy
IR	International Relations
KBL	Kredietbank Luxembourg (Credit Bank Luxembourg)
KGB	Komitet Gosudarstvennoy Bezopasnosti (Committee for State Security)
KOF	Konjunkturforschungsstelle Schweiz (Swiss economic research centre)
KPL	Kommunistesch Partei vu Lëtzebuerg (Communist Party of Luxembourg)
KPR	Kabinet Predsednika Republike (President's Cabinet)
KSZE	Konferenz über Sicherheit und Zusammenarbeit in Europa (Conference on Security and Cooperation in Europe)
LCY	League of Communists of Yugoslavia
LME	liberal market economy
LSAP	Lëtzebuerger Sozialistesch Aarbechterpartei (Luxembourg Socialist Workers' Party)
MFA	Ministry of Foreign Affairs

MPLA	Movimento Popular de Libertação de Angola (People's Movement for the Liberation of Angola)
MSZ/MSW	Ministry of Foreign Affairs and Interior Ministry
NA ČR	Národní archiv České republiky (Czech Republic National Archive)
NATO	North Atlantic Treaty Organization
OECD	Organisation for Economic Co-operation and Development
ÖGB	Österreichischer Gewerkschafts-Bund (Austrian Trade Union Federation)
OGBL	Onofhängege Gewerkschafts Bond Lëtzebuerg (Independent Luxembourg)
ÖStA/AdR	Österreichisches Staatsarchiv/Archiv der Republik (Austrian State Archives)
ÖVP	Österreichische Volkspartei – Austrian People's Party
PIH	Polska Izba Handlu – Polish Chamber of Trade
PPZ	Przedsiębiorstwa Polonijno-Zagraniczne (Polonia foreign companies)
PRL	Polska Rzeczpospolita Ludowa (Polish People's Republic)
PZPR	Polish United Workers' Party
Russian SFSR	Russian Soviet Federative Socialist Republic
RVHP	Rada vzájemné hospodářské pomoci (The Council for Mutual Economic Assistance)
SDPAG	Steyr-Daimler-Puch AG
SEA	Single European Act
SED	Sozialistische Einheitspartei Deutschlands (Socialist Unity Party of Germany)
SEZ	Special Economic Zone
SFRJ	Socialisticna Federativna Republika Jugoslavija (Socialist Federal Republic of Yugoslavia)
SIDA	Swedish International Development Cooperation
SIV	Savezno izvršno vijeće – Federal Executive Council
SOGERE	Sociedade geral de cervejas e refrigerantes de Moçambique (The general group of beer brewing and soft drinks of Mozambique)
SPÖ	Sozialistische Partei Österreichs (Socialist Party of Austria)
SR	Socialist Republic
SSIP	Saveznom sekretarijatu za inostrane poslove (Foreign Affairs Federal Secretariat)

SSR	Soviet Socialist Republic
SSST	Savezni Sekretarijat za Spoljnu Trgovinu (Federal Secretariat for External Trade)
STATEC	Institut national de la statistique et des études économiques (Government Statistics Service of Luxembourg)
UCITS	Undertakings for Collective Investment in Transferable Securities Directive
UNITA	União Nacional para a Independência Total de Angola (National Union for the Total Independence of Angola)
USD	US Dollar
USSR	Union of Soviet Socialist Republics
ÚV KSČ	Ústřední výbor Komunistické strany Československa (Central Committee of the Communist Party of Czechoslovakia)
VÖEST	Vereinigte Österreichische Eisen- und Stahlwerke (United Austrian Iron and Steelworks)

Introduction: Economic nationalism's plurality in discourse and practice in small (nation-)states

Adrian Brisku, Martin Gumiela and Lars Fredrik Stöcker

The Covid-19 pandemic, as German historian Andreas Wirsching claimed in a 2020 essay on nation states and their place in the global economy, marked the end of a half-century of accelerated globalization, internationalization and economic liberalism.[1] Reinforced by the ruptures of Russia's full-scale attack on Ukraine two years later, the growing schism between China and the United States and the swiftly escalating tensions between the Islamic world and the West, the 2020s indeed seem to herald a new era of economic 'deglobalization'. Accordingly, the term 'economic nationalism' has made a comeback in public and social science debates alike. As a concept, however, economic nationalism remains fuzzy. Traditionally equated with protectionist trade and monetary policies, economic nationalism is most often used in a Weberian sense to denote statist measures adopted in opposition to economic liberalism, that is, policies of free entrepreneurship, open markets and unhampered flows of capital, goods and workforce across state borders.[2] Similarly, the field of consumption psychology and marketing conceptualizes the term as an antipode to cosmopolitan consumption, framing the consumer's preference for home-grown over imported products.[3] Scholars of nationalism, on their part, have – in an attempt to liberate the concept of economic nationalism from the dominance of the international political economy (IPE) approach, which primarily conceives of it technocratically as a rational policy choice and a mere 'smokescreen for underlying material interests'[4] – applied the term to outline the connection between economic grievances and nationalist mobilization which, as is argued, has been neglected by mainstream nationalism studies.[5]

Our volume pursues a more general and pluralistic reading of the term that goes beyond its traditional, reductionist understanding as a mere synonym for 'a set of state practices challenging liberal principles of international economic exchange'.[6] Following a revisionist school of scholars, which emphasizes the 'need to look at the specific content of nationalist projects instead of simply labelling protectionist or autarkic policies as economic nationalism',[7] we employ the concept of economic nationalism as an umbrella term that hosts a wide variety of policies, ranging from inward-looking, protectionist impulses to ultraliberal, open-market paradigms. A paradox at first glance, liberal economic policies and voluntary dependence on economic exchange with outside markets indeed can serve a state's national interest, as some of the case studies in our volume will show, particularly if governments consider 'their economic dependence on some states as a security threat but on other states as mutually beneficial exchange'.[8] Hence, economic nationalism, as a crucial force behind the economic actions and decisions made by national societies and governments, encompasses a broad range of policy choices following the 'national purpose and direction', as critics of the realist approach in IPE scholarship have stressed.[9] Economic nationalism thereby manifests itself, as our volume illustrates, in various incarnations ranging from 'liberal/progressive' and 'conservative/defensive' to 'extreme aggressive/expansionist and/or autarkic' varieties.

On a second level, we aim to bridge the gap between nationalism studies and IPE scholarship, which has long neglected the impact of cultural and normative influences on the world political economy.[10] Our volume particularly focuses on the intrinsically dynamic, discursive nationalization of economic policymaking processes, which goes beyond the static focus on 'national identity' as a determining factor for foreign economic policy actions discussed by some IPE scholars.[11] The significance of the discursive level is highlighted by Thomas Fetzer who, in his revisionist reading of IPE literature on the topic, points to the, at first glance, seemingly contradictory nexus between accelerated globalization and the nationalization of domestic economic debates.[12] Given that strategic economic policy choices cannot be conceptually disconnected from the accompanying rhetoric that links these choices, be they exclusionary or inclusionary, to the benefit of (national) society, we conceptualize our understanding of economic nationalism as an intricate conglomerate of national interests, sentiments, motives and subsequent policy actions.

Informed by this perspective and recognizing that global economic ruptures and crises can boost nationalisms,[13] our edited collection investigates the trajectories of economic nationalism in late Cold War Europe, exploring the scope and limits of small (nation-)state actors pursuing and defending their national economic interests in times of large-scale political and economic changes, induced by the simultaneous crises of Western Keynesianism and Eastern Marxism-Leninism, the collapse of the 'Fordist model' of production, the oil and financial shocks, East-West détente and the interplay of global economic liberalization and decolonization. Our collection focuses on eight smaller (nation-)states – where nation refers also to sub-state entities in Yugoslavia and the USSR with their economic space but without political sovereignty – on both sides of the Iron Curtain, reconstructing their national economic discourses and policy objectives. Straddling the bipolar perspective on capitalist and state-socialist economies, which is still prevalent in the literature on small-state agency in divided Europe, we challenge the assumption that smaller national economies were inherently vulnerable and subjected to the geo-economic binaries of Cold War politics. Far from being powerless, small states in East and West were, as the contributions in our volume demonstrate, capable of genuine agency. This agency allowed them, in the wake of the large-scale political and economic watersheds from the late 1960s onwards, to forge their own strategies of economic survival beyond the constraints of Cold War alignments and to transform their smallness into a strategic asset employed to expand their room for manoeuvre in a quickly shifting global environment.

Small states, as is commonly assumed, are by definition 'rule-takers' rather than 'rule-makers'.[14] Cold War studies, however, have long refuted the assumption that small states, per definition, lack agency.[15] Particularly in the period examined in this volume, that is, from the 1960s onwards, the political room for manoeuvre increased considerably for small states. Neutral Sweden, for instance, exerted considerable influence on the world stage as a self-proclaimed 'humanitarian great power', while Finland successfully volunteered as a mediator in the process of European détente and host of the CSCE process in the early 1970s. Under the impact of East-West rapprochement, even mid-sized European states which do otherwise not correspond to the 'classical' definition of small states, such as the People's Republic of Poland, eventually managed to overcome their enforced small-state dependency in the strictly hierarchic Soviet bloc, which at least up to the early 1970s had left little space for autonomous satellite agency on the global stage. Even the 'proto-states' within the USSR and Yugoslavia, the ethno-national federal republics, considerably increased their economic scope of action through border trade and greater foreign economic autonomy, particularly the more industrially developed republics bordering the Western orbit.

Due to their minor size in relation to larger states or economic blocs, small states are, if we follow the approach of much IPE scholarship, unable to pursue traditional protectionist strategies and intrinsically forced to implement policies of strategic openness to survive. In other words, economic nationalism, at least if conceived exclusively as a 'defensive/protectionist' policy, is not considered a viable option for small economies and states. Peter Katzenstein makes this case for Western Europe during and after the Cold War in his 1985 monograph *Small States in World Markets*,[16] which examines the surviving and thriving political-economic strategies of Austria, Belgium, Denmark, the Netherlands, Norway, Sweden and Switzerland in Western markets during the long 1970s. A similar argument is made by Harald Baldersheim and Michael Keating who, in their 2015 volume *Small States in the Modern World*,[17] apart from the Scandinavian states plus Iceland, the Baltic states and New Zealand also include in their analysis the cases of Scotland and Quebec, which due to their strong quasi-national identities and status resemble sub-states of their own. According to this reading, small size in itself is not an obstacle to economic success. By contrast, smallness and the inherent flexibility of small economies and nation states offer a set of advantages over large states, as political economists Alberto Alesina and Enrico Spolaore claim, but only unless political borders do not hinder the free flow of goods, capital and people.[18]

A closer look at the economic history literature on the topic of small states and their economic flexibility (or lack thereof), however, reveals a significant discrepancy to the IPE approach. Economic historians tend to assign economic nationalism, in its traditional reading as a defensive strategic path towards a closed economy, exclusively to the histories of economic development of both large and small European states in the first half of the twentieth century. Ivan Berend expands on this trope in his 2022 piece 'Economic Nationalism in Historical Perspective',[19] extending the era of interwar protectionism into the Cold War period, yet only with regard to small(er) states in Soviet-controlled Central and Eastern Europe. While smaller states in the West thus are assumed to have been inherently subjected to external, macroeconomic exposure due to the minor size of their economies, as is illustrated by our volume's case study on Luxembourg, smaller states in the communist East could, as Berend argues, still afford protectionism, setting up tariffs and state subsidies to defend their domestic economies from global competition. By the early 1970s, however, this strategy had reached its limits. A combined effect of domestic and external market pressure forced the socialist orbit to make a course correction. Accompanied by increasingly nationalist and surprisingly undogmatic debates on domestic economic needs and interests, most socialist states now proactively promoted Western capital investments and the expansion of East-West trade relations in a new spirit of socialist 'proto-globalization'.[20] Angela Romano and Federico Romero's 2021 volume *European Socialist Regimes' Fateful Engagement with the West*[21] discusses this U-turn from near autarky to controlled openness performed by the communist regimes in Bulgaria, Czechoslovakia, Hungary, the GDR, Poland, Romania and non-aligned Yugoslavia through the long 1970s.

Our volume shares the focus on small-state agency and flexibility in times of economic changes with the above-mentioned scholarly works. Not unlike larger states and national economies, small states consistently discussed and applied a wide variety of economic measures, depending on the available options of how to best secure their national self-interest, ranging from 'liberal/progressive' (open/outward-looking) to 'conservative/defensive' (protectionist/inward-looking) policies, whereas both variants could either occur in 'extreme' (aggressive/expansionist or autarkic) forms or, as was the most common case, as a mix of protectionist and liberal economic measures in search of a 'middle way between isolation and expansion'.[22] We thus reject the implicit assumption that the oscillation of small states between globalizing and protectionist economic strategies should 'be seen in terms of a zero-sum game',[23] given that 'parties can be pro-market when it comes to domestic issues', as Italo Colantone and Piero Stanig state, 'while at the same time being isolationist and protectionist in terms of trade and international relations'[24] – or vice versa.

Following this vein, our volume sheds light on how small-state decision-makers made use of new openings while at the same time attempting to remain in control of market forces and their impact on the domestic economy by channelling and containing them through protectionist measures. As much as the period from the 1960s onwards was characterized by political and economic liberalization and economic decision-making driven by pragmatism and realpolitik – be it in Bruno Kreisky's firmly social democratic and neutral Austria, in junta-era Greece or in state-socialist Poland – (in)direct state interventions in economic activities that 'discriminated' in favour of 'national/ethnic' and 'geographic' grounds were pursued by the same actors simultaneously, irrespective of, or even because of, ideological and geopolitical divisions. At times, strategic economic choices were not dictated by mere pragmatism and market logic, but derived 'from a specific national identity, such as the "pro-Western/European" identity held by some nationalists in the former Soviet Union' which, as Eric Helleiner points out, explains the preference of the post-1991 Baltic governments for liberal, Western-oriented pathways over the traditional autarkic ideals of the Soviet era.[25] Exploring the motives for small states' choices of strategic economic policymaking during the highly volatile late Cold War era, we can thus not ignore the underlying cultural, historical and normative motives that largely determined the course of nationalizing economic debates and their transformation into viable policies, which argues in favour of our broader conceptualization of economic nationalism as a roof for analysing small-state behaviour in times of far-reaching economic changes.

This collaborative volume is informed by four methodological approaches. The first one is the interdisciplinary perspective of drawing from and integrating the disciplines of economic history, political economy, nationalism, national political histories and the history of the Cold War. The second one, related to the preceding one, is the historical approach of relying on new archival material as well as contextualizing economic positions and strategies in the discursive national, political and economic contexts of the time, linking them also to preceding economic historiographical narratives. The third approach is a comparative one, entailing juxtapositions not only of similarities and differences in political-economic discourses and practices between the two geopolitical power blocs but equally importantly between small states and sub-state entities within federal systems, whereby a 'loose' typology of varieties of economic nationalism is ascertained. And fourthly, and very distinctively, this work applies a novel small (nation-)state approach. With this perspective, the task of the contributors to the collected volume is neither to determine a political and economic entity's size in terms of its mode of production, GDP, population and territory, nor is it to take such an entity for granted. It rather consists of including – when reconstructing political-economic discourses and practices – pertinent discursive self-perceptions of state and non-state actors of being and acting as small (weak or active) and other actors outside of this particular entity perceiving them as such.

The following nine chapters elaborate on the conceptual ideas and impulses presented above, discussing the options and room for manoeuvre available to small states and proto-states from the 1960s through the 1970s and 1980s, before the end of the bipolar world overthrew the geopolitical chess board. In contrast to earlier works in the field of small-state scholarship, we not only juxtapose and compare the strategies and agency of size-wise comparable small states in the East and West but also widen our focus to include micro-states (the case of Luxembourg) and proto-states (as we have decided to call the federal constituents of the USSR and Yugoslavia) into our framework. Based on the hypothesis that all of our cases exhibit recognizable facets of small-state economic behaviour, our volume discusses the conceptual framework against the background of debates and policy choices in Luxembourg, Austria and Greece in the West, as well as Czechoslovakia, the Estonian SSR and Poland in the East, with Slovenia and Croatia representing non-aligned Yugoslavia. All of those 'small' (proto-)states and national economies – be it in relation to other countries or on the ground of their (self-)perception as small in size – similarly pursued, as we argue, their own 'variety' of economic nationalism, irrespective of the differing ideological and geopolitical conditions they operated in.

Adrian Brisku opens the first section with a conceptual historical account on economic nationalism and small-state governance, highlighting the controversial and contested position on this political-economic phenomenon in discussion of (political) economists as well as in debates among both economic historians and IPE scholars. Drawing on historical and recent, implicit and explicit framings of this political-economic phenomenon, Brisku reconceptualizes economic nationalism in terms of 'varieties': 'liberal/progressive', 'conservative/defensive' and 'extreme (aggressive/expansionist and/or autarkic)', with such strands often manifesting concurrently. The chapter by Lars Fredrik Stöcker shifts the focus to the constituent republics of Europe's communist federal states, where the intertwined dynamics of simultaneous marketization and embryonic globalization in the 1970s and 1980s triggered economic state-building processes that were fuelled by nationalizing economic debates and anticipated the multinational federation's dissolution along ethno-national lines, as is illustrated by the case of the Estonian SSR.

The following section discusses the opportunities and pitfalls of globalization. Although economic globalization played out very differently in the capitalist and state-socialist halves of Europe, small states on both sides of the Iron Curtain aimed to embrace it in order to increase their global impact and economic flexibility. Thomas Kolnberger offers a historical account of post-war Luxembourg's astonishing self-reinvention from heavy industrial steel producer to global finance hub. 'Hyper-liberal' economic policies and the self-perception of being small as a core identity aspect and key asset for national survival securely navigated Luxembourg, which balances on the threshold between small and micro-state, painlessly through the crises of the 1970s and 1980s into the post-industrial age. Barbora Menclová investigates the repercussions of globalizing economic policies on the other side of the Iron Curtain, in particular Czechoslovakia's attempts to increase its economic impact outside the Soviet bloc. Focusing on the 'alternative globalizations'[26] of the socialist states, which aimed at strengthening their cooperation with partners in the Global South, Menclová describes how Czechoslovakia pushed for the intensification of bilateral ties with Angola and Mozambique in the 1970s, a 'liberal' economic strategy that fit well into the mould of a historically 'export-oriented' nation.

The volume's third section juxtaposes three closely interlinked case studies on the effects of détente on bilateral trade relations of and between small (nation-)states in Cold War Europe. Although Austria under the rule of the social democratic icon Bruno Kreisky, Edward Gierek's crisis-ridden Poland of the 1970s and Greece under the regime of the colonels at first glance had little in common, their economic policy choices were shaped by a similar spirit of pragmatism that prioritized national economic interests over political and ideological dogmas. Ioannis Brigkos explores Greece's trade relations with Austria and the German Democratic Republic at a time when the junta was largely isolated internationally. Strange bedfellows at first sight, each of these states had its own national economic reasons for turning a blind eye on their trade partners' political and ideological stance. In the next chapter, Maximilian Graf discusses Austria's Eastern trade with Poland and East Germany, opening up their foreign economic policy eastwards to secure full employment in the state-owned industrial sector and the survival of the Keynesian, corporatist model through, as Vienna hoped for, predictable trade agreements. The People's Republic of Poland takes centre stage in Martin Gumiela's chapter. In his contribution on a Comecon state seeking to expand its economic room for manoeuvre outside the Soviet bloc, Gumiela outlines a strategy that differs from other discussed cases due to its particular focus on compatriots in the West as bridge-builders and mediators in Poland's nascent economic opening up to foreign capital investment.

The last section shifts attention to national economic state-building processes evolving in Yugoslavia and the USSR in the wake of the sweeping economic changes that proceeded much along similar lines in East and West during the last two decades of the Cold War. Unnoticed by most international observers, some of the Yugoslav and Soviet federal republics developed what might be labelled small-state-like strategies, nurtured by the intertwined policies of marketization, decentralization and globalization tested by many socialist regimes. Benedetto Zaccaria discusses how the globalizing markets of the 1960s and 1970s gradually eroded Socialist Yugoslavia's federal integrity. Framing Slovenia and Croatia as 'sub-state' entities with their own national economic agenda, this chapter elaborates on the concept of economic autonomy, which both federal republics tried to corroborate by pursuing closer integration with the (neighbouring) Western markets. Finally, Kevin Axe investigates the reform dynamics in the Estonian SSR, which under the impact of Moscow's course of globalization and perestroika yielded a new vision of a self-managing republican economy. Drafted by a small group of local economists and planners, the idea of economic home rule swiftly developed a life of its own, mobilizing Estonian society against the predominance of the central authorities.

Notes

This volume is the result of a workshop entitled 'Varieties of Economic Nationalism' held at the University of Vienna in September 2022, which gathered scholars from ten countries to discuss the economic options, choices and strategies of small European states during the latter half of the Cold War. The funding of this joint event was provided by the Austrian Science Fund (FWF) through Adrian Brisku's project 'National Economy-Building in Albania, Czechoslovakia and Georgia in the 1920s' (M 2847) and Lars Fredrik Stöcker's joint project 'A Breach in the System: The "Polonia Firms," 1976–1994' (I 4877-G), carried out in cooperation between the University of Vienna and the University of Warsaw. We would like to thank the FWF for also granting additional funding for the open access publication of this volume and our colleagues and co-authors as well as the anonymous reviewers for their ideas, impulses and creative contributions to our collaborative project.

1 Wirsching, 'Kaiser ohne Kleider?'.
2 Berger and Fetzer, 'Introduction', 4.
3 Fetzer, 'Nationalism and Economy', 969.
4 Suesse, *The Nationalist Dilemma*, 7.
5 Cf. Berger and Fetzer, *Nationalism and the Economy*.
6 Fetzer, 'Nationalism and Economy', 964.
7 Jensen Eriksen, 'Business, Economic Nationalism and Finnish Foreign Trade during the 19th and 20th Centuries', 41.
8 Abdelal, *National Purpose in the World Economy*, 2.
9 Ibid., 33.
10 Tsygankov, *Pathways after Empire*, 1.
11 Cf. Abdelal, *National Purpose in the World Economy*; Tsygankov, *Pathways after Empire*.
12 Fetzer, 'Beyond "Economic Nationalism"', 246.
13 Suesse, *The Nationalist Dilemma*, 326.
14 Kruizinga, 'Introduction', 2.
15 See, for instance, Crump and Erlandsson, *Margins for Manoeuvre in Cold War Europe*; Romano and Romero, *European Socialist Regimes' Fateful Engagement with the West*.

16 Katzenstein, *Small States in World Markets.*
17 Baldersheim and Keating, *Small States in the Modern World.* On the topic of 'small nations' in Western Europe like Scotland, Quebec and Catalonia and the linkage between globalization and nationalist mobilization, see also Paquin, *La revanche des petites nations.*
18 Alesina and Spolaore, *The Size of Nations*, 3–4.
19 Berend, 'Economic Nationalism in Historical Perspective'.
20 Pula, *Globalization under and after Socialism*, 78.
21 Romano and Romero, *European Socialist Regimes' Fateful Engagement with the West.*
22 Suesse, *The Nationalist Dilemma*, 5.
23 Pickel, 'Introduction', 11.
24 Colantone and Stanig, 'The Surge of Economic Nationalism in Western Europe', 133.
25 Helleiner, 'Conclusion', 224.
26 Mark, Kalinovsky and Marung, *Alternative Globalizations.*

Part I

Small State and Proto-State Agency in Times of Economic Changes

1

Varieties of economic nationalism in small (nation-)states

Adrian Brisku

Introduction: Economic nationalism reoccurring, economic nationalism avoided

Seemingly, economic nationalism – as a political-economic phenomenon, concept and discourse – has been reoccurring globally and reverberatingly 'worryingly' since the global financial and economic crises of 2008.[1] It is seemingly though for in taking a conceptual history approach[2] to modern economic ideas, one of which is economic nationalism, and their discursive practices, the concept has been in use since the late 1920s. And the phenomenon has been manifesting variously at least since the mid-nineteenth century. Such a continuity, however, is not obvious in the main scholarships that engage with it: economic history, international political economy (IPE) and nationalism studies. In fact, nationalism literature until recently has avoided/neglected the nexus been nation and the economy.[3]

Not only is it not obvious but there is an apparent paradox in its deployment in the economic history and the IPE scholarships. Such paradox emerges when juxtaposing its usage by economic historians and political economists. Economic historians have used it to account for the defensive economic policies of smaller and less developed countries of Central and East Europe[4] for national and social integration processes from the end of the First World War. Here, the phenomenon is present for 'almost the entire 20th century'.[5] Additionally, some historians have often associated it with these states' exclusionary economic policies towards their national and ethnic minorities, most egregiously perpetrated in the larger Nazi German economy.[6] Meanwhile, scholars of the political economy of small states – the wider IPE scholarship uses it as an analytical though still contested concept – have avoided it altogether. Such avoidance is premised upon a one-faceted understanding of economic nationalism as defensive/protectionist policies/practices, which contemporary small states – being inherently vulnerable to larger states – cannot afford pursuing. Consequently, such states have to remain open and adapt to the pressures (too small to be protectionist) of larger economies or economic blocs with which they interact or are a part of.[7]

And to be sure such an assumption would appear persuasive considering the post-2008, post-Brexit and post-pandemic global political-economic developments whereby the discourse and practices of economic nationalism returned with vigour only among the largest world economies and economic blocs. Such a return is exemplified with US President Biden Administration's announcement in April 2023 of a four-pronged strategy of a new industrial policy for 'Renewing American Economic Leadership' in the world.[8] And this US national economic strategy was itself a response to earlier economic strategies' renewed industrial policies of the other two largest economic zones: China and the EU. Thus, the moves of the world's three largest economic spaces pointed to a 'global return to industrial policy [read protectionist]'.[9] On such policy changes, particularly with regard to the United States, informed political commentators and economic historians have noted that the last two presidents, respectively, Donald Trump and Joe Biden – perhaps confusingly for the former rode on the right-wing populist wave in the United States, whereas the latter has been a centre-left Democrat – 'position[ed] themselves as economic nationalists'.[10]

Such a paradox as well as this apparent 'reversal' as to where the phenomenon is re-emerging – thus traditionally not among smaller nations and economies but larger ones – stems from negative associations with especially interwar extreme nationalism of Nazi Germany. It also derives from ideological interpretations[11] within the IPE literature. As one of 'the three main ideologies of modern political economy' – alongside economic liberalism and Marxism[12] – economic nationalism remained a controversial discourse and policy, perhaps 'subdued' and 'under the rugs' during the Cold War even as Soviet Marxism[13] and Keynesian liberalism[14] waned in the 1980, it resurfaced in vigour after nearly three decades of post-Cold War neoliberal global predominance and its subsequent crises.[15] Certainly, such ideological framings elucidate contested economic doctrines and practices of state and/or non-state actors, especially during the latter part of the Cold War period. However, they do not help in understanding why the political-economic phenomenon of economic nationalism, that is, intervention (in investment, production, redistribution and (de)regulation) within national economic contexts, reoccurs, in fact, persisting not only since the concept was coined in 1928 but even earlier.

This chapter posits two arguments. The first argument holds that as economic nationalism remains a problematic, controversial and ideologically contested concept in the global and national political discourses as well as in the aforementioned scholarships a reconceptualization as varieties of economic nationalism is warranted and thus advanced. This is so despite recent IPE scholarship's use of economic nationalism as an analytical framework to ascertain and illustrate liberal and defensive economic discourses, strategies, policy tools and practices – deployed by state actors and sought by non-state actors within (supra/sub)national contexts – and because of its enduring associations with particular historical political-economic practices of certain countries, of certain sizes. Such a reconceptualization, as *varieties of economic nationalism*, conceives of this political-economic phenomenon manifesting as a 'liberal/progressive' (open/redistributive/outward-looking) variant, a 'conservative/defensive' (protectionist/inward-looking) variant – often these two strands manifest concurrently – and an 'extreme' (aggressive/expansionist/outward-looking and/or autarkic/inward-looking) variant. This reconceptualization builds on historical and contemporary framings and categorizations – implicit and explicit – considered by (political) economists on the phenomenon since the late 1920s. And this reconceptualization is compounded with another concept: *national economy-building*, which, aside from this variety of policies and practices that state/non-state actors deploy/or seek to deploy in the process of constructing (supra/sub)national economic spaces and societies, entails a historical perspective in these strands' continuities and ruptures. The second argument is that such a variety is also manifested in small(er) (nation-)states in modern and contemporary history.

The trouble with economic nationalism: Historically and ideologically controversial

The first argument of this chapter is that a reframing as *varieties of economic nationalism* captures the controversies and reductionist uses[16] of economic nationalism as well as its historical practices, particularly when considering, as below, its continuities as a concept since its inception in the early twentieth century.

Indeed, when it was first coined and used by American economist Leo Pasvolsky, in his 1928 book *Economic Nationalism of the Danubian*

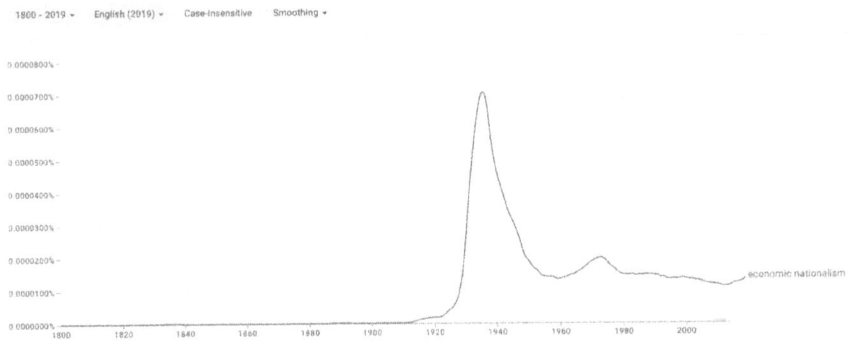

Figure 1 The sharp emergence and the steady usage of the concept since the 1920s. *Source*: Google ngram viewer.[17]

States – a 600-page work on the Austrian, Czechoslovakian, Hungarian, Romanian, Yugoslavian and Italian economies – economic nationalism referred not only to nineteenth-century protectionist policy tools (tariffs). It also referred to other interventionist practices deployed by such states during the early interwar period.[18] Other practices entailed nations engaging in economic cooperation – as opposed to being in competition – as the case of Nordic cooperation.[19]

For one of the first self-proclaimed scholars of economic nationalism, the Geneva School neoliberal thinker Michael A. Heilperin,[20] the aftermath of the Great Depression of 1929 had displaced economic nationalism's primary association with old-fashioned protectionism. The early 1930s Europe, with its extreme national policies of self-sufficiency and self-reliance,[21] as he elaborated in his 1960 work, *Studies in Economic Nationalism*, had ushered in 'virulent forms' of economic nationalism. Not conceptualizing it explicitly in terms of varieties, he pointed to its historical forms, historical origins (*avant la lettre*) spanning centuries, in the ideas of Calvin's Academy (1559) and the early practices in mercantilist and economic development policies pursued by some European states in the seventeenth and eighteenth centuries. Accordingly, in his time of writing *Studies*, that is, the late 1950s, the concept remained controversial not because of the historical variant, the 'old-fashioned protectionism', which had had a commendable role in the development of European economies. It was so because of its association with these 'virulent forms'. Crucially, it also remained globally pervasive: 'rife' in the United States, 'prevail[ing]' in underdeveloped countries and in 'the collectivism of the totalitarian countries of the communist bloc'. And despite vying for a return of 'economic internationalism' – he saw it as being revived in parts of Western Europe of the late 1950s – he thought that the future of international economic cooperation was 'largely depend[ed] upon the fate [and the type] of economic nationalism'.[22]

When discussing economic nationalism's 'virulent forms', Heilperin framed it also as a debate between John M. Keynes, as an opponent of the phenomenon – by referencing Keynes's 1933 piece titled 'National Self Sufficiency' – and F. H. Simmonds, with his 1939 book titled *The Great Powers in World Politics: International Relations and Economic Nationalism*, as its proponents.[23] On a closer reading however, Keynes did not entirely reject the phenomenon, even as/or because it was becoming associated with national self-sufficiency, and self-reliance projects of the early 1930s. Keynes – who did not operate with the concept of nationalism per se but rather with the question of how economic policies could promote national community where there was no need to talk about national identity – saw Soviet Russia, Fascist Italy and Nazi Germany's national self-sufficiency projects combined old-fashioned protectionist and new quota policies as examples of a kind of economic nationalism. Accordingly, they were illustrations of 'dangerous economic nationalism'.[24] And he was able to conceive of a different type of economic nationalism for the United Kingdom: one with 'some degree of self-sufficiency'. The rationale for this was less economic and more political: ensuring internal and external peace as the nineteenth-century 'ideal economic internationalism of our fathers',[25] Keynes noted, 'the maxims of the former faith ... non-interference with international division of labour, free trade, solving the problem of poverty for the whole world' did not help in avoiding the Great War.[26] Thus, if and when the purpose of economic ideas and policies was not only about profit-seeking and national economic development but also about ensuring peace among and within nations, he thought that a recalibration of such policies was needed. More concretely, such a recalibration, thus a pragmatic and flexible approach, entailed a minimization of 'economic entanglement between nations' and encouraging more national production, 'let goods be homespun, whenever it is reasonably and conveniently possible, and above all, let finance be primarily, national'.[27] For Great Britain, a 'greater national self-sufficiency and economic isolation [was a] luxury which we can afford if we happen to want it'. And this version was different from the 'dangerous economic nationalism' of the Soviet, Italian and German experiments.[28] The difference from these 'dangerous economic nationalisms' actually, aside from a sense of degrees, was not so much as the entailed policies. It was about who and how they would implement them. Accordingly, they were advanced by 'silly doctrinaires', and likely to become economically nonviable projects, especially when 'hastily and insanely' implemented, and when accompanied by the elimination of internal opposition to such policies, as with the Soviet economic nationalism.[29]

Despite Heilperin's underscoring of the phenomenon's global pervasiveness in the late 1950s, the concept sparked no significant research interests among social scientists in the 1960s. There were, nonetheless, economists such as Albert Bretton with a 1964 article, 'The Economics of Nationalism',[30] and Harry Johnson with a 1965 article, 'Economic Nationalism in New States',[31] who interestingly – both deploying a 'mainstream economics' perspective of cost-effectiveness of the phenomenon – did not conceive it as controversial and negatively. Indeed, both understood it as state interventionist policies that had an impact on national economy's full economic potential. And that politically it produced targeted effects. For Bretton, who contextualized his paper 'The Economics of Nationalism' as part of a larger study of Canadian nationalism, economic nationalism – understood as making 'investment in nationality or ethnicity' – was 'not [profitable] for everyone in society but for specific identifiable groups'. And thus, the effect of this 'investment in nationality was not so much income-creating as income-redistributing',[32] especially in 'favour of some parts or all of the middle class'.[33] For Johnson, too, contextualized his article in the decolonization processes of the 1960s, and developed a 'theory of nationalist economy' – meaning having a national 'economic program' – such national economic policies led to 'a reduction of material production below the economy's potential'.[34] Their political effects were redistributive too; 'the economic content of nationhood' entailed a transfer of wealth from masses to middle classes and/or about policies of confiscation or nationalization of foreign-owned enterprises. Accordingly, such economic policies were a feature of the early-twentieth-century state-building processes of the new Central Eastern European states as well as of the new decolonized states in the 1960s. They were not, however, economic policies for advanced economies,[35] hence Johnson's suggestion of leaving the study of the phenomenon to historians rather than 'mainstream economists'.[36]

'Mainstream economists' in the 1970s, however, continued to engage with the phenomenon because, as Heilperin had noted earlier, it remained prevalent in both advanced and developing economies. And the rationale for such engagement was to understand and underscore its danger to the international economic order of the time. As the editor of a 1980 edited volume, *The New Economic Nationalism*, Otto Hieronimy noted that a consensus had emerged among the contributors of the volume (the result of a three-day conference in June 1978 with prominent economists from the OECD countries). That consensus was about the emergence of a 'new economic nationalism' – akin to interwar European protectionism – that was 'concern[ing] for the future of the liberal economic order'.[37] Unsurprisingly linking the emergence of this 'new economic nationalism' to major crises, namely 'the disintegration of the post-war international monetary system' of the 1970s, Hieronimy thought that the phenomenon had been both the cause and the consequence of these crises. Interestingly, without conceptualizing it in terms of varieties, he distinguished between its 'traditional efforts' and 'contemporary manifestations'. The former's practices – aimed at protecting domestic production – consisted of tariffs, dumping, export subsidies and various forms of 'beggar-my-neighbour' policies. The latter's policy tools – intended at finding or 'expanding' markets for domestic production abroad – consisted of 'certain types of industrial policy, as well as so-called voluntary export or import agreements' and were a feature of developed market economies. What was undoubtedly similar to Hieronimy, between the interwar and the 1970s – there was no mentioning of Keynes's 'dangerous economic nationalism' or Heilperin's 'virulent forms' – was the pervasiveness of '*monetary nationalism* [sic; Keynes had made the point that finance needed to be primarily national] … [it being the] most disruptive manifestation'. In fact, he noted the pervasiveness of both variants – 'traditional' with practices for domestic market protection, 'contemporary' with practices for expanding domestic production abroad – not only in industrialized and developing countries. Such practices were part of the economic interactions 'within' the industrialized (OECD) countries, remarking that a language of 'strong and weak countries [had] become common'.[38]

Such a negative and/or controversial take on the phenomenon among some 'mainstream economists' – and not only – to some extent was consistent with positions in other disciplines of social sciences, whereby avoiding the concept altogether had become the norm. Generally, the understanding among modern societies, particularly after the Second World War, was they were of nations and states with their individual economic units but without nationalism, especially of the exclusionary one. Explicit associations with the marker of 'the national' and even more 'nationalist' became uncommon. For instance, twentieth-century historical sociology's unit of analysis – when discussing and/or analysing economic affairs of certain countries – became 'society' rather than 'national economy'.[39] Perhaps this was more explicit in German historical sociology whereby well-established nineteenth-century concepts of *Nationalökonomie* (the science of national economy) and *Volkswirtschaft* (the national economy itself) were replaced after the Second World War with *Wirtschaft* (the economic system)[40] rather than in historical sociology as such. An argument for this avoidance in the discipline of historical sociology might not be entirely linked to the experiences of the mid-twentieth-century extreme nationalisms. A post-Second World War linguistic adaptation in the German academic discourse to the now dominant Anglophone economic discourse might have played a role, too.[41] Furthermore, already a connection between 'society' and 'economy' – unlike the plea for a nexus between nationalism and economy made by nationalism scholars such as Berger and Fetzer in the late 2010s – had been drawn by the 'father' of sociology, Max Weber. His conceptual influence cannot be underestimated also with his 1922 book, *Economy and Society: An Outline of Interpretative Sociology*, published in English in 1968, which as prominent intellectual historian of economic thought Keith Tribe noted was his final contribution to twentieth-century social sciences.[42] Nationalism scholarship of the 1980s, too – most prominently Ernest Gellner who in his 1983 work, *Nation and Nationalism*, argued that industrialization had led to the rise of nationalism – kept the two concepts of nationalism and economy 'as analytically separate realms'. So did scholars within the Liberal and Marxist political-economic traditions.[43]

It would be from the late 1980s that economic nationalism would start to become less negatively charged but ideologically contested. This was so when it became a subject matter of inquiry in social sciences, especially in the newly established field of the IPE, where perhaps the way how American political scientist Robert Gilpin framed it in his 1987 book, *The Political Economy of International Relations*, had a role in this ideological contestation. Here, Gilpin conceived of economic nationalism as one of the three ideologies, alongside liberalism and Marxism, of the modern political-economic thought. But in doing so, he conflated the 'nationalist' perspective of the mid-nineteenth century – drawing on insights from the 'preeminent economic nationalist and theorist of the Nationalist tradition'[44] Friedrich List[45] that referred to societies which shared a national identity and were willing to sacrifice for long-term goals of national communities[46] – and the realist doctrine (the primacy of state interests in an anarchical order) of the IR scholarship. Accordingly, there was a 'realist or economic nationalist perspective on trade, monetary and investment relations', which Gilpin subscribed to – alongside the liberal interpretation of market efficiency and the Marxist critique of the market.[47] And of these three, economic nationalism was that ideology in which 'economic ideas are and should be subordinate to the goal of state building and the interests of the state'.[48]

Gilpin, who like Heilperin did not conceptualize the phenomenon in terms of varieties, considered it as historically reoccurring – manifested as mercantilism, statism, protectionism, the German Historical School and the New Protectionism. Significantly, he saw it crystallized as: 'benign' and 'malevolent' mercantilism. The former was a defensive strategy with policies protecting national economic interests within the domestic realm as the basis for the survival and security of the state. Meanwhile, the latter was an offensive and expansionist strategy (aggressive imperialist and national expansion) played out in the international economy. This coincided with Heilperin's 'virulent forms', more concretely with the policies of the Nazi minister of economy Hjalmar Schacht towards Eastern Europe in the 1930s. To Gilpin, the phenomenon was not static in terms of time, place and long-term goals espoused by 'economic nationalists', a point resonating with scholars of economic nationalism of the 1990s and 2000s. These scholars also subscribed to his insight that economic nationalism's ideological strength rested on its appeal of the geographic location and the distribution of economic activities.[49] Though, some, like Abdelal and Pickel, questioned his statist position that economic ideas and practices were and had to be subordinate to state-building and state interests[50] in order for them to be referred to as economic nationalism.

Indeed, from the 1990s, with a less controversial yet ideologically contested understanding, a distinct literature of economic nationalism emerged in the IPE, and neologisms such as 'economic patriotism' also making inroads in the public and scholarly discourses from the mid-2000s. This was one of the main points – changing the perception within the IPE and nationalism scholarships on economic nationalism and nationalism as 'anachronistic ideologies' – of the editors, Eric Helleiner and Andreas Pickel, of one of the most referenced edited volumes on the subject matter, *Economic Nationalism in a Globalizing World*, published in 2005. Accordingly, their volume – enlisting it within this distinct scholarship – offered new insights on the phenomenon, drawing a connection between national identity and economics. In so doing, it allowed them to argue – against the dominant neoliberal narrative in the 1990s – that economic nationalism represented no danger to globalization. In fact, the latter strengthened rather than weakened this connection.[51]

Pickel especially, in his contribution to the volume, 'False Oppositions: Recontextualizing Economic Nationalism in a Globalizing World', asserted that 'the neoliberal discourse [in the political sphere] treat[ed] economic nationalism as a pernicious doctrine, and its proponents as a political enemy', adding that an 'underlying dichotomy between "economic nationalist" and "economic liberal" [was] well established and widely shared – even among scholars'.[52] He largely traced the origins of this 'false' dichotomy in Gilpin's misreading of Friedrich

List's 'nationalist perspective' that accordingly was not an 'abstract economic framework'. Rather, it was a prism for analysing the phenomenon in 'historical, cultural and other contexts'.[53] Subsequently, Pickel remarked how even 'classical' works on nationalism such as those by Ernest Gellner's *Nations and Nationalism* (1983) and Liah Greenfeld's *The Spirit of Capitalism: Nationalism and Economic Growth* (2001) – explaining, respectively, how the rise of capitalism triggered nationalism and vice versa – could not place the phenomenon in such contexts and importantly provide a systematic account of how national identity affected economic processes.[54] Such a false dichotomy, Pickel suggested, begged for a rethinking of economic nationalism – which, accordingly, thanks to new insights in many disciplines in social sciences and the resilience of nation as a symbolic system and social structure – beyond such reductionism and antagonism.[55] And such a rethinking, on the one hand, entailed analysing the phenomenon within the general context of nation and nationalism of a particular country: a call which is closer to the perspective imparted in the concept of *national economy-building*. On the other hand, it meant considering it not only as an ideology/policy but also as political action and as structure.[56] Pickel reiterated such a reframing nearly two decades later in his introduction to the 2022 *Handbook of Economic Nationalism*, adding that the phenomenon remained 'part of our mostly unreflected social codes, contained in our national culture'.[57]

Meanwhile, unlike economic nationalism's scholarly origins with its apparent conceptual stability in the 2000s – illustrated also by a flurry of publications[58] – the genesis of 'economic patriotism' was in political discourse. First articulated by former French prime minister Dominique de Villepin in a 2005 speech – used with a similar understanding as Gilpin's 'benign mercantilism' – as a 'defence of local prerogatives [i.e., French economic interests] in integrated markets [i.e., within the European Union]',[59] the concept then became the analytical framework for Clift and Woll's 2013 edited volume, *Economic Patriotism in Open Economies*. Like previous scholars' observations about economic nationalism's pervasiveness as a phenomenon, they too maintained that economic patriotism was 'a universal phenomenon [but] endemic within interdependent markets and economic jurisdictions'.[60] Like Pickel, they thought that a liberally biased scholarship misused the concept, using it as a 'term of abuse'. And yet, to them both concepts exhibited common features: pursuing economic ideas and choices that discriminated in favour of particular social groups/economic actors, 'insiders', because of their territorial status. And the content of their long-term goals was malleable over time, especially in times of crises. Where the two concepts differed, however, was in that 'unlike economic *nation*alism [sic, and they considered it as old of a phenomenon as that of the nation-state], economic patriotism [was] agnostic about the precise nature of the unit claimed as *patrie* [sic]: it can also refer to supranational or sub-national economic citizenship'.[61]

In a similar manner to Heilperin's tracing of the origins of the phenomenon, *avant la lettre*, Clift and Woll found economic patriotism's initial manifestations in the crises-ridden, mid-1970s Western Europe – a period and economic space coinciding with Hieronimy's 'new economic nationalism', the latter thus not framing it as economic patriotism. Unable to afford 'defensive' economic strategies – the 'old-style industrial policies' – national economies within the European Community, they noted, did not discard such strategies. What they did was to create new and often 'offensive' strategies whereby long-term national goals expanded from the national to the supranational, thus the European, level. This meant that on the one hand national economic space opened, 'liberalized', whereas on the other hand supranational economic space came to be 'defended', protected, from outside economic actors and interests. As such, both the new strategy and the 'old one' were to further the interests of the 'territorial insiders'. Accordingly, this was an insight that a 'liberal-biased' IPE scholarship on economic patriotism, and by extension on economic nationalism, missed not only in analysing this 'universal phenomenon' in general but also in specific cases when 'politicians chose liberal economic policies as a selective strategy for further territorial "insider" interests'. Without explicitly framing their deployment of economic patriotism in terms of varieties, they nevertheless identified its two ideological strands: 'liberal' and 'conservative', alongside their categories derived from the nature of unit of *patria*: subnational/local patriotism, economic nationalism and supranational patriotism.[62]

Varieties of economic nationalism and 'national economy-building' as alternative concepts

Arguably, any past and contemporary engagement with attempts to reconceptualize the phenomenon, including its recent reincarnation as economic patriotism, would still have to grapple with historical controversies associated with it. Some IPE scholars, as shown above, would not draw past economic discursive continuities in their analysis. It still remains the case in social sciences analysing and critically reconstructing the phenomenon as well as in political discourses when the notion re-emerges in times of economic crises and change. However, so long as some economic activities take place – as they do – within a particular economic space/territory, especially national one, and various policies are enacted to promote, or legitimized under, 'the national interest', 'our economy', and importantly historical references and perspectives are drawn to them, it is possible to view the phenomenon as persisting variedly: in contradiction and/or in accord with economic globalism/globalization.

Hence, aside from and because of competing and contested discourses and practices regarding this political-economic phenomenon, the problem with it has been also – as elaborated above – conceptual, in the framing of it; thus, the need for capturing its various historical and contemporary manifestations. Such a problem remains even with those accounts and analyses that underscore its contested complexity, defensive and offensive strategies/policies (even some infusing a historical perspective on the phenomenon). This is because their framings remain 'trapped' to the singularity of meaning the concept of economic nationalism exudes prima facie, mostly controversial associations, or simply 'traditional' understandings. Those accounts or analyses that do not have or infuse such a historical perspective seem 'condemned' to reappear. Therefore, a reconceptualization that captures the phenomenon's varied manifestations as *varieties of economic nationalism*, and one that imparts a historical perspective to this variedness through another alternative concept, *national economy-building*, are warranted. And while the concept of *varieties of economic nationalism* builds on existing and emerging perspectives in the IPE and nationalism scholarships, which, respectively, account for economic and national phenomena in plural forms as well as on varied categorizations – implicit and explicit – by some of the aforementioned political economists and scholars, *national economy-building* was coined in the process of a comparative conceptual history research. The latter examined political-economic discourses in some small (nation-)states in the continent between the late nineteenth and early twentieth centuries.

Thus, the reconceptualization of *varieties of economic nationalism* builds on the IPE paradigm of variety of capitalism which insists on the multiple forms of economies and of their strategies of economic development. And here such multiple forms, starting with initial 'ideal types' of economies identified by the proponents of this paradigm, Peter A. Hall and David Soskice: liberal market economies (LMEs), 'co-ordinated market economies' (CMEs) and non-ideal type, 'the Mediterranean capitalism'[63] – largely corresponding with the OECD economies – over time came to include a third, the dependent market economy (DMEs) of post-socialist East Central European countries,[64] and a fourth type, hierarchical market economies (HMEs) in Latin America,[65] some economies in

East Asia[66] as well as Turkey.[67] It also builds on recent reconceptualization in nationalism literature that accounts for various forms of reproduction of 'the nation' as a pattern, globally.[68] Such a reframing would heed the early 1990s scholarly appeal, including that within economic nationalism scholarship, of moving beyond the dichotomy of 'good civic' and 'bad ethnic' nationalism.[69]

And crucially, it builds on the implicit and explicit framings of some of the aforementioned authors. Implicitly, Keynes's categorization pointed to three variants of economic nationalism: 'old-fashioned protectionist', 'dangerous' (extreme/self-sufficiency) and 'some/greater degree of self-sufficiency'. Heilperin's account reproduced the historical, the 'old-fashioned protectionist' economic nationalism on the one hand, and the 'virulent'/extreme economic nationalism of the 1930s on the other hand. Additionally, he observed its various manifestations in the socialist countries (their collectivism) as well as that in the United States. Hieronimy, too, etched out the 'traditional, protectionist' and the new manifestations of 'expansionary' economic nationalisms, leaving out the 'extreme'/dangerous version of the 1930s. Explicitly, Gilpin generated the dichotomy of 'benign' (protectionist/defensive) and 'malevolent' (expansionist/aggressive) mercantilism. Pickel – in his reframing of it as idea/ideology/policy – distinguished between the 'generic/banal' (which was the liberal's bias and thus the 'conventional view' on economic nationalism) and 'substantive' economic nationalism. On 'substantive' economic nationalism which occurred at the policy level, he identified two other categories: 'progressive' and 'reactionary' (this also being the liberal's bias, 'conventional view' at this level) economic nationalism. And thus, as one of the most ardent scholars for reframing economic nationalism, considering his assertion that within a national economic policy context there were always substantial debates between 'economic liberals' and 'economic nationalists', Pickel argued for a 'conceptual shift' whereby 'economic liberalism' was to be considered analytically as a 'particular form of economic nationalism'.[70] Such a call for a 'conceptual shift' resonates with the reconceptualization as varieties of economic nationalism advanced here.

Clift and Woll, too, though primarily concerned with economic patriotism – which unlike economic nationalism had a wider meaning of territoriality (as an imagined common economic space): thus, aside from the national, there were the subnational and supranational economic spaces – identified three 'territorial' types: local economic patriotism, economic nationalism and supranational economic patriotism. And at the ideological/policy level, they discerned a variety, or at least a dichotomy, between 'conservative' and 'liberal' economic patriotism/nationalism. And lacking a deeper historical perspective in their account, the 'extreme' variant of economic nationalism was not in. The 'conservative' strategy meant inward-looking and defensive economic policies preserving the status quo: discursively articulated as fending off competition at 'home'. The 'liberal' strategy entailed 'offensive, outward-looking' policies with new ways of supporting national firms and/or citizens abroad, including selective or strategic liberalization strategies that helped a certain group of economic actors.[71] Accordingly, what the proponents of 'conservative' and 'liberal' economic patriotism/nationalism had in common was their favouring of 'territorial insiders'. Where they differed was in how they articulated their views and designed their policies, whereby 'conservative' economic nationalists/patriotists were explicit in their discourses and policies of favouring territorial insiders and resisting outsiders. The 'liberal' ones, meanwhile, were implicit, designing policies that 'support[ed] insiders without in principle excluding outsiders', ultimately 'strengthen[ing] the position of national or regional target groups'. And because of their implicit nature, the effects of such 'liberal' economic nationalist/patriotic policies became evident in practice rather than in discourse.[72]

Arguably thus, discursively as well as in practice the phenomenon appears varied, manifesting as 'liberal/progressive' (open and simultaneously outward-/inward-looking), 'conservative/defensive' (protectionist/inward-looking) and 'extreme' (aggressive/expansionist/outward-looking and/or autarkic/inward-looking) economic nationalism. Such a variety has not been outlined in the IPE scholarship that remains caught in the dichotomy of 'going beyond' the 'conservative/defensive' variant, while dissociating from its 'extreme' manifestations. A recent and impressive global historical account on economic nationalism by IPE scholar Martin Suesse titled *The Nationalist Dilemma: A Global History of Economic Nationalism, 1776 to Present* (2023) also argues for thinking 'of different kinds of economic nationalism' as a reaction to economic inequality[73] and does name the 'going beyond' as 'expansionist economic nationalism'. But his suggestion for thinking as such still remains a dichotomy rather than a variety: the two variants of 'expansionist economic nationalism' and the 'isolationalist economic nationalism'[74] that are closer to the two variants advanced here, respectively, the 'liberal/progressive' economic nationalism and the 'conservative/defensive'. Such a variety has not been outlined also in the economic history literature that in fact latches onto either the 'extreme' or onto the 'conservative/defensive' variants.

It is in this light – of an incongruity between these two scholarships – that varieties of economic nationalism necessitate another concept, *national economy-building* which imparts a historical plurality of economic discourses/doctrines and practices in a particular national economic space and context. Echoing Pickel's plea for a reframing of economic nationalism, *national economy-building* was coined when comparing late nineteenth century and early interwar political-economic thinking of influential Habsburg-Bohemian/Czechoslovak, Tsarist-Georgian/Georgian and Ottoman-Albanian/Albanian intellectual and political figures. It was premised upon the idea that the rise of the discipline of political economy – from the second half of the nineteenth century[75] – including the notion of national economy, precipitated the emergence of various economic doctrines and political-economic vocabularies. And thus, those figures in the comparison – in advancing their views for viable national economies in the period when the respective emerging national and economic spaces were under respective imperial rule and in the period when they became independent national states – articulated 'liberal/progressive' and 'conservative/defensive' economic discourses and policies.[76] Over time, other political-economic doctrines emerged and became embedded, even marginalizing other ones, as in the case of 'extreme' self-reliant economic nationalism of late socialist Albania.

In some respects, this concept draws on an insight from the nineteenth-century German Historical School – which incidentally used the notion of nation-building, not in the sense used in nationalism scholarship (as studying the use of state power to construct national identities)[77] but as a 'redefined mercantilism'[78] – that 'the validity of economic doctrines depends on circumstances. What might be good for a nation at one time might be quite unsuitable for it at another'.[79] And similarly to List's 'national system' of nations in cooperation through custom unions, it differs – in it being wider – to the concept of 'national economies' deployed by economic historian Kreutzmüller. The latter specifically uses it to account for and reconstruct 'nationalist and racist convictions and practices as – at times – prevailing factors in the economy' of interwar countries in the European continent,[80] focusing thus only on the 'extreme' variant of economic nationalism and therefore also rendering it static.

With these two alternative concepts, it is therefore possible to capture the varieties of the phenomenon both in its contemporaneous and historical dimensions in a particular and/or in a comparative context(s). In this light, a scanty account of the contemporaneous 'return' of economic nationalism in a large and a mid-sized state – respectively, the United States and the United Kingdom – points to its plurality and contested-ness of discourses and policy options. Such a contestation often draws on historical manifestations of each variant. In the UK, the pre- and post-Brexit economic discourses and policies reveal a contestation between the 'defensive/conservative' economic nationalism – articulated under the narrative of 'taking back control', manifested with protectionist policies of 'tearing off trade agreement', 'economic disintegration' from the EU as well as a closing of its labour market to foreign workers and the variant of 'liberal' economic nationalism. Proponents of the latter variant criticized how this 'defensive/conservative' variant undermined the existing post-Second World War 'rule bound liberal economic order', and also – harkening back to the deeper past – disregarding Adam Smith's tenets of 'forgoing the gains from trade would harm the wealth of nation'.[81] They also contested the 'progressive' economic nationalism of the Labor Party's 2022 economic policy[82] of 'Investing in Britain' – a 'three-part … plan to get Britain's economy back on track' with 'a long-term approach to economic growth and security' – that ensured 'we buy, make and sell more in Britain, and partner with businesses to make Britain a world leader in the industries of the future'. 'Investing in Britain' entailed concrete policies in 'reshoring, ensuring more public contracts go to British companies, and standing up for domestic industries … developing an industrial strategy, working hand in hand with trade union and businesses… secure[ing] the future of our steel industry by winning the global race for green steel production'.[83] Thus, within the recent British political-economic discourses, this 'progressive' variant sets it apart from the others, while chiming with historical discourses, notably with Keynes's 'version' of economic nationalism.

In the United States, this contemporaneous variety is manifested with the 'defensive/conservative' variant of the Trump Administration – his 'embrace of protectionism and restrictionism … steep tariffs on steel and aluminum imports… very much in keeping with his [Trump] mercantilist instincts … more stringent limits on the low-skill migration'[84] – and the Biden Administration's 'liberal/progressive' variant. Like the British Labor discourse, Biden's economic nationalism, articulated as 'Investing in America Agenda', garnered policies for 'mobilizing … private sector investments in the United States, bringing manufacturing back to America after decades of offshoring, and creating new good paying jobs, including union jobs … rebuilding our roads and bridges, using Made in America materials, built by American workers'.[85] And similarly to the (neo)liberal critique in the British context, political commentators in the American context drew historical references and analogies on Biden's 'progressive' economic nationalism, especially one of its doctrines, 'Buy American', seen as harking it back to 'The Buy American Act of 1933 … [the e]conomic nationalism that triggered and prolonged the Great Depression'.[86] Other commentators also have seen Biden's variant, the use of

> government power to bring about major economic transformation … invest[ing] vast amounts in American industries … [representing] a shift toward the kind of economic nationalism that has over the decades, found support, across the ideological spectrum … [as] a rethinking of the country's economic posture: seeking to promote certain sectors … so as not to cede them to competitors in Europe and Asia.

Accordingly, such a shift marked a 'deviation from the free trade gospel … [and a rekindling of Biden's 1988 presidential campaign call for a "new era of American economic nationalism" and as] a form of chauvinism in some ways more ambitious than Trump's as manifested through haphazard tariffs and trade wars'.[87]

Economic nationalisms in small (nation-)states

The second argument of this chapter is that economic nationalisms, thus varieties of the phenomenon – 'liberal/progressive', 'conservative/defensive' and 'extreme' – manifest historically and contemporaneously also among small(er) national economic spaces. Smallness within the conceptual framework of economic nationalism is understood from a *functional/relational* standpoint regarding how an economic space relates to other (supra)national economic territories regarding its mode of production, market conditions and security regimes.[88] It is also conceived from a *discursive/performative* perspective of how state and non-state economic/social actors of a polity – recognized internally and externally as small – generate policies or economic activities from such a recognition.[89] This argument bridges the reductionism in economic historians' accounts whereby the main variant associated with small states is that of 'conservative/defensive' economic nationalism with the avoidance of the concept of economic nationalism in the small states' IPE scholarship. The latter – generally analysing advanced small state economies in the 'West' which does not see analytical value in the use of economic nationalism as a discourse and assumes that small economies are inherently vulnerable, such economies, thus, need to find modes of adaptation to survive, modes of strategies characterized as 'neo-liberal' and 'social-democratic' – does not see them as capable of 'conservative/defensive' economic policies.

Undoubtedly then, juxtaposing both concepts: *varieties of economic nationalism* and *national economy-building*, with accounts and analyses of economic historians and political economists on small national economies, not only the dissonance between these two scholarships but crucially the variedness of the phenomenon in small (nation-)states becomes clearer. For instance, in prominent economic historian Ivan T. Berend's accounts, the only variant that historically could be associated with small or weaker national economies was the 'conservative/defensive' one. In his 2022 historical overview of the phenomenon, tracing its intellectual origins and influence in the nineteenth century and its dominance as an economic policy in Europe in the first half of the twentieth century – as with the concept of national economy-building – and for most of the twentieth century in Central and Eastern Europe, he understood economic nationalism as representing the idea, theory and the practices of 'self-defence of the weaker nations'. He contrasted this ideology of 'weak, later starter, agricultural economies', from the second half of the nineteenth century, to the pre-nineteenth-century mercantilism (mercantilist policies) of 'the much stronger competitors of the most advanced industrial powers'.[90]

Berend's views stand in sharp contrast to Keynes's insight on interwar economic nationalism of small states, which he did as a side note in his discussion of the viability of 'dangerous/extreme' economic nationalisms of Fascist Italy, Soviet Russia and Nazi Germany. Indeed, when implicitly discussing the two types of economic nationalism – from the perspective of self-sufficiency/autarkic policies – Keynes thought that weaker and smaller nations were not capable of pursuing the 'conservative/defensive' and even more so 'extreme' variant of self-sufficiency and self-reliance. The small and weak nation he had in mind in this discussion was the free Irish state. As he put it, 'a unit much too small for a high degree of national insufficiency [sic] except at crushing economic costs, is discussing plans which might, if they were carried out, would be ruinous'.[91] Keynes's side note on the non-viability of 'extreme' economic nationalism indeed proved ruinous for the only small state implementing national self-sufficiency/autarkic policies such as late-1970s socialist Albania.[92] It also 'proved', together with socialist Albania's implementation of it – for the purpose of the second argument of this chapter – that small states could and did embrace an 'extreme' version of economic nationalism.

Between Berend's perspective of associating 'conservative/defensive' variant with smaller and weaker states in Central and Eastern Europe in the late nineteenth and twentieth centuries and Keynes's suspicion, especially of the 'extreme' variant as in the case of Ireland in the interwar power, stands Hieronimy's confirmation, similar to the chapter's second argument, that varieties of economic nationalism manifested not only in larger but also in smaller developed Western economies of the late 1970s. In his implicit discussion of the two categories – the 'traditional', that is, 'conservative/defensive' variant, of protectionist policies and practices for domestic market protection and the 'contemporary manifestations', that is, 'liberal/progressive' variant of economic practices by states in expanding domestic production abroad – he pointed out how the 'new economic nationalism' of the late 1970s was 'not limited to the "weak" countries'. Moreover, he asserted that 'nor can a sharp separation be drawn according to the size. Small *and* [italics in original] liberal countries [such as Switzerland] can also be nationalistic'.[93]

And to a large extent, the presence of both variants in Hieronimy's edited volume, a volume that did not discuss the smaller states in the Eastern bloc – a variety missing in Berend's historical perspective – was 'confirmed' in Romano and Romero's 2021 edited volume, *European Socialist Regimes' Fateful Engagement with the West: National Strategies in the Long 1970s*. This volume, examining national economic debates and strategies in Poland, Czechoslovakia, GDR, Bulgaria, Romania and Yugoslavia throughout the 1970s and the early 1980s, showed that these 'smaller European socialist regimes' not only had 'conservative/defensive' economic policies.[94] They also pursued a similar strategy of opening up and engagement in economic and trade relations with their capitalistic neighbours. Thus, rather than only having 'defensive/conservative' policies, they similarly embraced a 'liberal/progressive' policy of opening: import-led growth and integration in the world economy. It was an economic strategy that ultimately proved to be a failure,[95] as was the 'extreme/autarkic' variant of socialist Albania. Nevertheless, both variants – together with the 'conservative/defensive' one – illustrated that there were varieties of economic nationalism among small(er) states on both sides of the Iron Curtain.

Varieties of economic nationalism are also present in the small states especially when also deploying the national economy-building concept given the avoidance of economic nationalism in the IPE scholarship on small states. Indeed, this scholarship despite experiencing a 'revival' in the post-Cold War and the emergence of small new states with the implosions of the Soviet Union, Yugoslavia,[96] the amicable dissolution of Czechoslovakia and the apparent conceptual stability of economic nationalism did not engage with the latter. This was the case with one of the earliest comparative monographs, Katzenstein's 1985 book, *Small States in World Markets*. This work incidentally and fittingly to Romano and Romero's volume examined and compared the industrial policies of seven small states (Sweden, Norway, Denmark, the Netherlands, Belgium, Austria and Switzerland) in the western side of the Iron Curtain during 'the long

1970s'. The argument advanced here was these small economies despite their small size – hence the assumption about small economies' inherent vulnerabilities to larger ones – were not only able to survive but also able to thrive in times of economic crises and change. Without significantly contextualizing historical trajectories and economic narratives of these countries, Katzenstein argued that they were able to do so because they had a similar corporatist model of public policy-making, allowing them to successfully pursue modes or strategies of adaptations.[97] Thus, these strategies of successful adaptation were not framed in terms of varieties, but with inferences drawn for texts of the same period, such as Hieronimy's, such varieties are evident.

Similar inferences to draw are possible in Baldersheim and Keating's 2015 edited volume, *Small States in the Modern World: Vulnerabilities and Opportunities*.[98] Building on Katzenstein's argument – in their analysis of the advanced industrial and welfare states of Scandinavia, Ireland, Iceland, New Zealand, as well as autonomous entities of Scotland and Quebec – that smaller economies were more vulnerable than larger ones and therefore had to adjust, Keating added to Katzenstein's argument that there were various modes of adaptation. With all these small (nation-)states, concerned with economic competitiveness and social cohesion in the changing neoliberal, geo-economic context of European and global economic zones during the 2000s and 2010s, Keating, however, noted that two modes/strategies stood out. There was the neoliberal one: being open to the world market and accepting global competition and rules, deregulating capital and labour markets, and downsizing the government, a strategy/policy generating income and wealth inequality for a national economy. And the other strategy, the social-democratic one, opened to global economy but pursuing policies of social investment in human capital via education (research and development), and by providing support in health provisions, a strategy that renewed the national economy and increased its economic productivity.[99]

Keating did not engage with economic nationalism per se. And clearly his two modes/strategies of adaptation would fall within the 'liberal/progressive' variant. Nevertheless, he suggested – akin to the insight of the historical plurality of economic discourse in the concept of national economy-building – that such paths of adaptations of small (nation-)states were informed by 'legacies of policies and institutions' as well as 'national imaginary'. Keen to underscore when considering such legacies that there was no 'historical determinist[m]' as advanced by 'path dependency theorists' and not be overwhelmed by 'the national imaginary … [and] national myths',[100] he nevertheless remarked that national imaginary and discourses played a significant role on how a national polity of a small country reconstituted itself. Accordingly, 'the national imaginary is … compounded by what happened and how it is interpreted. Small nations faced with big neighbours may be particularly attached to their national myths and, while these are not objective reality, they are important elements in the construction and reproduction of the polity.'[101]

Conclusion

This chapter has detailed – from a conceptual history perspective – how and why the political-economic phenomenon of economic nationalism, historically and contemporaneously, remains a controversial and contested concept, discourse and practice. In doing so, it underscored the discrepancies between the continuity of the various forms of the phenomenon – 'the universality' of it observed by numerous scholars and (political) economists especially after the Second World War – the reoccurring 'warnings' about the dangers it posed to the international/global economic order, the avoidance and neglect to engage with the concept by other scholars and economic historians' contextualization of it with only specific historical periods and variants.

Moving beyond the confines of conceptual history approach, by arguing for a reconceptualization of economic nationalism – based on historical patterns of framing the phenomenon – it advanced two arguments. It argued that to overcome the aforementioned discrepancies, economic nationalism ought to be reconceptualized in terms of its discernible, various forms: 'liberal' (nations in competition) and 'progressive' (nations in cooperation), 'conservative/defensive' (nations in a zero-sum game) and 'extreme' (aggressive/expansionist and/or autarchic nations). Such a reconceptualization may also shed light as to why the two 'planetary perspectives', exquisitely accounted by prominent historian Bo Stråth: the Brandt Commission's vision for 'global Keynesianism' of the late 1970s and early 1980s and global corporations' ideal, the neoliberal grand narrative, for 'a planetary enterprise in a single world' taking hold in the 1990s until the multiple global crises that began in 2008,[102] did not succeed. It also asserted that this political-economic phenomenon, with its various forms – often synchronically and diachronically – is present also in small(er) (nation-) states in modern and contemporary European and global history.

Notes

This research is part of my project 'National Economy-Building in Albania, Czechoslovakia and Georgia in the 1920s' (M 2847) supported by the Austrian Science Fund (FWF).

1 Bohle, Scepanovic and Rennwald, 'The Return of Economic Nationalism?', Bronz, Frieden and Weymouth, 'Populism in Place'; Wolf, *The Crisis of Democratic Capitalism*, 66.

2 This approach assumes that modern concepts are politically and socially charged. See Koselleck, *Futures Past*.

3 Berger and Fetzer (eds), *Nationalism and the Economy*.

4 See Kofman, *Economic Nationalism and Development*; Schulz and Kubu (eds), *History and Culture of Economic Nationalism*.

5 Berend, 'Economic Nationalism in Historical Perspective', 2.

6 Kreutzmüller, 'Introduction', 2.

7 Keating, 'The Political Economy of Small States in Europe', 7; Bishop, 'The Political Economy of Small States'.

8 The White House, 'Remarks by National Security Advisor Jake Sullivan'.

9 The United States was faced with China's

> use of full arsenal of state-directed, economic national policies … first under Donald Trump and now Joe Biden is employing state-directed industrial development, protectionism, the subsidised reshoring manufacturing, and trade war strategies more effectively and aggressively than Trump. The EU is following the same path … [in fact], [t]he global return to industrial policy began with China's Made in China 2025 plan, announced in 2015, and was followed by the EU Green Deal Investment Plan in 2020, then the US responded with the 2022 Chips Act and the Inflation Reduction Act.

See Nagle, 'The Washington Consensus Is Dead'.

10 Foer, 'The New Washington Consensus'; Berend, 'Economic Nationalism in Historical Perspective'.

11 Here this notion is understood similarly to that put forward recently by Piketty, namely in a 'positive and constructive sense [of] … a set of priori plausible ideas and discourses describing how society should be structured [which] has social, economic, and political dimensions [and that] … ideological conflict and disagreement are inherent in the very notion of ideology'. See Piketty, *Capital and Ideology*, 3.

12 Nakano, 'Theorizing Economic Nationalism', 211.

13 Åslund, *How Capitalism Was Built*, 20.

14 Skidelsky, *Money and Government*, 167.

15 Wolf, *The Crisis of Democratic Capitalism.*
16 Pickel, 'Introduction', 3.
17 https://books.google.com/ngrams/graph?content=economic+nationalism+&year_start=1800&year_end=2019&corpus=en-2019&smoothing=3, 9 June 2023.
18 Paslovsky, *Economic Nationalism of the Danubian States.*
19 Hemstad, 'Promoting *Norden* and the Nordic Cooperation in the 1930s'.
20 Slobodian, *Globalist*, 8.
21 Heilperin, *Studies in Economic Nationalism*, 16–18.
22 Ibid., 10.
23 Levi-Faur, 'Economic Nationalism'.
24 Keynes, 'National Self-Sufficiency', 6.
25 Ibid.
26 Ibid., 1–2.
27 Ibid., 2; for a more recent reference to this quote see also Zahra, *Against the World*, xviii.
28 Ibid., 6.
29 Ibid., 7.
30 Bretton, 'The Economics of Nationalism'.
31 Johnson, 'Economic Nationalism in New States', 240.
32 Bretton, 'The Economics of Nationalism', 376.
33 Ibid., 386.
34 Ibid.
35 Johnson, 'Economic Nationalism in New States', 238–9.
36 Pickel, 'Introduction', 3.
37 Hieronimy (ed.), *The New Economic Nationalism*, 1.
38 Ibid.
39 Tooze, 'Imagining National Economies'.
40 Ibid.
41 *The Quarterly Journal of Economics* (established in 1886) kept its title, the *Zeitschrift für die gesamte Staatswissenschaft* (1844) became the *Journal of Institutional and Theoretical Economics* in 1986, without changing the subject or issues.
42 Tribe, 'Preface', vii.
43 Fetzer, 'Nationalism and the Economy', 963.
44 Abdelal, 'Nationalism and International Political Economy in Eurasia', 25.
45 The juxtaposition of List's vision for a cosmopolitical-economic system, with his 'national system', as a critique of Smith's vision of a liberal cosmopolitan one is a long, well-established one in the modern political-economic thought. Less attention, though, had been drawn on how the notions of *national* and *nations*, respectively, feature in the very titles of their works. See List, *National System of*

Political Economy; Smith, *An Inquiry into the Nature and Causes of the Wealth of Nations.*

46 Gilpin, *The Political Economy of International Relations*, 31–4.

47 Ibid., xiii.

48 Ibid., 31.

49 Ibid., 31–3.

50 Abdelal, 'Nationalism and International Political Economy in Eurasia', 25–6, which in fact remains a prominent conceptual framework of analysing cases of state-building of new or old states after enduring war. See Berdal and Zaum, *The Political Economy of Statebuilding.*

51 Helleiner and Pickel (eds), *Economic Nationalism in a Globalizing World*, 1.

52 Pickel, 'Introduction', 2–3.

53 Ibid., 3.

54 Ibid., 3–4. This latter point, or task, was taken up in a 2019 edited volume, titled *Nationalism and the Economy: Explorations into a Neglected Relationship*, whereby its editors, Stefan Berger and Thomas Fetzer, argued that there was a widespread historical and contemporary interaction – particularly in the European continent – between national identity or 'subjective characteristics' and economic processes or 'objective characteristics', an interaction they referred to as 'nationalism-economy nexus'. And in this, their definition of economic nationalism – not framed in terms of its varieties – entailed 'more than protectionist strategies of raising trade tariffs and investment barriers'. Furthermore, Fetzer in his contribution, titled 'Economic Europeanness', by applying a constructivist approach (discourse and practices) argued that such a nexus – 'territorially-based "imagined economies"' – was observable in an EU context (Fetzer, 'Economic Europeanness', 277).

55 Pickel, 'Introduction', 6–9.

56 Ibid., 12.

57 Pickel, 'Introduction to the Handbook of Economic Nationalism', xv–xvi.

58 Indeed, the scholarship is vast, see Baughn and Yaprak, 'Economic Nationalism', Levi-Faur, 'Economic Nationalism'; Crane, 'Bringing the Nation Back In'; Helleiner, 'Economic Nationalism as a Challenge to Economic Liberalism'?; Nakano, 'Theorizing Economic Nationalism'; Pryke, 'Economic Nationalism'.

59 Clift and Woll, 'Economic Patriotism: Reinventing Control over Open Markets', 2.

60 Ibid., 3.

61 Ibid., 2.

62 Ibid., 3.

63 Hall and Soskice (eds), *Varieties of Capitalism*, 2–28; For a critique to this approach, see Allen, 'The Varieties of Capitalism Paradigm'.

64 Nölke and Vliegenthart, 'Enlarging the Varieties of Capitalism'.

65 Schneider, 'Hierarchical Market Economies and Varieties of Capitalism in Latin America'.
66 Carney, 'Varieties of Hierarchical Capitalism'.
67 Kiran, 'Expanding the Framework of the Varieties of Capitalism'.
68 Mylonas and Tudor in their edited volume demonstrate the empirical and conceptual diversity (five categories) of nationalism. See Mylonas and Tudor (eds), *Varieties of Nationalism*; see also Decker, 'Varieties of Nationalism in the Political Discourse of Habsburg Austria'.
69 Pickel, 'Introduction', 7–8.
70 Ibid., 12.
71 Clift and Woll, 'Economic Patriotism', 8–9.
72 Ibid., 10.
73 Suesse, *The Nationalist Dilemma*, 11.
74 Ibid., 323–4.
75 See Tribe, *Constructing Economic Science*.
76 See Brisku, 'Renegotiating the Empire, Forging the Nation-State'; Brisku, 'Renegotiating the Empire, Forging the Nation-State', Brisku, 'Renegotiating the Empire, Forging the Nation-State'. For a more systematic account of the national economic discourses and policies of these three entities as small independent states after the First World War, see Brisku, *'National Economy-Building' in Albania, Czechoslovakia and Georgia in the 1920s*.
77 Mylonas, 'Nation-Building'.
78 Skidelsky, *Money and Government*, 88.
79 Ibid.
80 Kreutzmüller, 'Introduction', 2.
81 Born et al., 'The Cost of Economic Nationalism'.
82 Lynn, 'Labor's Disastrous Switch to Economic Nationalism'.
83 Reeves, 'Labor's Plan for a Stronger, More Secure Economy'.
84 Salam, 'Trump Can't Have It Both Ways'.
85 The White House, 'President Joe Biden Investing in America'.
86 Frum, 'This Is No Time for Protectionism'.
87 Scheiber, 'The Biden Team Wants to Transform the Economy'.
88 Keating, 'Preface', xi.
89 Kruizinga (ed.), *The Politics of Smallness Modern Europe*, 6–7.
90 Berend, 'Economic Nationalism in Historical Perspective', 2. See also Szlajfer (ed.), *Economic Nationalism in East Central Europe and South America, 1919–1939*.
91 Keynes, 'National Self-Sufficiency', 6.
92 Biberaj, *Albania*.
93 Hieronimy (ed.), *The New Economic Nationalism*, 2.

94 While not engaging with the concept of economic nationalism per se, Roman Szporluk, similarly to Berend, suggests that the early-twentieth-century forms of nationalism in the Central East European states had Marxist elements in their national platforms, whereas Marxist states in post-Second World War Europe adopted elements of nationalist creed. See Szporluk, *Communism and Nationalism.*

95 Romano and Romero, *European Socialist Regimes' Fateful Engagement with the West*, 1–5.

96 Keating, 'The Political Economy of Small States in Europe', 7.

97 Katzenstein, *Small States in World Markets*, 21–2.

98 Baldersheim and Keating (eds), *Small States in the Modern World.*

99 Keating, 'The Political Economy of Small States in Europe', 9–11.

100 Ibid., 19.

101 Ibid. For Rioux, however, who in his 2020 monograph, *Small Nations, High Ambitions*, compared economic interventions – capital investment – by the two regional governments of Quebec and Scotland, not only were national imaginaries important elements in the construction and reproduction of these respective small polities, they were crucial also in generating the interventionist economic policies of these two 'subnational' entities. Thus, contrasting the 'minority economic nationalism' of Quebec and Scotland – same entities as in the analysis in Baldersheim and Keating's volume – Rioux found their nationalisms affected their economic policies, generating a kind of economic nationalism different from the protectionist policies. As he put it, 'Quebecois and Scottish nationalisms fuelled state [regional government] intervention and the crafting of policies geared toward the development and preservation of *local* [sic] production and ownership in key industries, notably in technology-intensive, high-value-added sectors' (6).

102 Stråth, *The Brandt Commission and the Multinationals*, 347.

2

Becoming 'masters of their own house': Economic nationalism and small-state building in communist federations

Lars Fredrik Stöcker

Introduction

'State dissolution and reconstruction', as political science teaches, 'are relatively rare events in the modern state system'.[1] In Europe's chequered twentieth-century history, however, the continent's political map became fragmented along ethno-national lines twice over: first as a consequence of the dismantling of the European land empires in the aftermath of the First World War, and once again after the collapse of communism, which marked the end of 'Yalta Europe' and the break-up of Yugoslavia, the USSR and the Czechoslovak Socialist Republic. Already at the dusk of the Great War, however, the pre-1914 empires featured 'regional integration patterns shaped by nationalist sentiment'[2] that anticipated the post-war demarcations. Similarly, ethnic fragmentation was manifest in the communist federations long before their decline, driven by nationalist mobilization and increasingly vocal claims for ethno-territorial self-determination by the federal republics' titular nations.

The Cold War era marked a prolonged period of 'proto-state formation',[3] which long remained concealed by the ideological cloak of communism. The ethno-national federal republics, endowed with their own political, cultural and, by time, even economic institutions, consolidated their proto-statehood through the 1980s, when nationalizing debates strengthened demands for greater autonomy and, eventually, secession in Yugoslavia and the USSR, whereas the Czechoslovak divorce unfolded first amidst the turmoil of post-socialist transformation. Europe's communist federations thus served as incubators for a range of aspiring future nation states, which showed increasing assertiveness on the domestic and international front. A major catalyst was the manifold efforts to reform the socialist planning system, which unintentionally laid the ground for nascent (proto-)national economies along ethno-territorial lines. Confronted with inefficient economic institutions, rising consumerism and an increasing technological backlog, all state-socialist regimes eventually succumbed to global market pressures. A combined cure of marketization and economic decentralization gradually empowered the federal republics which, as the socialist orbit opened up to Western markets and capital, gained an unprecedented level of autonomy in foreign economic affairs. The intertwined dynamics of socialist 'proto-globalization'[4] and the domestic push for decentralization stand out as key drivers behind these economic state-building processes, which effectively challenged federal cohesion. Instead of stabilizing the fragile federations, the reform attempts amplified existing economic and fiscal imbalances and fuelled lingering grievances that swiftly took a nationalist tone. Feelings of relative economic deprivation, which are often at the root of ethnic conflict and separatist mobilization,[5] underpinned disintegrative forces that eventually led to the break-up of the communist federations into a range of smaller successor states.

While our volume primarily explores the policy choices of sovereign small states in a swiftly changing global economic environment, this chapter aims to prove the usefulness of extending our approach to small-state agency in late-Cold War Europe to the communist federal units. Some of the constituent republics of Yugoslavia and the USSR indeed developed economic strategies to protect their pronouncedly *national* interests that were not essentially different from those of Europe's nominally sovereign small states, many of which, in a similar vein, tried to use the new openings of East-West rapprochement to gain more leeway in the bipolar post-war world. This is especially true for the Baltic SSRs which, much like Slovenia or Croatia, marked showcase examples of communist federal republics displaying clearly defined small-state-like features by the dawn of Soviet power. In contrast to earlier international political economy (IPE) scholarship on the divergent paths of economic transformation among the post-Soviet successor states, which proceeds from a rather static idea of national identity as a determining cultural force,[6] this chapter investigates the way in which collective feelings of economic deprivation first exacerbated the simmering 'tension between economic strength and political power'[7] and how the ensuing, gradually nationalizing reform debates eventually were translated into (proto-)national economic policies.

Conceptually, this chapter addresses two strands of literature on the phenomenon of economic nationalism. On the one hand, it discusses the often-neglected correlation between economic grievances and nationalist political resurgence by taking a closer look at the rhetorical framing of economic discrepancies in nationalizing public debates on centre-republic relations and its impact on the Baltic 'national reawakening'. Economic historian Helga Schultz explained the abovementioned neglect with the 'new culturalism' gaining upper hand in mainstream nationalism studies after the 1990s Balkan War, which consolidated the traditional primacy of culture and politics over economics in studies on ethnic conflict in multinational states and empires.[8] On the other hand, this contribution investigates how the nationalizing reform discourse affected economic policymaking, focusing particularly on the case of Soviet Estonia which, following the sovereignty declaration of November 1988, pursued a clearly nationally defined foreign economic policy. Political economists, on their part, have failed to fully grasp the impact of nationalist political mobilization on strategic economic policy choices, referring to the allegedly intangible rationale behind it.[9] Following our 'varieties of economic nationalism' approach, this chapter concludes with a comparative outlook, relating Estonia's national economic strategies, which, as those of other small nation states discussed in this volume, combined statist-protectionist with hyper-liberal measures, to those of its Baltic neighbours, which developed a similar small-state-like behaviour under the conditions of perestroika.

National rights and economic disempowerment

As the world's first communist state, the USSR was by its 1922 constitution conceived as a multinational federation, based on the idea of the equality of its constituent nationalities and structured into nominally sovereign ethno-territorial units. Although the Bolsheviks promoted the vision of a 'new man' with a post-national identity, later pejoratively dubbed as *homo sovieticus*, they purposefully turned to the nationalist toolbox to engineer one of the biggest socio-economic experiments in the history of mankind. A paradox at first glance, the Marxist-Leninist playbook considered the consolidation of national awareness a key precondition for the realization of internationalist goals. Once all Soviet ethnicities had reached national consciousness, the reasoning went, this would eventually be replaced by a class consciousness that superseded ethno-national divides. Hence, the Leninist regime proceeded to 'implement the principle of ethnofederalism on an unparalleled scale and to an unprecedented degree of systematization',[10] forging tactical alliances with separatist movements harbouring own state-building aspirations and ethnic groups that counted among the former colonial subjects of the czars. Replacing the supranational imperial regime, in which all ethnic groups, including the Russians themselves, had been subject to an autocratic monarch, Soviet ethno-federalism provided the illusion of a kind of home rule, simulated by a systematically replicated corpus of autochthonous educational and cultural institutions.

In the Stalinist USSR, its official status as a voluntary federation of equal ethno-national republics remained unchanged. In practice, however, the logic of strict power hierarchies prevailed, feeding on the heritage of centuries of centralist rule over territories acquired by military conquest. When the Red Army invaded, occupied and annexed the neutral Baltic states during the Second World War, the attempts of upholding any semblance of voluntary accession were half-hearted. Strategic key posts of republican rule were filled with emissaries from Moscow and the former political elites killed, deported or muted by other means. The agricultural and industrial landscape was distorted beyond recognition through collectivization and nationalization, while exports were redirected from Western Europe to the domestic market, lastingly binding the Baltic SSRs to the other federal republics to a degree that by far surpassed 'normal conditions in market economies'.[11] Many of the Baltic states' pre-war achievements, by contrast, such as educational systems up to university level in the local languages, were preserved in the spirit of Leninism. Estonians, Latvians and Lithuanians were formally recognized as the titular nationalities of three new federal subjects, which with slight territorial modifications mimicked the geographical contours of the formerly sovereign republics. Although these national attributes essentially remained an empty shell, the false semblance of sovereignty would turn out to have 'unanticipated consequences for ethnic mobilization'.[12]

The sovereign statehood of Estonia, Latvia and Lithuania had been systematically destroyed, but the interwar republics lived an afterlife as a kind of 'ghost states', whose forced incorporation into the USSR had never been legally recognized by most Western democracies, within a federation of ethno-territorial republics, the majority of which lacked a similar historical heritage of nation and state building. This did not seem to have any practical significance during the Stalinist period, which left little 'room for articulation, left alone full-scale pursuit, of national and territorial interests'.[13] As the country woke up from paralysis after Joseph Stalin's death in 1953 and a new leadership aimed at getting out of the deadlock, however, the situation changed. While the strong political verticality of the party state remained sacrosanct, the post-Stalinist Thaw left limited space for critical debates about the command economy system and the harmful effects of over-bureaucratization, which was identified as a major obstacle to economic growth and plan fulfilment. Unlike in Poland or Hungary, where home-grown communist elites attempted a thorough reform of the Marxist-Leninist model, economists in the USSR remained restricted by ideological mind cuffs. Soviet economic reforms did not expand beyond the field of management and administration, leaving the intrinsic dysfunctionalities of central planning untouched. However, given that every administrative reform contained an inherent regional component, this small opening was enough to reveal the corrosive potential of the ethno-federal model, as was demonstrated by the so-called *sovnarkhoz* experiment, which for a limited period elevated the union republics to the level of economic units in their own right.

Nikita Khrushchev's reform programme, which was launched in 1957, owed its name to the regional economic councils (*sovety narodnogo khozyaistva*) that were appointed to supervise a set of newly established, spatially defined economic entities. The transition towards a territorial system of economic administration revolutionized the Soviet tradition of subdividing the domestic economy into industrial branches and largely followed the demarcations of the USSR's ethno-territorial polities with the exception of Russia proper, Kazakhstan, Ukraine and Uzbekistan, which were further split into smaller units. All other regional economic councils, or *sovnarkhozes*, were directly subordinated to their respective republic's Council of Ministers, which granted the republican elites an unprecedented degree of economic autonomy. For the first time since their occupation and annexation, also the Baltic SSRs were granted decision-making authority over their own industrial production, which, within a decade after the onset of the *sovnarkhoz* reform, enabled them to double their productivity and to 'equal their pre-war level of production and standard of living'.[14] The Balts thus convincingly illustrated how administrative decentralization could help to overcome the detrimental impact of the 'bureaucratic dead-weight'[15] of the central ministries in Moscow and its unwanted side effects, such as inefficient resource allocation and industrial stagnation.

The operational autonomy of the republican governments remained restricted by a string of regulations. At the sub-level of districts and rayons, by contrast, which were often dominated by autochthons, economic power increasingly shifted to the non-Russian republics' constituent nationalities.[16] Although the *sovnarkhoz* reform efficiently channelled the dammed-up frustration among local leaders, who under the old economic regime had been held accountable for their republics' economic performance without possessing the necessary control and resources to fulfil the targets set by the centre, there was another side to the medal. Early into the reform process, regional economic councils from Latvia through Ukraine to Georgia displayed tendencies of over-allocating centrally supplied resources to their own republics and hoarding them, thus mimicking the economic survival strategy employed by most Soviet enterprise managers vis-à-vis the industrial ministries in Moscow.[17] The non-Russian republics, which due to their institutional skeleton of political and cultural institutions shared many traits with sovereign states, thus gradually metamorphosed into what Yoshiko Herrera has labelled 'imagined economies',[18] filling the empty shell of republican proto-statehood with new meaning as the peripheral elites started to actively 'bolster their *national* economies'[19] (emphasis added).

Fearing for the internal cohesion of the federation, Moscow eventually halted the experiment in order to hinder further national fragmentation of economic interests and governance. Starting from 1962, republican authority was heavily curtailed and smaller *sovnarkhozes* merged into supra-republican regional economic councils to prevent similar forms of localist particularism. After Khrushchev's replacement with hardliner Leonid Brezhnev in 1964, the reinstallation of the old economic order, based on the administration of production branches rather than territorial units, gathered pace. Special commissions tasked with the liquidation of the *sovnarkhozes* organized the re-subordination of enterprises to their respective industrial branch ministries, thereby ensuring that most of the decision-making power remained with the central authorities.[20] The Communist Party leadership in Moscow even went as far as discussing the abolition of the ethno-territorial model altogether, assessing proposals opting for the administrative redivision of the Soviet land mass along strictly economic lines or the merging of the three Baltic SSRs into a single supranational entity.[21] At the end of the day, the constitutionally grounded 'formal political architecture of the state as a federation of sovereign national republics'[22] remained intact, although it would repeatedly come under scrutiny even in the following decades. The ephemeral experience of quasi-national economic autonomy thus taught the non-Russian elites the important lesson that Moscow always prized its political self-interest above economic arguments, even at the cost of inefficiency and stagnation.

The nationalizing rhetoric of economic state building

Despite the curtailing of nationalist expression, which hindered the emergence of national communisms of the Polish or Hungarian type in the Soviet Union, 'the state related features of economic nationalism developed strongly' in the Baltic SSRs.[23] The long-serving chairman of the Lithuanian Communist Party Antanas Sniečkus in particular managed to shield his republic from the most harmful effects of Soviet over-industrialization and successfully used his good standing in Moscow's corridors of power to promote Lithuanian industries and production.[24] Even Estonia, which had suffered much more from Stalin's megalomaniac industrialization policies and experienced greater Russification through the ensuing mass influx of blue-collar workers from other parts of the USSR, managed, at least to a certain degree, to stake out an own economic agenda. The *sovnarkhoz* experiment had not only proven the superiority of local management schemes in terms of efficiency and output but also ignited a 'renaissance' of Estonian economic thought and the formation of republican expert cadres.[25] Economic experiments, developed by Estonian economists and planners, were conducted on a smaller scale throughout the 1970s and 1980s within selected branches, mostly in Estonia's agricultural and light-industry sectors. As the industrially and technologically most advanced republic with the highest living standards in the Soviet Union, Estonia soon developed into Moscow's favourite laboratory of economic reform. Considered to be too small to fail, it provided an ideal testing ground for experimental pilot projects that, if their outcome turned out favourably, could be expanded to the USSR as a whole. Little surprisingly, it was thus in Estonia that the idea of economic home rule resurfaced after the advent of perestroika, although in a much more radical form and under considerably more advantageous political circumstances.

The master narrative of Estonia's Singing Revolution is primarily focused on the dissident-led mass gatherings and the role of heritage activists and collective counter-memory as powerful antidotes to the official Soviet myths of voluntary accession to the USSR and age-old Estonian-Russian friendship. One of its most emblematic symbols remains the Baltic Way, a human chain that on the fiftieth anniversary of the Molotov-Ribbentrop Pact in August 1989 stretched from Vilnius through Riga to Tallinn over a distance of six hundred kilometres, with Estonians, Latvians and Lithuanians jointly waving their pre-war tricolours and singing patriotic tunes in a peaceful protest for the restoration of their lost statehood. The significance of relative economic deprivation as a key factor behind popular mobilization features less prominently in this narrative, although it was precisely the imbalances of the command economy system and the preponderance of the industrial ministries in Moscow that ignited the initial spark for a mass movement whose centrifugal forces would eventually contribute to bringing down the USSR.

The seminal event was a live broadcast aired on Estonian television in February 1987, in which a Moscow official announced the central government's plan to launch a gigantic mining project to explore the rich phosphorite deposits in Estonia's northeast. Unofficial expert reports of respiratory diseases among children living in the vicinity of the Maardu phosphorite mines near Tallinn were already circulating.[26] Concerns were soon openly voiced by an ever-broader coalition of university students, intellectuals and local Communist Party officials, who feared that large swaths of Estonian land would be turned into a moonscape if Moscow's plans were to be implemented. Societal discontent eventually erupted into the first non-dissident mass protest in Soviet Estonia, which went into history as the 'phosphorite war'.[27] Similarly as in neighbouring Latvia, where protesters mobilized against the plan of the central ministries to erect a giant hydroelectric power plant on the river Daugava near Daugavpils, the 'phosphorite war' turned into a trailblazer of glasnost. The focus of the increasingly critical public debate soon shifted away from the phosphorite issue to a more general discussion on the nature of centre-republic relations. The mining project, the argument went, would only reinforce Estonia's 'exaggerated and thus inadvisable [industrial] specialization' within the Soviet economy, which reminded, as a protest letter signed by the rector of Tartu State University claimed, of the lopsided economic development in many Third World countries.[28]

Mikhail Gorbachev's visit to Estonia that same month did little to appease public anger. The Soviet leader lauded Estonia's economic performance in his encounters with local workers, enterprise directors and nomenklatura members. Yet he did not refrain from mentioning the generous subsidies from the central budget that, as he insinuated, worked to the advantage of the republic. The net worth of Estonian exports to the all-union market, he claimed, amounted up to two and a half million roubles, while resources and commodities worth three million roubles reached the Estonian SSR via interrepublican barter.[29] Gorbachev's statement was a prime example of the 'imperial view' that Moscow shared with other metropolises of multinational empires, highlighting the alleged inherent benefits for small areas of being part of larger economic polities.[30] For the Estonians, however, the claim that their republic despite its record-breaking output numbers constituted a financial burden was nothing but an insult. Local experts contested the accuracy of the figures, although they had little concrete evidence at hand to disprove them, as federal republics did not exist as autonomous economic units in Soviet statistics and reliable data on interrepublican commodity exchange were lacking.[31] With an annual deficit of five hundred million roubles, however, as an Estonian Communist Party official calculated, the republic would have accumulated an estimated debt of twenty billion roubles during the past four decades which, as he pointed out, would surmount the indebtedness of any developing country in the world.[32]

The unfolding controversy about who was subsidizing whom shared common traits with the long-simmering tensions in the Yugoslav federation, where all constituent republics, Serbia included, felt constantly economically deprived.[33] In the Soviet context, by contrast, where factual political and economic federalism remained a chimera, it was first under the impact of glasnost that union republics could be discursively imagined as a 'measurable economic space'.[34] The conceptualization of the Estonian SSR as an economic entity in its own right was manifested and elaborated in a reform proposal drafted by a group of 'closet reformers within the establishment',[35] which was published in the Soviet Estonian daily *Edasi* in September 1987 and became commonly known as the 'Four-Man Proposal' (*nelja mehe ettepanek*).[36] Designed as a constructive contribution to Gorbachev's programmatic goal of decentralizing the overregulated Soviet economy, the proposal recommended the abolishment of interrepublican barter in favour of monetary trade for the sake of greater transparency, the expansion of the union republics' autonomous foreign economic relations and the introduction of a convertible currency.[37] In practice, however, the reform outline aimed for nothing less than the 're-establish[ment of] the Estonian nation as master of the Estonian territory'.[38] Evoking the inherently ethno-federal structure of the USSR, the vividly debated proposal 'provided a sense of territoriality'[39] that had been largely absent from economic debates since the dissolution of the regional economic councils two decades earlier.

The economic demarcation vis-à-vis the domestic Soviet market, which started from the 'Four-Man Proposal' and picked up pace with the establishment of the Estonian Popular Front by the proposal's initiator Edgar Savisaar in spring 1988, was accompanied by an increasingly nationalizing rhetoric that paved the way for the Western-oriented economic reform path of late- and post-Soviet Estonia. The gap between centre and periphery widened in the course of Gorbachev's ambitious reform agenda, which also included the introduction of cooperatives. Designed as collectively owned businesses based on 'socialist property', as the regime highlighted in an effort to gloss over the de facto legalization of private economic activity,[40] these micro-enterprises were to raise the overall efficiency in the country by offering economic incentives to its citizens. Soon after the first cooperatives started to emerge in late 1986, the Estonian, Lithuanian, Latvian and Moldavian SSRs, all of which had been forcibly annexed to the USSR during the Second World War, topped the list of union republics with the highest per capita number of cooperatives.[41] Ideological resistance against the taboo-breaking reform, by contrast, was particularly evident in the Soviet heartland, where the strong Marxist-Leninist stand against 'non-labour profit', earned by many cooperatives by simply buying and reselling goods, merged with the traditional 'dislike of pure moneymaking' in Christian Orthodoxy.[42]

Many Estonians remained suspicious of the anti-capitalist reflexes and the rejection of entrepreneurial initiative among the sizeable Russian-speaking community in their republic. 'We Baltic people', as an Estonian teacher put it, 'are more accustomed to making our own decisions and running our own lives than the Slavs'. Russians, by contrast, knew only 'serfdom and communism', lacking the formative historical experience of free enterprise.[43] Opinions of this kind frequently occurred in the unfolding debate on economic imbalances, which not only fostered the transformation of the Estonian SSR into an 'imagined economy', to once again use the concept proposed by Herrera, but also yielded an 'imagined national economic "culture" '[44] as a key factor of economic state-building processes at the dusk of Soviet power. On the one hand, this nationalizing rhetoric reflected the experience of living in a showcase republic of economic innovation with an own tradition of thinking outside the Soviet box. On the other hand, it highlighted the long-term impact of historical trajectories, which distinguished the Balts from the Russians. Estonians cultivated their self-image as a hard-working nation with a centuries-old mercantile tradition, which, as a Western correspondent sensed, lived on in the guise of a still prevalent air of 'pleasant, almost Germanic efficiency',[45] and living memories of sovereign statehood and market economy.

Given Estonia's advanced level of industrial development and high living standards compared to most other union republics, some authors doubt that economic grievances had a major mobilizing effect during the Singing Revolution.[46] Yet for most Estonians, being the 'best pupils in an admittedly very bad class'[47] was hardly satisfactory, particularly as they considered neither Russia proper nor the Caucasus or Central Asia as a point of reference for assessing their level of economic advancement. Much like Hungarians or Czechs, they tended to compare their situation to that of their capitalist neighbours, in particular the Finns, with whom they shared linguistic and cultural similarities. Finnish television could be received in northern Estonia and weekenders from nearby Helsinki were a common sight on the streets of Tallinn since the resumption of the ferry route across the narrow Gulf in 1965. Finland thus served as a kind of 'mirror, mirror, on the wall'[48] for Estonia, similarly as West Germany did for the

GDR, not least as the Finnish and Estonian economies had been at a comparable level before the outbreak of the Second World War. Seen from this perspective, the promise of progress and modernity, a cornerstone of the Soviet regime's self-imposed civilizing mission, faltered. A look north across the Gulf exposed the tangible misery and drabness of the Soviet smokestack industries, economic mismanagement and chronic shortages, but it also gave a glimpse into the life that Estonians might have lived if they had been spared the tragedy of Soviet occupation.[49] The 'stolen future' narrative became an effective rhetoric tool to frame the annexation as a historical injustice and the Soviet economic model as alien to Estonian traditions and intrinsically detrimental to local interests.

The public debate about the imbalances between core and periphery not only questioned the USSR's self-image as a bearer of civilization, which in itself was a remnant of the imperial Russian tradition. Evoking another parallel to czarist autocracy, it also targeted directly at the very core of Marxist-Leninist ideology. Already during the first street rallies of the 'phosphorite war', protesters openly accused the industrial ministries in Moscow of 'colonial thinking',[50] which accentuated the perception of the central government as an extractive empire that showed complete disregard for local interests and grievances. The topos of the Soviet Union as a colonial power originally emerged in the West in the 1950s, at the peak of the Cold War, and resurfaced in the writings of the Ukrainian nationalist underground at the onset of Brezhnev's reign.[51] From the early 1970s onwards, even Estonian dissidents frequently addressed the persistent aftermath of 'Russian imperialism', linking their own liberation struggle to the fight for national self-determination in the decolonizing Third World. Under the impact of glasnost, eventually, nationalities across the USSR 'became more conscious of being subjects within an empire rather than perceiving themselves as voluntary participants within a state'.[52] From the industrially more developed republics, such as the Baltic SSRs, to the Central Asian republics with their '"neo-colonial" cotton monoculture',[53] the rhetoric of colonial exploitation took root as a device to express dammed-up discontent with economic imbalances against the central government.

Anti-imperialism had been a cornerstone of Soviet propaganda since the USSR's foundation. Soviet ethno federalism was praised as a way to illuminate post-revolutionary Russia's nations-to-be and to elevate them to the level of national self-determination, offering an alternative to the subjugation of subordinate ethnicities as practised by Western imperial-colonial powers.[54] Estonian writer Aivo Lõhmus, however, did not consider Soviet colonialism to be an oxymoron. 'I am not an economist, so I don't know what is required to define a country as a colony', he stated at a public plenary in Tallinn in April 1988. 'But a republic in which ninety percent of the economy is not controlled by the republican government still seems to be a colony to me. Whether it is a matter of socialist or capitalist colonialism is of secondary importance.'[55] Hence, while Moscow adhered to an 'imperial view', stressing the economic benefits for small nations being part of larger multinational polities, local actors primarily focused on the entailing 'costs of domination in material and cultural life'.[56] Seen from the perspective of the small Baltic SSRs, a worrying side effect of Moscow's megalomaniac industrial development projects was, apart from the catastrophic ecological repercussions, the massive influx of Russian-speakers, which since the 1940s had changed the ethnic composition to the disadvantage of the autochthons particularly in Estonia and Latvia. Vilified as the '"civil garrison" of the occupying power',[57] the nationalizing Estonian debate framed the Russian-speaking immigrant workers as a privileged cast, highlighting their unjust preferential treatment regarding the allotment of modern apartments or the overall predominance of the Russian language in public life. In this vein, the predominantly Russian-speaking 'red barons' on Estonian collective and state farms inherited the traditional supremacy of the Baltic Germans as the 'new landlords',[58] which rhetorically linked the older, national-romantic topos of age-old oppression by foreign powers since the conquest of the Teutonic Order to current life under hammer and sickle.

'Small is beautiful'

The Estonian SSR was famed throughout the Soviet Union for its well-developed infrastructure and production sites that yielded consumer goods of relatively high quality and unusually attractive design. The colonial trope thus served a different discursive function than in, for instance, the Central Asian SSRs, which despite their integration into a nominally federalist system as mere raw material producers experienced a similar level of dependency on the metropolitan centre as Europe's former overseas colonies, and where popular discontent, accordingly, morphed into what might be categorized as classical 'anticolonial nationalism'.[59] By contrast, the Estonian debate about Moscow's allegedly extractive policies evoked a collective feeling of largely *perceived* relative economic deprivation, amplified by the highly ethnicized 'us and them' rhetoric and the 'stolen future' discourse. As sociologists following the internal colonial school have claimed, 'the strength of separatist orientation is seen to depend more on perception of relative deprivation than on demonstrable evidence of exploitation',[60] which explains why the erosion of the USSR, similarly as in Yugoslavia, started from the most developed parts of the federation. In the Estonian case, the very real experience of Brezhnev's Russification campaigns and the Russian 'elder-brother patronization of the USSR's smaller peoples'[61] merged with bottled-up frustration over the palpable consequences of the strictly centralized hierarchies of economic decision-making. This mixture developed a life of its own, triggering vocal public support for the ideas presented in the 'Four-Man Proposal', which argued for injecting the empty shell of republican quasi-statehood with new meaning.

The debate on greater economic and, as the limits of the discourse expanded, even political autonomy moved towards a peak in autumn 1988, following a long summer of mass gatherings and patriotic song festivals that earned the Singing Revolution its name. The, at first glance, rather technocratic nature of the discussion on how to revive the ailing Soviet economy through regional initiative barely masked its underlying anti-imperial implications. Echoing the formative experience of centuries of domination by alien economic elites, which the Estonians shared with many other nations of Central and Eastern Europe, the initially rational tone of the reformers gave way to a much more radical 'ideology of becoming "master of one's own house"',[62] fuelled by the harshly anti-Soviet rhetoric of the dissident-led opposition movement which increasingly set the agenda of the public discourse. The point of culmination was the adoption of a declaration on sovereignty by the Soviet Estonian Supreme Soviet in November 1988, which turned the established hierarchy upside down by authorizing the republic's highest state, governmental and judicial organs to wield power over the territory of the Estonian SSR. While the USSR Constitution, which guaranteed the formal sovereignty of the federal units, equated state ownership with ownership of the supranational Soviet people, the Estonian declaration employed the notion of republican and thus, implicitly, national ownership, subordinating all of Estonia's natural resources, industries and the entire building stock and infrastructure to local control. Unilaterally shifting the 'standing of "sovereignty" from a vertical (class struggle) to horizontal (inter-state) plane',[63] the local government thus converted the formalized but largely insignificant borders of the ethno-territorial republic into the contours of a politically subordinate yet economically autonomous polity.

The 1988 declaration, which swiftly found favour with republican elites across the USSR's non-Russian peripheries, largely followed the ideas outlined in the 1987 'Four-Man Proposal' as a blueprint for the protectionist vision of a closed, proto-national economy within the Soviet framework. Only full local control, as the reform-oriented republican leadership argued, would allow Estonia to reach a level of progress and efficiency that matched the economic potential of its workforce and production units. A new set of economic laws, which partly contradicted all-union legislation, continued Gorbachev's by then increasingly hesitant reform path of decentralization and marketization. Putting private entrepreneurs on an equal legal footing with state-owned companies, Estonia was first in the USSR to initiate the turn from 'big factory thinking' to small entrepreneurship, laying the foundation for Estonia's future reputation as a trailblazer of post-Soviet transformation. Already at an early stage of perestroika, Estonian economists had launched the so-called small enterprise reform, a pilot project in the light-industry sector setting up production units with a maximum of fifty employees to test their efficiency in competition with larger enterprises.[64] By autumn 1988, however, small entrepreneurship had acquired a highly symbolic significance beyond the logics of efficiency and productivity. Stalinist smokestack modernization, as one of the signatories of the 'Four-Man Proposal' stated, had littered the republic with giant dinosaur industries that were at odds with the 'Estonian tradition of production'.[65] Estonia's turn towards an economic model based on small and medium-sized enterprises thus not only marked a reorientation towards the 'developed economies' in the West, where this form of economic activity prevailed, as Estonian economist and reform advocate Erik Terk highlighted.[66] The broad public support for the bottom-up rise of small entrepreneurship also reflected the long-term persistence of the 'petty bourgeois ideal of peasants, craftsmen, and shopkeepers that represented the normality of the interwar period'[67] among Estonian society. 'Small is beautiful' was thus essentially an economic credo as much as a political one, which cemented the inherent incompatibility of Estonia's national economic interests with those of the Soviet federation as a whole.

One of the revolutionary features of perestroika was the opening up of the Soviet market to global capital. Domestic economic change thus went hand in hand with embryonic globalization processes. The Kremlin had begun to realize that large-scale technological transfers and hard-currency inflows through foreign direct investments were the only way out of a deadlock of stagnation that had begun to threaten the stability of the regime. Compared to pioneers such as Poland or Hungary, the USSR was certainly a late bloomer of socialist globalization. However, as it coincided with Gorbachev's mission to decentralize the Soviet economy, the combined effect was tremendous, especially along the Soviet Union's western peripheries. The Baltic SSRs with their relatively sophisticated production apparatuses and operating sea ports, which channelled much of the USSR's exports to the West, were naturally suited to stand at the vanguard of Soviet globalization. Accordingly, Estonia was the first federal republic with an own foreign trade association established in early 1987, with Latvia and Lithuania following suit. Although these associations only supervised a small section of local exports, they reinforced the standing of the Baltic republics as self-managing economic entities, which significantly boosted the ongoing state-building processes in the region.

In Gorbachev's USSR, geography again mattered. The Balts thus primarily focused on neighbouring Sweden and Finland as their preferred economic partners, not least as they could draw on an already existing network of economic linkages across the Baltic Sea. Estonia in particular had gathered ample experience in dealing with partners from capitalist countries due to its uniquely close connection with Finland. In the years preceding perestroika, leading Estonian light-industry enterprises had engaged in several joint production schemes as contractors for Finnish companies, and even the transnationally operating Swedish furniture retailer IKEA regularly commissioned Estonian manufacturers to produce wooden bookshelves on its behalf.[68] The roots of Nordic-Baltic border trade stretched even further back in time. As in the case of Slovenia's and Croatia's border trade with Austria and Italy,[69] first bilateral agreements between Finland and the Baltic SSRs had been signed already in the late 1960s. Similar treaties with Sweden entered into force in early 1985. Being net importers of processed food and soft goods, the Nordic neighbours offered an outlet for the Baltic textile and agri-food industries, while scarce foodstuff, paper pulp and building material were imported in return via barter.[70] From 1988 onwards, the trade turnover exponentially grew, as did the Finnish and Swedish inflow of capital investments into the region, particularly to Estonia, which established much closer ties across the Baltic Sea than Latvia with its large Moscow-controlled heavy industry sector and still primarily agricultural Lithuania.

Estonia thus became one of the most vibrant laboratories of Soviet globalization which, seen from the Baltic perspective, was rather a process of macro-regionalization that laid the ground for the nascent Nordic-Baltic market. The rapid economic integration across political divides eminently served the small-state interests of Sweden and Finland as well, as both were looking for a new role in a rapidly changing world. Losing its monopoly as one of Moscow's key foreign economic partners, Finland expanded its presence on the Baltic market in an effort to maintain its traditional position as an 'East-West trading giant'.[71]

Sweden, on the other hand, aimed at securing its influence and soft power on the continent in view of the dynamic rapprochement between the blocs, using its historical links and strategic gateways to the Baltic region. Although Sweden in many respects acted as a 'great power' vis-à-vis the three (re-)emerging Baltic nation states,[72] echoing its imperial presence in the region centuries earlier, the swiftly intensifying Nordic-Baltic economic and trade relations established a new pattern of mutually beneficial small-state cooperation already before the independence of the Baltic republics was formally restored in August 1991. Sweden and Finland came to play a key role in the economic but also political transformation of Estonia, Latvia and Lithuania (in that order), leaving distinctly 'Nordic hallmarks' on the normative and legislative foundations of the three nascent market economies and parliamentary democracies.[73]

Soviet Estonia's path of economic globalization, which threw the republican economy wide open to Nordic investors, trade partners and economic expert advisers,[74] stood in stark contrast to its Eastern 'foreign' economic policies. Beginning from the sovereignty declaration, the republican leadership pursued a policy of demarcation from the all-union market, although it turned out to be a Herculean task to dissolve the intricate economic interdependencies between the Soviet Union's federal units. One of the first measures was to halt the unabated influx of Russian-speaking workers into the republic, which threatened to thwart any effort to increase local economic autonomy. Already from early 1988 onwards, Estonia imposed a penalty tax of 16,000 roubles on local companies for each recruited newcomer,[75] which was unparalleled anywhere else in the USSR. Further protectionist measures aimed at rationing scarce products by restricting their uncontrolled outflow and sale to non-residents.[76] This directly affected particularly the masses of Leningraders accustomed to stocking up their pantries during shopping trips across the Narva river, which marked the border between the Estonian SSR and the Leningrad Oblast. Vilnius applied similar measures, distributing buyer's cards among local residents to prevent commodities from being brought out of Lithuania.[77] From January 1990 onwards, all three Baltic republics started quoting and regulating the import and export of goods across republican borders by legal means.[78] The erection of customs barriers and tariff walls in the Baltic SSRs sharply contrasted with the global trend towards a liberal international order and the ongoing efforts by the European Community member states to create a single internal market. Setting up frontier customs posts along the republican borders, however, was a key element of economic state building in the region, further accelerating the transformation of the Baltic 'imagined economies' into fully fledged national economies in their own right.

With Moscow effectively controlling the external borders of the Baltic republics through the all-union customs agencies at airports and commercial harbours, the republican governments still lacked the means to gain complete economic sovereignty, which prevented them from fully realizing their potential of trade and economic cooperation with the West. Many of the protectionist measures thus had a merely declarative-political character. Accordingly, the vast majority of respondents in a representative survey carried out among leading Estonian managers and top executives in 1990 declared that closing the internal Soviet border should be the number one priority of Tallinn's economic reform policies.[79] With increasingly determined separatist movements mushrooming across the USSR, a series of 'economic wars' eventually broke out throughout the Soviet peripheries. Republican governments from Tallinn to Tashkent increasingly refused to participate in the strictly centralized Soviet system of redistribution, applying a variety of measures to halt the outflow of republican production for the artificially low prices set by Moscow.[80] Throughout 1991, these demarcation processes contributed to consolidating the Baltic republics' land borders, until the turmoil following the failed Moscow coup and the subsequent restoration of Estonia's, Latvia's and Lithuania's pre-war statehood in August that same year sealed their ultimate economic and political divorce from the Soviet federation.

Conclusion

The sudden collapse of Europe's communist federations in the aftermath of the 1989 revolution and the virulent nationalist backlash took even well-informed outside observers by surprise. The ethno-national fault lines along which the federations eventually split up, however, had emerged much earlier, defying the officially propagated victory of communist internationalism over nationalist antagonisms. In the USSR, the constitution promised federal horizontality and granted each republic the right to secede, at least on paper. Yet unlike Yugoslavia, where the highly decentralizing 1974 constitution enabled its constituent republics to accumulate 'the resources necessary to act as virtually independent economic and political agents', the Soviet Union retained its 'asymmetric federalism' almost up to its dissolution.[81] Constituting the dominant Soviet ethnicity, Russians lacked their own ethno-national republic, given that the Russian SFSR itself mirrored the Soviet '*matryoshka* model of sovereignty' (emphasis in original),[82] hosting a multitude of autonomous republics and oblasts granted to minority groups that did not qualify for a union republic of their own due to their size or lack of national consciousness. As a consequence, Russian national identity merged with a supranational, pointedly 'Soviet' identity, cementing de facto Russian supremacy over the nominally sovereign non-Russian peoples. With the advent of glasnost, the rifts in the faux-federal system eventually came out in the open as dammed-up local grievances over economic imbalances morphed into nationalizing political disputes. The Estonian case serves as a perfect example of how a collective feeling of relative economic deprivation fuelled local demands for 'real' autonomy in both economic and political issues, thereby reanimating the original federal idea.

The nascent state-building processes in the perestroika-era USSR disproved the fundamental assumption of Leninism that the removal of the basis for capitalist exploitation also entailed the elimination of the roots of national conflicts.[83] Similarly as during the *sovnarkhoz* experiment, it was the Kremlin itself that unintentionally strengthened ethno-particularist tendencies along the Soviet fringes by partially empowering the republican governments in domestic and, in line with Moscow's globalizing ambitions, even foreign economic matters. The Soviet Union's ethno-territorial foundation now worked in favour of the non-Russian nationalities, which were increasingly determined to bring their constitutionally granted sovereignty to life. From 1990 onwards, as separatist mobilization accelerated from the Baltic Sea to the Central Asian steppes, the USSR eventually transformed, similarly as Yugoslavia, into a 'state of states'.[84] The erosion of central authority was particularly tangible in the Baltic SSRs, which by spring 1990 had shed the attribute 'Soviet' in their self-designation, reinstated their pre-war tricolours, elevated their native tongues to the status of official languages and transformed their Soviet-era puppet foreign ministries into institutions that efficiently served distinctly national and not all-union interests on an international stage. The creation of quasi-national economies was the last missing step towards proto-statehood for the Baltic republics, which now displayed 'the full characteristics of independent states that have lost their independence'.[85]

Gorbachev's dual reform agenda of decentralizing and globalizing the Soviet economy revealed the vast 'differences in economic development and market readiness'[86] in the USSR, which even exceeded the already substantial North-South gap in the Yugoslav federation. Far from all union republics were capable of developing proto-state-like features before the collapse of the Soviet Union in 1991. Particularly the Central Asian economies were so inextricably linked to the all-union distribution and supply chain that local demands for greater autonomy stopped short of sovereign statehood.[87] Hence, the case of the Baltic SSRs, just like that of Slovenia or Croatia, suggests that there is a close correlation between economic advancement and the degree of separatist mobilization in multinational states. While less developed regions risked 'cutting themselves off from technology transfer, across to high-value added jobs and development subsidies',[88] economically superior parts were more likely to conclude that they might be better off without the stagnant rest of the federation. Successful (proto-)national economy-building also presupposed a number of favourable conditions such as the ability to produce exportable goods, a functioning infrastructure and proximity to potential new markets. There is also reason to assume that size was a determining factor. It is certainly no coincidence that Estonia and Slovenia, which counted among the smallest republics of their respective federations, came closest to resemble fully fledged national economies by the end of the 1980s and gained a similar reputation as foreriders of transformation in the entire post-socialist space after 1991. Despite Western scepticism regarding the ability of the small Baltic economies to survive on the rapidly globalizing world market, smallness proved to be a strategic advantage in times of comprehensive economic and political changes, while less flexible larger entities such as Ukraine, which in terms of resources and industrial potential had much better starting conditions than the Baltic republics, remained firmly stuck in the federal superstructure.

Estonia, Latvia and Lithuania coordinated their agendas to a degree that the vision of a self-managing republican economy outlined in the 'Four-Man Proposal' soon came to figure as the 'Baltic model' in the pan-Soviet reform discourse. Accordingly, the Baltic SSRs are often summarily treated in the literature on perestroika, which is mirrored by the generalizing approach of transitologists and IPE scholars to the post-1991 transformation paths of Estonia, Latvia and Lithuania.[89] The economic strategies implemented by the republican governments to secure their national interests vis-à-vis the central government, however, differed in a number of key respects. The question whether small nations thrive best as open or closed economies has for centuries been a matter of scholarly dispute.[90] Estonia's strategy, by contrast, followed a dual approach, combining ultra-protectionist with hyper liberal measures. Opening up its economy to primarily Nordic investors from 1988 onwards, Estonia not only showed a clear determination to reintegrate into a macro-region it considered itself and aspired to be part of historically and culturally. Amidst the geopolitical turbulences of the late 1980s, Nordic investments also served as a necessary life insurance in troubled and unpredictable times following the credo of Poland's

President Lech Wałęsa, who famously stated that 'having a Frenchman or Englishman here with his factory is like having a division of troops'.[91]

Tallinn held on to its firm belief in free trade and capital movement even during privatization, although the habit of Nordic investors to buy up and close down some of the largest local enterprises not always seemed to benefit national economic interest,[92] which illustrates that Estonia's economic U-turn to the West did not necessarily follow the logic of the market alone but was also considered a precondition for national survival. The parallel, strictly protectionist stance towards the Soviet market followed a different logic. Protecting the domestic market and industries necessitated the erection of an economic curtain eastwards to shield Estonia from Moscow's harmful influence. Throughout the early 1990s, Estonia determinedly continued the dismantling of its economic ties with the post-Soviet space, 'even in cases where economic reasoning suggested that they should be maintained'.[93] Hence, by 1993, Estonia had become the first post-Soviet successor state with a number one trading partner outside the former USSR.[94] A contradiction at first glance, this dual approach between isolationism and expansionism, echoing Marvin Suesse's concept of the 'national dilemma' that defines this balancing act as the classical challenge faced by all economic nationalists,[95] reflected the cultural compass of most Estonians and the traditional 'belief of the Baltic peoples that they are more "advanced," more "western" and more "cultural" ' than their eastern neighbours, which went hand in hand with the self-image of being an 'extremely important bulwark against Russification'.[96] The Estonian case thus reaffirms the 'significant role that ideational factors play in economic policy',[97] shedding light on a nexus that is still underestimated in much of the political economy literature.

Lithuania's economic strategies followed a fundamentally different approach, despite the close cooperation and continuous exchange of ideas between the Baltic SSRs. Lithuanian reformers remained split over the sequence and nature of economic measures, which, as a consequence, lacked coherence and coordination. Moreover, the 'cruder manifestations of nationalism' in the southernmost Baltic republic threatened to thwart the transition towards an open-trade regime, which was indispensable for an economy of that size, as Western expert observers warned early on.[98] Yet the Lithuanian leadership developed a consistently protectionist mindset, at least in the initial state of Lithuania's path of economic transformation. With no ferry connection to the Nordic states and sharing only a small common border with Poland's structurally weak and impoverished northeast, Lithuania lacked the advantageous geography of its northern Baltic neighbour. Prior to 1991, investment and trade cooperation with

Western partners remained thus marginal, mirroring the neglectable position of the republic in earlier border trade arrangements with Finland and Sweden. Retreating into self-sufficiency, Lithuania dwelled in its 'Albanized'[99] state well into the 1990s and retained a sceptical distance towards foreign investments, nurtured by fears of selling out the homeland.[100] This hesitant attitude widened the North-South gap in the Baltics, delaying Lithuania's economic transformation and, subsequently, the decoupling from the Russian economy by several years.[101]

The contrasting cases of Estonia and Lithuania illustrate how largely similar nationalizing economic discourses were translated into diametrically opposed practical policies and foreign economic strategies. Fuelled by experiences of economic deprivation, nationalist mobilization can thus foster openness, innovation and transformation, but also erect walls and barriers that hamper economic progress, which strengthens the claim that economic nationalism as a term 'can be associated with a wide variety of politics'.[102] At the end of the day, however, Lithuania managed, just as Latvia, to catch up with Estonia, which had taken the lead as the USSR's primary laboratory of economic East-West cooperation. Joining the thriving Nordic-Baltic market, Lithuania proved, as Estonia had done before, that a small-state status in times of global economic changes not necessarily has to be synonymous with vulnerability and subjection to external forces. As several of the chapters in this volume corroborate, cross-border alliances between small states can actively contribute to cushioning the shockwaves of geopolitical and macroeconomic changes and to increasing their room of manoeuvre in a swiftly changing world.

Notes

The research was supported by the Swedish Research Council (grant number 2014–176) and the Anniversary Fund of the Austrian Central Bank (grant number 18271).

1 Leff, 'Democratization and Disintegration in Multinational States', 205.
2 Schulze and Wolf, 'Economic Nationalism and Economic Integration', 2.
3 Griffiths, *Age of Secession*, 119.
4 Pula, *Globalization under and after Socialism*, 78.
5 Berger and Fetzer, 'Introduction', 2.
6 Abdelal, *National Purpose in the World Economy*, 18; Tsygankov, *Pathways after Empire*, 205.
7 Albrecht, 'Economic Nationalism among German Bohemians', 17.

8 Schultz, 'Introduction', 9–10.
9 Lan and Li, 'The Economics of Nationalism', 296.
10 Roshwald, *Ethnic Nationalism and the Fall of Empires*, 171.
11 Hogan, 'Economic Reforms in the Sovereign States of the Soviet Union', 307.
12 Leff, 'Democratization and Disintegration in Multinational States', 210.
13 Herrera, *Imagined Economies*, 106.
14 Kasekamp, *A History of the Baltic States*, 136.
15 Brown, *The Gorbachev Factor*, 134.
16 Ericson, 'Soviet Economic Structure and the National Question', 246.
17 Nove, *An Economic History of the USSR*, 368.
18 Herrera, *Imagined Economies*.
19 Pihlamägi, 'Administrative Shakeup in Industry and Construction', 247.
20 The reversal of the *sovnarkhoz* reform, however, did not succeed to suffocate all forms of 'economic patriotism' among the republican elites in the non-Russian SSRs, as is illustrated by the Georgian kinship networks and the Uzbek cotton cartel which continued to thrive from the 1960s onwards. Suesse, *The Nationalist Dilemma*, 229.
21 Misiunas and Taagepera, *The Baltic States*, 150.
22 Roshwald, *Ethnic Nationalism and the Fall of Empires*, 176.
23 Schultz, 'Introduction', 24. As in much of the literature produced on the topic by economic historians and IPE scholars, Schultz here applies the traditional reductionist reading of economic nationalism as a synonym for protectionism.
24 Ibid., 25.
25 Juurak, 'Nii nagu see oli', 17.
26 Gerner and Hedlund, *The Baltic States and the End of the Soviet Empire*, 70–1.
27 Liivik, 'Glasnost Policy Reaching Estonia', 124.
28 Küng, *Estland vaknar*, 118.
29 'Estonia – Brief Review', report by the Socialist Union of Central-Eastern Europe for the Socialist International, March 1987. Arbetarrörelsens arkiv och bibliotek [The Labor Movement's Archive and Library], Stockholm, Johannes Mihkelson papers, archival number 2268, box 19, folder 2, p. 1.
30 Spechler, 'The Economic Advantages of Being Peripheral', 449.
31 Ahde and Rajasalu, 'On the Economic Structure of Estonia and Finland before the 1990s', 89–90.
32 'Ideed edasi areneda' (1987), *Edasi*, 16 October.
33 Lazarević, 'Economy and Nationalism in Yugoslavia', 275.
34 Fetzer, 'Nationalism and Economy', 968.
35 Taagepera, 'Estonia's Road to Independence', 16.
36 For a more detailed discussion of the proposal and its genesis, see Kevin Axe's contribution in this volume.

37 'Ettepanek: Kogu Eesti NSV täielikule isemajandamisele' (1987), *Edasi*, 26 September.
38 Miljan, 'The Proposal to Establish Economic Autonomy in Estonia', 151.
39 Beissinger, *Nationalist Mobilization and the Collapse of the Soviet State*, 119.
40 Peet Kask, 'Väikekooperatiivide päevaprobleeme', *Edasi*, 19 January 1987.
41 Sten Sjöström, 'Sovjets jantelag broms för företagsamhet', *Dagens Industri*, 4 February 1988.
42 Baysha, *The Mythologies of Capitalism and the End of the Soviet Project*, 94.
43 Lloyd Garrison, 'Old Nationalism, New Profits', *Time Magazine*, 15 December 1986.
44 Fetzer, 'Nationalism and Economy', 968.
45 Conor O'Clery, 'German-Style Efficiency Gets a Russian's Blessing', *The Irish Times*, 17 October 1988.
46 Emizet and Hesli, 'The Disposition to Secede', 501.
47 Lainela and Sutela, *The Baltic Economies in Transition*, 18.
48 Bren, 'Mirror, Mirror, on the Wall', 191.
49 Nielsen-Stokkeby, *Baltische Erinnerungen*, 281.
50 Küng, *Estland vaknar*, 117.
51 Zisserman-Brodsky, *Constructing Ethnopolitics in the Soviet Union*, 70.
52 Emizet and Hesli, 'The Disposition to Secede', 505.
53 Leff, 'Democratization and Disintegration in Multinational States', 212.
54 Roshwald, *Ethnic Nationalism and the Fall of Empires*, 177.
55 Küng, *Estland vaknar*, 97.
56 Spechler, 'The Economic Advantages of Being Peripheral', 449.
57 Smith, 'The Resurgence of Nationalism', 135.
58 Made, *Eesti ärkab*, 173.
59 Go and Watson, 'Anticolonial Nationalism', 36.
60 Emizet and Hesli, 'The Disposition to Secede', 496.
61 Lieven, 'Russian Empires', 33.
62 Schultz, 'Introduction', 9, 15.
63 Suyarkulova, 'Reluctant Sovereigns?' 131.
64 Venesaar and Vitsur, 'Development of Entrepreneurship in Estonia', 6.
65 Made, *Eesti ärkab*, 22.
66 *IME Bülletään* no. 15, Tallinn: Eesti Majandusministeerium, Eesti Majandusarengu Instituut, 5.
67 Åslund, *How Capitalism Was Built*, 188.
68 *Sveriges handel med Östeuropa och Sovjetunionen*, 106.
69 See Benedetto Zaccaria's contribution in this volume.
70 *Marknadsguide Sovjetunionen*, 92.
71 Reinikainen and Kivikari, 'On the Theory of East-West Economic Relations', 8.

72 As Janne Holmén states, 'a country can be a small state in relation to a larger state but act like a great power in relation to a smaller one'. Holmén, *Den politiska läroboken*, 17.
73 Bergman, 'Adjacent Internationalism', 73.
74 Stöcker, 'In the Spirit of Perestroika?' 599.
75 Piirimäe, 'Estonia "Has No Time"', 34.
76 'Economic Survey of the Baltic Republics', draft version of a report commissioned by the Swedish Foreign Ministry, June 1991. Immigration History Research Center Archives, University of Minnesota, Minneapolis, Joint Baltic American National Committee records, archival number 1143, box 49, folder 10, p. 58.
77 Ibid., 44.
78 A. Skoblov, 'Kaup sisse, kaup välja', *Äripäev*, 7–13 November 1990.
79 Nurmi and Üksvärav, 'How Estonian Managers Experienced the Transformation to Independence and Market Economy in 1990–1991', 175.
80 Suyarkulova, 'Reluctant Sovereigns?' 137.
81 Bunce, 'Peaceful Versus Violent State Dismemberment', 220.
82 Suyarkulova, 'Reluctant Sovereigns?' 130.
83 Connor, 'Eco- or Ethno-nationalism?' 348.
84 Leff, 'Democratization and Disintegration in Multinational States', 220.
85 Boris Strugatsky quoted in Sherlock, *Historical Narratives in the Soviet Union and Post-Soviet Russia*, 128.
86 Leff, 'Democratization and Disintegration in Multinational States', 217.
87 Suyarkulova, 'Reluctant Sovereigns?' 137.
88 Henry Hale quoted in Herrera, *Imagined Economies*, 39–40.
89 See, for instance, Tsygankov's clear distinction between the three Baltic peoples' consolidated national identity and the comparatively less marked national consciousness of Ukraine and Belarus and his approach to the connection between the rootedness of national otherness and foreign economic policymaking in *Pathways after Empire*.
90 Spechler, 'The Economic Advantages of Being Peripheral', 448.
91 Quoted in Šćepanović, 'National Interests and Foreign Direct Investments in East Central Europe after 1989', 215–16.
92 Kõll, 'Economy and Ethnicity in the Hands of the State', 377.
93 Jensen-Eriksen, 'Business, Economic Nationalism and Finnish Foreign Trade during the 19th and 20th Centuries', 54.
94 Ilves, 'Iseseisev Eesti riik maailmas', 340.
95 Suesse, *The Nationalist Dilemma*, 5.
96 Report entitled 'Nepasiduosim! 50 Years and Continuing', drafted by Jouzas A. Kazlas, 28 January 1988. Väliseesti Muuseum [Museum of Estonians Abroad], Toronto, Tõnu Parming papers, untitled folder, p. 1.

97 Helleiner, 'Conclusion', 220.
98 'Economic Survey of the Baltic Republics', 58.
99 Kokk, Aavo (1990), 'Kazimiera Prunskiene majandusprogramm võib lahendada Leedu sisepoliitilise kriisi', *Edasi*, 30 June.
100 Abdelal, *National Purpose in the World Economy*, 99.
101 Norkus, 'Võrdlev pilguheit Eesti, Läti ja Leedu postkommunistlikule arengule', 27, 29.
102 Helleiner, 'Conclusion', 220.

Part II

Going Global

3

'No games, just business': Luxembourg's varieties of economic nationalism

Thomas Kolnberger

Introduction

In socio-economic terms the 1960s–1980s marked an era of significant change in the history of Luxembourg. Until the oil price shock of 1973, an unprecedented period of economic growth known as 'The Glorious Thirty' (*Les Trente Glorieuses*) was in full swing.[1] During the 1970s, the Western world plunged into an international recession, putting an end to decades of overall post-war economic expansion. In Luxembourg, these years are not so much associated with the oil shock but the steel crisis. The recession in the global steel market hit the Grand Duchy's heavy industry sector hard in two consecutive waves in 1973–5 and again in the early 1980s. However, in hindsight this (in ancient Greek) *krísis* of the 1970s turned into *kairos*, 'the right, critical, or opportune moment' for structural change in the country: finance and service replaced steel as Luxembourg's economic lead sector while the importance of the heavy industry decreased significantly. The shared conviction that the recession was the prime mover, indeed, the actual driver for change led Luxembourg's political and economic elites to adopt a double strategy to achieve a viable solution for the national steel crisis. On the one hand, they sought to internationalize the challenge – in practice, to 'Europeanize' it. On the other hand, the smallness and cooperative tradition of the country made a closing of the ranks of all stakeholders – government and all political parties; employers and employees – in support for a shrunken and modernized primary industry possible.

Luxembourgers experienced the ensuing decades from the mid-1980s to the Global Financial Crisis of 2007/8 as *Les Vingt Splendides*. These 'twenty splendid years' represent another, though this time specific Luxembourgish era of economic upswing surpassing even the average economic growth rate of the post-war decades.[2] Revenues were (partly) redistributed in the guise of expanding welfare service as well as rising individual salaries and wages, trickling down into the pockets of the Grand Duchy's nationals and the growing number of foreign residents alike. This 'trickle-down' of national income was based on positive externalities generated by the node of global finance, which Luxembourg had become. Still, the lion's share of the profits has ever since been fed back into the relentless circulation of global capital flows in order to buttress Luxembourg's comparative advantage as an international financial centre (IFC).

This chapter reviews Luxembourg's economic history and the variety of capitalism the national economy adapted to during the transformation of the 1960s–1980s. The guiding question of the chapter is the 'classical' subject of Small State-Studies: Does Size Matter or Not?[3] This question includes an often overlooked corollary, namely the economy or diseconomy of scales. The simple meaning of economies of scales is doing things more efficiently with increasing or decreasing size. Dealing with the changes of economic strategies of the country during these decades, the chapter investigates, besides discussing advantages or disadvantages of being small, how strategies of adaption played out in the national economic discourses.

In general, the discussion of 'varieties of capitalism' seeks to fathom institutional foundations of comparative institutional advantages as a style of governance between liberal and coordinated market economies.[4] What this approach does not consider adequately enough is the question of how various branches of the economy may be treated differently – both in terms of national economy-building and in selling that economic policy to the public and to their partners and neighbouring states (economic nationalism).[5] This chapter shows that some industries have the inherent potential to be loaded with nationalistic sentiment while other sectors or divisions cannot raise a national agenda or remain emotionally sterile (or even disdained). In Western Europe, country-wise preferences demonstrate a wide range of such sectoral inclinations *pro patria*: agriculture policy, for example, has been a constant major issue in France but its national framing is different from the lobbyism of German carmakers or Finnish shipbuilding. All three cases are dealing with national pride, identity and perceived importance for each economy but in very different ways.[6] Thus, a central argument of this chapter is that the type of industry makes a difference to how economic nationalism plays out – based on the case study of Luxembourg's shift from steel to finance as the national major industry.

In both cases (steel and finance) Luxembourg is an insightful example of how long enduring strategy of maximal internationalization, understood as selective *de*-nationalization, institutionalized supranationalism and integration on common political ground, can ensure survival and prosperity of a small nation state. This – on first sight rather paradoxical – economic nationalism is based on (a) exogenic and (b) endogenic factors: (a) the economic nationalism of other countries created the very niches and opportunities for Luxembourg to exploit in the first place. Luxembourg seized these windows of opportunity for economic self-empowerment by exercising legitimate national interest; (b) Luxembourg's small state structure shaped the capacity of individual agents or interest groups to react to the steel crisis in the same way as to the emergent financial market: the result is free market corporatism as the 'lesser ideology' of a small democracy's political economy. In this context, the history of national economy-building matters and the particulars of this course – and the discourse about it – need to be presented in some detail.

Luxembourg's dis/courses of national smallness: Past and present

Historiographically speaking, Luxembourg has been perceived as an archetypical small state in the national public and traditional academic discourse: threatened by bigger neighbours since the demise of the powerful House of Luxembourg in the Late Middle Ages. The constant menace of being partitioned or annexed is a recurring topic of national identity-discussion ranging from the topos of 'foreign dominations' from the fifteenth to the nineteenth century, the popular imagination of three consecutive 'dismemberments' (in 1659, 1815 and 1839) to the occupation during the First World War by Imperial Germany. The brutal annexation by Nazi-Germany, which has wiped Luxembourg off the map by denying its independent historical development, is commemorated as a political and cultural trauma until now.[7]

Contrary to older or newer post-colonial micro-states Luxembourg's state building experience has been in line with the Western type of modernization since the nineteenth century. Created by the Congress of Vienna in 1815, the Grand Duchy is 'too big' to be classified as a micro-state, and it has remained on the threshold to a micro-state ever since. In line with Miroslav Hroch's classical model, the formation of state capabilities (administration, infrastructure, schooling, industries, etc.) came first, handicapped by *capacity* problems only.[8] 'We live in a small country' is a self-understanding and experience on a daily basis and a defining factor for Luxembourg's style of governance.[9]

Luxembourg's practice of its traditional trilingualism is a unique feature. After secession due to the Belgian Revolution of 1830–9, the use of High-German, French and Luxembourgish (a West Central German variant) has become a 'dispersed' language routine. There are no demarcated and exclusive linguistic areas within one state like in Belgium or Spain, which could nurture separatist attitudes.[10] Thus, beside smallness, 'in-betweenness' is the next dominant feature of Luxembourgish identity discourse along with the desire to keep the status quo.[11]

One can preliminarily conclude that Luxembourg's nationalism from the mid-nineteenth century onwards centred upon sovereignty as a specific defensive state patriotism. This notion holds that the state, as a territorial delineated political entity with a constitution, should govern itself, free from outside interference, unless the obligation to uphold independence outweighs the capacities of the small state or endangers its economic prosperity. To put it differently: it is up to the *Staatsräson*/*raison d'état*/national interest to decide when and where, and to whom parts of the nation's sovereignty should be delegated as ultimate sovereign choice to uphold sovereignty by chartered integration. Common nationalistic-patriotic sentiments, actions and ressentiments are part of Luxembourg's history. However, and due to the European integration process, its already blunt edges were further sanded down to the 'banal nationalism' of our days. 'Banal nationalism' describes nationalistic-patriotic sentiments in the context of international status competition in sport, environmental awareness, technological progress, competitiveness, etc.[12] Luxembourg's ongoing nation-branding campaign ('Let's make it happen')[13] catches an observer's eye as the logical continuation of the Grand Duchy's liberal elites' commitment for the preservation and development of the country's competitive advantage in economic affairs: economy first!

The following tabular comparison illustrates the social-economic transformation and the impact on the country's profile as a 'now-and-then' of certain key indicators (Table 1).

Luxembourg's 'liberal' economic nationalism before the international steel crisis

'Luxembourg has lived of steel like Egypt has lived of the Nile', Luxembourg's former prime minister Pierre Werner declared, still in present perfect tense,

Table 1 Luxembourg before and after the transformation

Key indicators	1960s	1990s	2000s
Total area (since 1839 in km²) (world rank/sovereign states)	**2,586.4**	**2,586.4**	**2,586.4** (168/195)
Total population (world rank of all sovereign states in year)	**314,585***	**381,850** (140/173 in 1990)	**645,397** (163/195 in 2022)
GDP per capita world rank (year)	**3rd** (1960)	**1st**** (1999)	**1st-3rd** (2000–22)
Employees per sector (%) (primary:secondary:tertiary)	**11.6:45.7:42.7** (1969)	**3.7:32.5:63.8** (1989)	**2.6:26.7:70.7** (1999)
Official ***languages*** (unofficial)	French, German (**Luxembourgish**, Italian)	**F, G, Lux***** (Portuguese, English)	**F, Lux, G** **(E, P)**
Nationals:foreigners (%) (year)	**86.8:13.2** (1961)	**70.3:29.7** (1991)	**52.5:47.5** (2022)
KOF *Index of Globalization* (year)	****	**1st** (1970s–2000)	**1st-3rd** (2000–2010)

* For reasons of decolonization and rising number of states/territories, figures for a world ranking are statistically too volatile.

** There was a significant drop in the 1980s, however caused rather by the rise of other small states (e.g. Singapore or Ireland) than by the overall economic performance.

*** Third official language since 1984. Loi du 24 février 1984 sur le régime des langues – Mémorial-A n° 16 du 27/02/1984.

**** Data available since the 1970s only. In the 2021 ranking (for 2019), Luxembourg figures in the category "de jure" on place 2; in "de facto" on 41; in "overall" on 20 (see KOF Globalization Index).

Sources: World Economic Outlooks of World Bank and IMF; United Nations Statistics Division; STATEC.[14]

in his speech on the state of the nation, given at Luxembourg's Chamber of Deputies on 8 March 1983. In 1983, the end of the steel crisis was finally in sight and Luxembourg's tertiarization was in full take-off. That very year the steel sector still represented 50 per cent of the industrial production, 60 per cent of the total exports and 12 per cent of the total workforce even after a slump in production of 23.4 percentage points.[15] Werner's elegy underlined the importance of steel for the country's national development and sought to justify the efforts undertaken by his and previous administrations to keep the shaking industry alive.[16]

Steel represents a 'mythical' substance, not only for Luxembourgers. It is the world's most important engineering and construction material up to our days. Progress was once measured in national steel output and the modern world of the industrial age perhaps started with mechanic textile manufacturing but was ultimately built on iron ore. The Soviets designed their new image of man around steel and according to a Japanese saying, 'steel is the rice of industry'. A country without its own steel industry was not regarded as a full-grown member in the family of modern states.

In Luxembourg, working-class and blue-collar culture was particularly associated with mining and steel production. When the last mine closed in 1981 and the last blast furnace shut down in 1997, the industrial South of the Grand Duchy, *De Minett* in Luxembourgish, 'lost its name'. Even more, the whole country lost a fundamental part of its identity, as a prominent writer mourned – most Luxembourgers would have agreed.[17] In Luxembourg, steel played a key role in the national narrative carried along by both grassroots pride and by the elites' conviction that steel embodied *the* national interest. Until these days, schoolbooks inform Luxembourgish pupils that the steel industry of the South also improved the living conditions of farmers in the rural North because of the Thomas meal, a basic slag ground and by-product of the Gilchrist-Thomas process for refining pig iron (patented in 1877). Indeed, from 1880 to 1914, the state-sponsored distribution of this phosphate fertilizer increased the Grand Duchy's agricultural yield by 60 per cent, celebrated as uniting the peasant with the steelworker; the field with the furnace.[18] To guarantee the proliferation of heavy industry on national soil would call for and justify economic protectionism in times of crisis.

The refining of low-grade phosphor-rich iron ore (the *Minette*) in southern Luxembourg (and neighbouring Lorraine, incorporated into the German Reich in 1871) took place in a particular setting: the German Customs Union. This *Zollverein* (1834–1919), a coalition of independent German states and city republics under the leadership of Prussia, was formed to coordinate tariffs and common economic policies. The implementation of a joint customs border control and regulation strengthened the splintered German territories in economic terms. In joining this unprecedented single market in 1842, Luxembourg was granted a share of the annually redistributed collective customs revenues too. The agreement of the union with Luxembourg was periodically renewed. The membership ensured not only a vast export market for the iron ore mined in Luxembourg but also attracted German investment in banks, railways and mines – 'it takes a mine to run a mine' as the adage goes.[19] Much-needed capital and expertise was brought in, not only by German industrialists and bankers but also by Belgian and French investors. This golden age of industrialization, or *Hochindustrialisierung*, would not have been possible without a 'proto'-internationalization and 'proto'-Europeanization of Luxembourg's economy. Despite conjunctural crises linked to the German *Gründerzeit* in the 1870s, these decades are generally recounted as a success story. To state leadership it was apparent that supranational integration and small state sovereignty were not a contradiction in terms.[20]

About two-thirds of the ore was exported to the bordering Prussian Rhineland and to Belgium by the newly built railway system.[21] In view of rising foreign demands for mining concession and following 'the impulse of self-preservation' (Friedrich List), Luxembourg's government passed laws that would have pleased List's idea of economies based on nations under a system of protection to foster the nation's development: 'It is the task of national economy to accomplish *the economical development of the nation*, and to prepare it for admission into the universal society of the future.'[22] The government's measures were, so to say, 'upside-down', because the restrictions aimed against exports (of raw ore), not imports: a law of 1870 nationalized the property rights of *Minette* reserves down to a certain deposit depth.[23] Further national laws and international concession agreements since the 1870s, which became cherished ex post as 'Verhüttungsklausel' (smelting proviso), stipulated that mining was only granted (to nationals or foreigners alike) under the condition that a certain part of the iron ore had to be processed in Luxembourg.[24] As a result, five large steel companies were founded with local and foreign capital from the 1870s to the 1880s.

Based on these decisions, one already can identify a blueprint of small state management for understanding future developments in Luxembourg. The Grand Duchy had emancipated itself stepwise from being a subnational jurisdiction of a larger state (the so-called United Kingdom of the Netherlands, 1814–1830/39). Geopolitically speaking, Luxembourg was assigned the role of a 'neutralized' buffer state (alongside Belgium and Switzerland) by the Great Powers in 1867. To overcome the national limits of a domestic market far too small, the government accepted the waiver of selected national rights to gain access to bigger markets. Active location policy (as in the smelting provision) ensured added value. Export of iron ore and steel products was important but Luxembourg was far from being a single crop economy. Luxembourg already developed proactively niche sovereignty strategies and economic policies as evident in its currency management, which formed the seedbed for Luxembourg's rise as IFC one hundred years later.[25]

As iron ore deposits cross state borders, Luxembourg's *Minett* was 'naturally' part of an inter- and transnational industrial zone on mainland Europe (later known as 'Saar-Lor-Lux'[26]), in size and importance next only to the Ruhrgebiet. The mixed ownership of the enterprises, both in terms of capital *and* of intermarried elites' family interest of Luxembourgish, German, Belgian or

French origin, made border-crossing routine a basic requirement. Additionally, the predominant type of integrated steel mills, that is, mining, founding and processing in task-sharing order run by one enterprise on different work and extraction sites, supported the need for transnational cooperation. Furthermore, a small workforce hired itself out as (daily) cross-border commuters for Luxembourg's *Terres Rouges*.[27]

This example of early *transfrontaliers*, as they are called today, points not only to limitation of the national market but also to the inadequacy of the country's human capital, which was underdeveloped in number and qualification. With the rise of heavy industry, Luxembourg's negative migration balance of a widely agrarian society turned to an immigration surplus, mainly through German and then Italian migrants, who came as skilled or unskilled labour force in search for work into the southern industrial belt. Many of them stayed, married and became Luxembourg nationals.

Luxembourg's structural advantage in times of crisis like the 1970s–1980s is a perfect match for Katzenstein's six defining characteristics of small (European) states: (1) they have relatively homogeneous populations; (2) they are open to international economies; (3) they create niches in global economies; (4) they promote social solidarity due to perceived notions of vulnerability to external shocks; (5) they amplify their influence through regions, unions and alliances; and (6) they possess efficient and effective governments because of their propensity for interpersonal relations.[28]

The second and sixth points are linked: in Luxembourg a mixture of structural constraints and opportunistic pursuits of comparative advantages played in favour of capitalistic 'internationalism'. Because of the small administrative apparatus, it was possible to overcome bureaucratic inertia much quicker than in bigger states, where national interest is more dispersed, players more numerous and group particularism more pronounced. This holds true even for relatively small states such as Belgium – a true Leviathan in comparison to the Grand Duchy, where laws were tailor-made in line with specific business requirements. These 'quick fixes' had potential repercussions on the administration as a whole. For instance, the creation of one administration to deal with the multiple infrastructure projects related to the steel industry on the national and local level: the *Travaux Publics* ('Public Works'). This administration was able to find solutions in close coordination with different stakeholders (private and public). The slim number of bureaucratic personnel usually attributed to small and micro-states is generally listed as 'dysfunctionality'.[29] This structural constraint (where one person has to wear many, sometimes too many hats) may be a potential hotbed for clientelism and corruption, but a lean bureaucratic management is advantageous for conducting business. Indeed this factor has, time and again, been accounted as a specific quality of the country, particularly in the context of the evolving IFC Luxembourg or in the case of solving the steel crisis. Thus, smallness is not an absolute category and its true signification depends on the (dis)economies of scale.

Luxembourg's 'defensive' economic nationalism and the international steel crisis (1974–84)

In winter 1983–4, Western Europe's steel industry was in a disastrous state. The 1973 first oil shock had triggered a global recession and decline in the demand for steel, above all for mass steel. The rise of new (and older) players in Japan, South Korea, Brazil, USSR and China affected the output of steel and changed the 'geography of iron and steel'.[30] Europe's main production line was no longer competitive. While the initial conditions were quite similar, exit strategies and escape routes from and outcomes of the crisis were rather different, state by state. Mény and Wright conclude 'there are many reasons *why* the state become so involved: the first might be called psycho-national: it was contended that no country worthy of note should be without a steel industry'.[31] How states became involved depended on their style of governance along a spectrum ranging from more consensus-oriented cooperativism to more conflict-oriented majoritarian/competitive democracies.

In the case of Luxembourg's anti-crisis framework, there was a bilateral concentration process and the ad hoc creation of a national steering committee as pivot for national corporatism. By comparison, Austria's famous 'Sozialpartnerschaft', an example well known in Luxembourg, is rooted in the political crisis of a civil war and designed to overcome deep cleavages of partisanism ('Lagertheorie') after the Second World War. This cooperativism led to a quota design for *enduring* extra-democratic power sharing. Luxembourg's more informal cooperativism, known as the 'Stahltripartite', was only put in place when faced with existential economic threat. Consecutive meetings were set up as 'institutionalized dialogue in social affairs'. Three groups of stakeholders were thus brought to the negotiating table and formed a task force: employer, employees and state representatives. The law of 24 December 1977 formalized this form of cooperativism.[32] On the corporate side, the steel industry put modernization, specialization and higher productivity on the agenda and further acquisition of steel companies abroad as 'survival by growth' – in other words, they ventured more competitive internationalization (by economies of scale). The employees closed ranks on a national level. In 1979, a general union, the OGBL ('Independent Luxembourg Trade Union Confederation'), was chartered to raise the bargaining power of the employees.[33] The state as third party of this historical sprint in the evolution of cooperation[34] coordinated the common efforts. Luxembourg's government, as founding member of the European Coal and Steel Community (the actual driver to deepen the BENELUX initiative[35]) and the European Economic Community (EEC) accorded national actions on a supranational level: protectionism (against non-member states) and massive state subsidies.[36] The EEC launched an ambitious industrial policy programme (for the first and only time in its history) from 1977 to 1984.

Thus, to overcome the crisis and to secure its export-markets, the Grand Duchy made sure to be firmly embedded in transnational measures and international agreements – Luxembourg's geopolitical 'fetish' after the Second World War.

On a national and subnational level the loss of the steel industry would have had catastrophic consequences for the economy. Here, the economy of scales worked in two ways: the whole country, and not only a region (like Lorraine, far away from Paris, for example; or a small Federal State of Germany, like neighbouring Saarland) would have been affected – that was a self-evident fact for the population and all political parties.[37] A series of interviews with key actors[38] illustrate to all this need to pull together in the same direction.[39] The collapse of Luxembourg's industrial key player ARBED[40] would have been the 'beginning of the end of the nation', assured Jacques Santer, then minister for finance and labour. The members of the tripartite's heavyweight round successfully communicated the need for a common effort to their constituencies. The invoked 'Luxembourg Way' to preserve social peace without any violent strikes as in neighbouring industrial sites of France and Belgium was, he said, also accepted by the trade unions. This quest for a 'peaceful' transition was supported by most national press outlets (with the exception of the Communist daily). This may seem euphemistical, considering the 1976 workers strike and the 1982 general strike in favour of price indexation, but unemployment rates were kept to a minimum. Additionally, a general confidence that the rising IFC of the 1980s would further cross-subsidize the survival of the quasi-nationalized ARBED, a buy-out by state credits, became manifest. Consequently the government could build on a broad consensus for exceptional measures playing the patriotic tone needed. A special tax earmarked to pay for the social measures and state support was soon nicknamed 'Arbedsteier' ('ARBED taxation'). After its take-over of HADIR (Hauts-Fourneaux et Acièries de Differdange) in 1967, ARBED was *the* Luxembourg-based steel and iron producing company, and 'tout ce qui est bon pour l'ARBED est aussi bon pour le pays', as Luxembourg's eminent historian Gilbert Trausch was citing a contemporary motto in his corporate history.[41] Technically speaking, the ARBED taxation[42] represented an indiscriminating raise of certain excise and income taxes. Politically speaking, this temporary solidarity surcharge resembled a national-patriotic offertory. The master narrative now paid off: the transfer payments for the whole country originating in the industrial South had always figured prominently. Now, in times of crisis, it was time for rest of the country to honour this 'debt'. Such a rhetorical strategy of two complementary halves did not work in Belgium because of the deep nationalistic divide between the French-speaking southern industrial 'rusting' belt and the prospering Flemish North.

By contrast, Luxembourg's size and sociopolitical scale allowed for distributive and redistributive policies ensuring full employment and keeping afloat the welfare state.[43] The DAC ('Division anti-crise') task force[44] implemented an unseen labour hoarding during these years of crisis known from the Austrian example of the Kreisky era (1970–83). The 'excess number' of steel worker were first kept as a human resource-reserve in case of a (rather unlikely) massive rebound of the steel sector. When their expertise and know-how was not relevant anymore, a retraining and employment programme ('Travaux extraordinaires d'intérêt general'), accompanied by an early retirement scheme, reduced the sectoral working force from 24,000 in 1974 to 11,000 in 1987 without social friction. In the same time period the productivity increased rapidly (the average time spent on producing one tonne of sheet steel was reduced from 9.54 hours in 1975 to 3.36 in 1991) while the share of the steel sector in the GDP dropped from 25.3 to 7.6 per cent.

The 'material nature' of steel (i.e. the imprint it had on people and landscapes) had a clear bearing on its potential for generating economic nationalism. At the same time, Luxembourg's main trade depended for over a century on open(ing) markets. It is no coincidence that smaller European states like Belgium and the Netherlands also 'followed' the requirements of coal and steel industry as driver for integration, that is, initially joining small(er) domestic markets to form bigger transnational ones by customs unions, initiatives which outgrow into a sociopolitical agenda later on known as the European integration process. However, economic integration (be it within the BENELUX or the ECC) left enough room for manoeuvre to defend national interest.[45]

Luxembourg mobilized the means to ship through the calamity by riding the crest of that crisis on patriotic sentiment, to declare a national emergency and to communicate the need for joint efforts of a small country to close the ranks, even against bigger economies. However, even large national economies of Europe could 'dictate' the terms of steel trade and industry of their national economy for some time only. Ultimately, economic nationalism hit its limits when transnational markets and their brainchild – big and bigger trans- and multinational steel companies – took the lead. Interestingly enough, open nationalistic sentiments briefly surged when ARBED, after merging smoothly with Spanish Aceralia and French Usinor into Areclor in 2002, was incorporated by Indian-owned Mittal Steel in 2006, creating the multinational ArcelorMittal S.A. In the media and politics, this short take-over battle was styled 'national vs. global'; '*modèle social luxembourgeois* vs. *capitalism sauvage*' and 'European project vs. neoliberal globalization'.[46] In the end, at this stage of mergers, the only question left open for national interest was the location for the headquarters and tax domicile. The patriotic framing of the steel industry was much more difficult for the financial sector, which started as extended workbench for European, then global financial centres.

'Liberal' national economy-building again? The rise of the IFC Luxembourg in times of crisis

'When I first came to Luxembourg, finance was seen as something akin to gambling, a lottery. Steel, meanwhile, was seen as something solid, stable, that produced tangible results', said the Belgian banker and economist Philippe Duvieusart, describing the poor image the banking sector had with some political leaders and with public opinion, when he was appointed deputy director of KBL (Kredietbank Luxembourg) in 1965.[47] Although the financial centre's take-off coincided with the years of the steel crisis, the very same circumstances and political ensemble gave way to a very different form of national economic interest. Luxembourg's elites programme (to seize opportunities and) to develop a financial centre struggled to put down roots as deep and broad as steel and mining. It should even be argued that the opposite is true and finance is Luxembourg's unloved child, however a Golden Girl for its GDP.

By contrast, the financial locational politics of the 1960s brought back the idea of being an 'island'. That is a notion which the country expressly abstains in geopolitical affairs or in advancing a common market for goods, mobility, other services or much-needed brain gain. Basically, this 'bordered' understanding is founded on the modus operandi of international finance which is quite dissimilar to steel in three ways, namely that transnational finance's locational praxis can be above all defined as a continuous onshore/offshore relation between centres and peripheries; secondly, in global financial affairs Luxembourg could reap the luck of being a 'newly industrializing' country – a newcomer of sorts. Last but not least, the already mentioned disparity of the perceived 'immoral' character, the widely shared negative image of international finance and profits in public opinion on the one hand, and its actual contribution to the Luxembourgish welfare system, on the other.

Luxembourg's financial service industry has a long history.[48] Initially, it was custom-made for the small industrial nation. Already in 1915, in the second year of the 'Great War' and under imperial German occupation, the 'law for national and foreign founders' stipulated equal right and duties for any local or foreign private business or capital company in Luxembourg. Business partnerships and cooperation in the Grand Duchy registered abroad were subject to (favourable) Luxembourgish law and jurisdiction.[49] The local banking sector was established to attract investments in infrastructure and to support the development of the mining and steel industry. Already during the interwar period, Luxembourg followed its strategy to make the country bigger as it was. The economic union with Belgium (BLEU) had created not only a customs union but also a fixed exchange rate system between Belgian and Luxembourg franc in 1922. To encourage international activities, the stock exchange (*Bourse de Luxembourg*) was established in 1928 as a political statement that should help to transform little Luxembourg into an international finance centre. Financial operations were to be domiciled in the country, therefore the law initiative of 31 July 1929 which allowed holding companies a permanent legal residence in Luxembourg. This initiative is also an example for the above-mentioned 'quick fixes' to attract foreign investments, however in a proactive way. Others may conclude that this law purposely laid the basis to divert more money to the Grand Duchy, which rightfully should have been paid into other states' coffers.[50]

Reaping the comparative advantage, facing the national egoism of others

The beginning of Luxembourg as a global financial node was moderate and linked to its foremost industry. The country's export-depending steel and mining industry of the 1950s, 1960s and 1970s could only function with foreign currency advances. Export credits of the post-war boom period issued in various currencies and transferred from Luxembourg's European partners accumulated in the Grand Duchy, disproportionally to its political-demographic size. First, German banks began to use Luxembourg's expertise in multi-currency cash management, facilitated by the country's multi-lingualism and unbureaucratic channels, and started to transfer import and export credits to partner banks or in-house agencies in Luxembourg to clear liabilities from their own balance sheets. Other banks followed this cost-and-time-saving outsourcing strategy. Continuous balancing of credit and debt created bottom lines and the possibility for short-term current account credits – the birth of the so-called Eurocredits. These are loans whose denominated currency is not the lending bank's national currency, that is, German marks and above all US dollars. Luxembourg grew into an operative centre for this management and credit lines, charging small processing fees in return. Ironically, the so-called Werner Plan, presented by Luxembourg's then Prime Minister Pierre Werner in October 1970s for the adoption of a single currency, also intended to deepen the European Communities (1958–72), would have 'killed' this nascent financial centre building. National interests of other countries, France in particular, put this vision on hold.[51]

Another boost or serendipity occurred by an initiative of the US government.[52] The Kennedy administration implemented a protectionist tax measure in 1963. The Interest Equalization Tax, as it was called, targeted US investments abroad. This 'toll' was meant to make it less profitable to purchase foreign securities. As an at-source levy of 15 per cent, the tax's main purpose was to decrease the US balance of payments deficit. Marshall Plan, Vietnam War expenses, the Latin American debt crisis and private investors had dispersed the dollar (in cash and as book-money) around the world – and out of the jurisdiction of the United States and the Federal Reserve. When the project of a London-based banker to make that hidden treasure of 'stateless dollars' work was not perceived enthusiastically enough by the city, this very high financier Siegmund G. Warburg nearly single-handedly initiated the so-called Eurodollar market (Eurobonds) in Luxembourg.[53] Soon, he found many helping hands in the Grand Duchy.[54] Such bonds are held and traded in electronic book-entry form with clearing systems; one, Clearstream, originated in September 1970 in Luxembourg (founded as Cedel – *Centrale de Livraison de Valeurs Mobilières*) to minimize risk in settlement of cross-border securities trading. At this time, Luxembourg's financial sector soared in number of banks, turn-over and financial innovation, changing from being the mere extended financial workbench of London to a centre for investment funds, securities and private equity management in its own right.[55] Still, compared to the big profits made in London or New York, Luxembourg's profits were peanuts, however nuggets considering the economies of scale.

As we know today, the 1980s were particularly important for the relations between East and West. The decade marks a period of intensive reawakening of Cold War tensions and later of a thaw in relations. Economic stagnation and recession on both sides contributed to the change of minds. Western European states experienced a relaunch of the integration process with the completion of the common market by 1992 in their minds. Financial deregulation became a centrepiece and the 'mutual recognition principle' of the EEC with its ensuing directive after the so-called White Paper of 1985.[56]

In 1988, Luxembourg was the first member state of the EU to transpose the UCITS directive (Undertakings for Collective Investment in Transferable Securities Directive (UCITS) 2009/65/EC), allowing collective investment schemes to operate freely throughout the common market on the basis of an individual authorization from *one* of the members.[57] The small state structure enabled Luxembourg to be the first mover, its mix typical: outsourcing and commercialization of sovereign rights, however embedded in common market rules.[58]

In contrast to industrial production, financial activities are off-stage activities for the public – and, particularly in the case of Luxembourg, a furthermore 'unwritten chapter' for historians.[59] Accordingly, discourses are ambivalent: 'Über Geld spricht man nicht, man hat es' ('One doesn't talk about money, one have it'), this German saying represents one side quite literally. In Luxembourg, not even the architecture of money is 'heroic' and landmarking like the skyscraping financial districts of London, New York, Hong Kong, Singapore or even Dublin is missing.[60] In opposition to this cultivated inconspicuousness and discretion, a 'scandalizing' narrative of tax evasion ('tax haven') and financial machinations is latent, both in public and in academia (and among envious competitors). In recent years – and in a way characteristic for Luxembourg reading the signs of times correctly – the government (pro-)actively changed course to transparency policy in (over-) fulfilment with EU regulations to rebrand the IFC as 'clean and green' for attracting responsible investors. In course of this, the Grand Duchy listed the 'world's first Green Bond' and assesses herself as 'leading platform for sustainable finance'.[61]

Conclusion

In a common effort and under the watchful eyes of the public, Luxembourg's government, economic leaders and employee representatives managed the national steel crisis comparatively well – combining varieties of economic nationalism, rooted in the country's 'national economy-building'[62] discourses and strategies: liberal and market-guided principles for the steel branch; sectoral management for labour relations; and a state-led coordinated transitional economic regime were set in place. Luxembourg's small state building process and the transnational establishment of its national steel industry made this ephemeral mix possible. In a longue durée perspective, the history of national economy-building matters, as Hall and Soskice affirm, meaning that 'institutions of a nation's political economy are inextricably bound up with its history in two respects'. On the one hand, they are created by actions, statutory or otherwise, that establish formal institutions and their operating procedures. On the other, repeated historical experience builds up a set of common expectations that allow the actors to coordinate effectively with each other.[63]

Luxembourg is also a prime example for how economies of scales may work for small countries. As a small state, Luxembourg could realize external economies of scale by growing in size relative to its competitors by integration and internationalization. The country could master the international steel crises by reorganizing its political economy in a way bigger countries were not able to. Luxembourg also demonstrates how a small national economy (in the European context) survived and even thrived after/with an economic crisis not by embarking on 'traditional' protectionist policies, which small economies can ill-afford, but by adopting hyper-liberal economic policies. Nevertheless, it was necessary to appeal to solidarity and national sacrifice on the one hand. On the other, national interest and egoism of the others, respectively the outsourcing strategy of their financial and banking sector, created a niche that made Luxembourg a node in global financial affairs by the Grand Duchy's commercialization of sovereignty.[64] Ultimately, in both cases – steel and finance – the supranational level took over the lead, when national interest was best preserved by being trans- and internationally embedded.

Notes

1 This term was coined by Jean Fourastié, *Les Trente Glorieuses*, in 1979 to mark a silent, however profound, revolution in socio-economic affaires in France.

2 Zahlen, 'Le Luxembourg 1960–2010'. The average growth rate of the Grand Duchy in those years was 1.3 percentage points higher than during its 4 per cent growth of

the *Trente Glorieuse* period, leaving the slow growth of saturated Western European economies way behind; Zahlen, *The Luxembourg Economy*, 9–70.

3 Thorhallsson, 'Studying Small States'.

4 Clift and Woll, 'Economic Patriotism'.

5 See the presentation of the concept by Adrian Brisku in this volume.

6 Tracy, *Farmer and Politics*; Guy Chazan, '"Carmakers" troubles shake Germany's national psyche'; for the Finnish shipbuilding, see Matala, *A History of Cold War Industrialization*.

7 The 'trois démembrements' topos was presented on the official government website ('Apropos ... de l'histoire du Luxembourg') until 2022. For Luxembourg, see Péporté, Kmec et al. *Inventing Luxembourg*, Kolnberger, 'Forever small', for a general debate see Kolnberger and Koff, *Agency, security and governance of small states* or Kruizinga, *The Politics of Smallness*.

8 Hroch, *European Nation*.

9 Idiomatic expression often used in statements, press, etc. See Linden, 'Un beau petit pays?'

10 To bring the Belgian Revolution and secession (1830–9) to a diplomatic solution, the new Belgian state was entitled by the European Great Powers to annex the mostly French-speaking quarters of the Grand Duchy (today's Belgium *Province* de Luxembourg).

11 'We want to stay what we are' (in archaic Luxembourgish spelling *Mir wölle bleiwe wat mir sin*) is rated as motto (now in three languages). Among others, Batty Weber, Luxembourg's leading feuilletonists proposed a 'Mischkultur' (a mixture of French and German) as constitutive for Luxembourg's identity, see Kmec, 'Batty Weber'.

12 Reicher, 'Wettbewerb und Nation', compare Billig, *Banal Nationalism*.

13 This is the slogan of a campaign to promote the Grand Duchy's overall reputation with 'trois thèmes prioritaires: [...] la créativité, la diversité, la durabilité', see Carette,'Le Luxembourg relifte son 'nation branding'.

14 https://statistiques.public.lu/fr/actualites/population/population/2022/04/20220411.html; Angus Maddison. The World Economy: Historical Statistics. Paris: OECD Publishing Development Centre Studies. 2003, KOF Globalisation Index, https://kof.ethz.ch (accessed 10 December 2022). L'Economie luxembourgeoise au 20e siècle, edited by Robert Weides (for STATEC), Luxembourg: Editpress 1999.

15 'Le Luxembourg vivait de l'acier comme l'Egypte vivait du Nil', Lemaitre, 'Luxembourg: des banques hyperdynamiques'.

16 The authorship of the comparison (alluding to Herodotius) is usually awarded to Carlo Hemmer (1913–1988), a former president of Luxembourg's Stock Exchange (Bourse) and of Chamber of Commerce, and general secretary of the Business Federation Luxembourg, etc., in the 1950s: 'Luxembourg is a gift of steel as Egypt is a gift of Nile' (original in French), Overbeck, 'Montanarchäologie'.

17 'Réflexions sur un pays qui a perdu son nom' of Jean Portante in: Bassin minier. Traces et mutations, photographies, edited by John Braun et al., Luxembourg 1994.
18 Pauly, *Geschichte*, 81, Quasten, *Wirtschaftsformation*, 191, Wagner, *Thomasmehl.*
19 For the US context, see King, 'It takes a mine to run a mine.'
20 Pohl, 'Grundzüge'.
21 Van de Kerkhof, 'Die Industrialisierung'.
22 List, *The National System*, 142 (original italics).
23 Loi du 15 mars 1870 sur les gisements de mine de fer oolithique du canton d'Esch, Mémorial (du Grand-Duché du Luxembourg) n°4, 15/3/1870.
24 Loi du 12 juin 1874 sur le régime des mines et des minières de fer, in 'Mémorial' n°15, 13/6/1874 and Loi du 2 avril 1892, qui approuve les conventions des 10 avril 1891 et 13 février 1892, portant octrois d'une concession minière à trois sociétés de hauts-fourneaux luxembourgeois, in 'Mémorial' n°19, 9/4/1892.
25 Kolnberger, 'Geldpolitik.'
26 German Saarland, French/German Lorraine and Luxembourg.
27 For the origin of the name, see: Tschacher, 'Landschaftsnamen'.
28 Katzenstein, 'Small States'.
29 Simpson, *Theory of Disfunctionality.*
30 D'Acosta, 'Steel Industry'.
31 Mény and Wright, 'State and Steel', 23 (my emphasis).
32 Hirsch, 'The Luxembourg model', Huberty, 'Luxembourg'.
33 OGBL, '1976. Einheitsfront gegen die Stahlkrise'. This umbrella organization (its statute a 'very Luxembourgish copy & paste' of the ready-made ÖGB, the 1945 code of the Austrian Trade Union Federation) is the socialist and most important of the three nation-wide unions with the largest membership.
34 Axelrod, *The Evolution.*
35 After the First World War and the termination of the Zollverein, Luxembourg and Belgium established the Belgium-Luxembourg Economic Union (BLEU) on 25 July 1921, compare Kaiser, 'Transnational Practises'.
36 Gieseck, *Krisenmanagement*, 32–61.
37 Analysing the various party programmes of the conservative party (CSV), the Socialists (LSAP), the Communists (KPL) and even the Liberals (DP) and the Greens (Déi Gréng/Alternativ) of 1968, 1974, 1979, 1984, 1989 in view of the steel crises reveals a clear commitment to keep a Luxembourgish steel industry alive, see Manifesto project database, available at: https://manifestoproject.wzb.eu/ (accessed 5 March 2023).
38 *Lëtzebuerger Stolkris, 1975–1984* (DVD).
39 For the factor of political participation, see Vetterle, *Die Teilhabe am Politischen.*
40 Acronym for *Aciéries Réunies* [literally 'United Steelworks'] *de Burbach-Eich-Dudelange.*

41 Trausch, *ARBED*, 10. The ARBED was created in 1911 after an international merger – the last one established the multinational ArcelorMittal, headquartered in Luxembourg in 2006 as the second largest steel producer in the world (2022).
42 De Lëtzeburger Merkur, 'Antikrisengesetz vom 1 Juli 1983', 4.
43 Schmidt, 'Politik der inneren Reform', 243–4.
44 Krieps and Krieps, 'La crise sidérurgique'.
45 Ahrens and Eckert, 'Industrial Policy'.
46 Besch, 'ArcelorMittal'.
47 Duvieusart later became general director of KBL (since 2020 Quintete Privat Bank) from 1969 to 1973, see Moyse et al., 'The Architects', 53, 'Inventaire des papiers Philippe Duviesart', DIAL, available at: file:///C:/Users/Thomas/Downloads/Papiers_Philippe_Duvieusart.pdf (accessed 16 December 2022).
48 Franz, 'Der Finanzplatz Luxemburg'.
49 Loi du 10 août 1915, concernant les sociétés commerciales. In 'Mémorial' n°90, 30/October 1915, compare: Calabrese and Majerus, 'Treasure Island'.
50 Calabrese, *The Fund Code*.
51 CVCE, 'A Rereading'.
52 Other egoisms and 'text-book economic nationalism going wrong' creating flight capital which fostered the IFC include a 25 per cent levy on securities income in Belgium, imposed during the national financial crisis of 1957–8; a 25 per cent levy on bond coupons held in Germany by foreigners, introduced in 1965, and the so-called 'Bardepot' of 1970, requiring banks to place a share of their deposits with the German Bundesbank.
53 Bonds are in bearer form (the buyer can remain anonymous) and they are mostly free of withholding taxes at source. For the key players of the Eurobond-market before the rise of Luxembourg, see Burke, 'Witness Seminar', 70: 'The quintessential Eurobond buyer in the early days was the only half-mythical figure of the Belgian dentist – a high-earning individual, living in a country with a bureaucratic tax system where domestic bonds were subject to tax at source, and where there was a limited choice of investment opportunities.'
54 Ferguson, *High Financier*, 201–32.
55 The best overview of the establishment of Luxembourg's IFC is given by Moyse et al., 'The Architects'.
56 Drach, 'Removing Obstacles'.
57 Gentili et al., *The SIVACs*.
58 See Walther, Schulz and Dörry, 'Specialised International Financial Centres'.
59 Majerus, 'Écrire l'histoire'.
60 For the producers of the action thriller 'The International' (2009 film) the buildings in real Luxembourg as movie location for the HQ of the fictional (and corrupt) merchant bank, based in Luxembourg, were too moderate. Until very recently,

high-rise buildings accommodated state administrations, EU institutions and housing only, see Thewes, 'La silhouette'.

61 See https://www.luxembourgforfinance.com/en/homepage/ (accessed 8 September 2023).

62 See Brisku's conceptual proposal in this volume.

63 Hall and Soskice, 'Varieties', 13, compare Pickel, 'Explaining', 1 and Fetzer, 'Nationalism', 59.

64 Bauler, *Les fruits*.

4

Czechoslovak experts in independent Lusophone Africa as a variant of economic nationalism

Barbora Menclová

Introduction

British historian Tony Judt called the 1970s in Europe 'the most dismal decade of the 20th century'.[1] He was referring to the numerous economic and social crises caused, among others, by the two oil shocks, which contrasted sharply with the long post-war era of economic growth and rising living standards. In Western European countries, they manifested themselves, for example, in increased political violence and mass unemployment.[2] Initially, the East seemed to be spared from these adverse effects, but a few years later, they manifested themselves with much greater force. The growing debt, technological backwardness and the increasing dominance of the West forced the states of the Soviet bloc to seek new solutions in their foreign policy strategies.

Czechoslovakia was, together with East Germany, one of the most economically developed countries of the Comecon member states. Its economy was based on its export-oriented industry since its foundation in 1918.[3] In the discussion about economic nationalism, Czechoslovak policies can be defined as liberal/outward-looking, which sought to strengthen relations with foreign actors for most of the twentieth century.[4] One of the short exceptions was the consolidation period following the suppression of the Prague Spring at the end of the 1960s, where there were visible tendencies to the protectionist/inward-looking measures,[5] which can be defined as a conservative variant of economic nationalism.[6] However, this approach did not last long. In response to its deteriorating economy from the mid-1970s, Prague abandoned them and promoted a new form of economic nationalism to protect its economy from global challenges, which, unlike its previous variant, was based on deepening cooperation with the West and the Global South.[7] Economic growth was supposed to support the import of technology from Western countries. Due to the lack of hard currency, it was necessary to borrow from foreign creditors.[8] The result was an increasing national debt, although in the Czechoslovak case, it did not reach the same dimensions as in neighbouring Poland or East Germany. On the contrary, until the end of the Cold War, Czechoslovakia was one of the least indebted members of the Soviet bloc.[9]

Further, some state socialist countries sought to deepen their alliances with the Global South, especially Africa and the Middle East, after 1975. There, one of Prague's critical foreign policy strategies became the dispatch of its experts in the factories and other institutions abroad. This strategy brought or should have brought various economic benefits.[10] It also concerned two former Portuguese colonies in Africa, Angola and Mozambique, whose decolonization occurred in the mid-1970s. Both newly independent states became priorities for Czechoslovak foreign policy in sub-Saharan Africa,[11] and the number of Czechoslovak experts there belonged to the highest in the Global South.[12]

Despite researchers' growing interest in economic relations between East, West and South in the late Cold War.[13] Little attention has been paid to the strategies of smaller socialist states.[14] An exception is a publication by editors Angela Romano and Frederick Romero, including Pavel Szobi's chapter on Czechoslovakia.[15] Pavel Szobi also published his study on Czechoslovak economic cooperation with Angola as part of another monograph.[16] An overview of the development of the Czechoslovak economy in the twentieth century is offered by the work of a collective of authors led by Václav Průcha.[17] Also, the sending of Czechoslovak experts to the countries of the Global South, despite its significant role in the foreign policy of Czechoslovakia in the late Cold War, has not attracted the greater academic attention. It is in contrast to the situation abroad, where it is the subject of various research.[18] The exception is a dissertation of the Slovak historian Barbora Buzássyová, focused on education[19] or a specialized issue of the Prague Papers Journal dedicated to selected African countries, including Angola.[20] However, these publications do not explicitly question whether the sending of Czechoslovak experts to the countries of the Global South could also be a response to the new global economic challenges that Prague had to face.

This chapter overcomes the research gap and contributes to the academic discussion about the varieties of economic nationalism of smaller socialist states in the late Cold War on the example of the dispatch of Czechoslovak experts in Angola and Mozambique. In particular, it explores what economic interests Czechoslovakia pursued with this strategy, the expectations of the Czechoslovak authorities and its results. Further, it examines whether the Cold War rivalry and the Czechoslovak alliance with the Soviet Union influenced relations with both Lusophone African states. Finally, the dispatch of the Czechoslovak experts is represented in the broader context of the academic discussion about varieties of economic nationalism.

The research is based on declassified archival documents completed by interviews with former experts and other stakeholders, their memoirs, diaries and print. Concerning the archives, the research was conducted namely in the Archive of Ministry of Foreign Affairs (Archiv ministerstva zahraničních věcí, AMZV), in the National Archive (Národní archiv České republiky, NA ČR) and in the Archive of Security Services (Archiv bezpečnostních složek, ABS ČR). Concerning the interviews, eleven interviews were conducted and recorded with former Czechoslovak experts working in independent Angola and Mozambique and one interview with a former Czech lecturer of the Portuguese language in the years 2019–21. The records are available in the author's personal archive.

East-South cooperation and Czechoslovakia in the 1970s and 1980s

The beginning of the 1970s seemed favourable for promoting economic interests of the socialist states on a global level. Although the socialist countries lost their key ally Egypt at that time, they still maintained their influence in the Middle East, and the loss of Egypt was balanced by the 'gain' of Vietnam. The decolonization of the Portuguese colonies of Angola and Mozambique in sub-Saharan Africa and the coup in Ethiopia then became essential.[21] As Eric Burton points out, the revolutionary enthusiasm of African countries was combined with the need of the Soviet Union and other state socialist countries to secure new sources of raw materials.[22] The high prices of raw materials on world markets, together with generous loans from foreign donors, stimulated an economic boom in Africa in the 1970s. This was also reflected in trade exchange increase with the East when African exports consisted primarily of raw materials and its imports of products from the European socialist countries,[23] although, as Lorenzini states, even the increase in the mutual trade in this period did not threaten the dominant position of the West.[24]

On the other hand, in the 1970s, numerous economic and social crises and new global threats, including energy dependence and environmental problems, led to the questioning in both the West and the East if limitless progress could be achieved through modernization based on industrialization.[25] Another important question was how to face new economic and social challenges. The increasingly visible technological lag of the East behind the West led to an increase in importing these commodities from Western European countries on credit. The growing indebtedness of socialist governments to their capitalist counterparts led to deepening economic interdependence, the adverse effects of which became fully apparent a decade later.[26]

The search for new sources of raw materials, especially in African countries and the Middle East, became another essential aspect of the 1970s for the Soviet bloc. In addition to oil, these included, for example, phosphates, which were crucial to increasing agricultural production, exotic wood or cotton.[27] One reason was the USSR's announcement at the beginning of this decade that it could no longer meet the oil demand of its European allies.[28] In the 1980s, the need for new sources of raw materials deepened after the Soviet Union, due to its economic difficulties, stopped supplying oil to other socialist states at discounted prices and instead began to sell it on world markets.[29]

The other phenomenon was the reduction of the technological progress between the East and some countries of the Global South, such as India or Brazil, which became competitors of socialist countries there in some cases.[30] Rapprochement with the West and technological backwardness were also manifested in the willingness of the East to participate in joint projects in the countries of the Global South, so-called tripartite cooperation. The West supplied advanced technologies and highly qualified management, the East middle management and equipment, and the South raw materials and unskilled labour.[31]

In the 1980s, the economic difficulties of the Soviet bloc, including the technological backwardness and indebtedness mentioned above, deepened. It was also caused by a change in the West towards its foreign debtors. The economic crisis in the 1970s led capitalist states to tighten the provision of loans and increase interest rates. These measures hit the countries of the Global South very hard. Many African states, including Mozambique, became insolvent and stopped paying their debts to socialist countries. The consequence of increasing indebtedness was a reduction and, in many cases, a complete trade collapse between the two actors.[32]

The development of relations between the East and the South outlined above also reflected, to a certain extent, the attitude of Czechoslovakia. Since the end of the 1950s, Prague has been Moscow's main ally in its global ambitions, when one of the Czechoslovak foreign policy strategies towards the Global South has been sending experts to factories, agricultural enterprises and other institutions there. To coordinate this cooperation, the Czechoslovak foreign trade corporation Polytechna was established in 1959, subordinate to the ministry of the same name. In addition to sending Czechoslovaks to job positions abroad, its task included hiring foreign workers for domestic companies or selling licences.[33] But the Polytechna was not the only institution with the authority to send Czechoslovak citizens to work abroad. It could be individual ministries or other foreign trade corporations like Motokov.[34]

However, according to some current studies, already in the mid-1960s, disillusionment with the results of cooperation with African states was already reflected in Czechoslovakia, which was also deepened by its economic recession.[35] In response to these factors, according to Barbora Buzássyová, the Czechoslovak authorities have been striving since the end of the decade for a greater return on the costs incurred to the Global South.[36] After the Warsaw Pact troops invaded Czechoslovakia in August 1968, efforts to make more fundamental changes in Czechoslovak foreign policy officially ended. Still, some trends remained, such as the preference for sending specialists over other Czechoslovak aid to the Global South. According to Buzássyová, the reason for prioritizing this cooperation was its significant economic contribution to the Czechoslovak state budget. At the same time, the state authorities were well aware that experts could, thanks to their work directly at the workplace in a foreign country and contact with its key representatives, mediate new business contracts for Prague.[37]

At the beginning of the 1970s, after the economic recession in the 1960s, Czechoslovakia experienced a relative economic boom like other socialist states. Foreign debt was minimal, and trade turnover with other countries grew. The previous orientation was also preserved. Its main trading partners continued to be the socialist states with around 70 per cent, followed by the countries of the West with 22 per cent, and only 7 to 8 per cent of the total annual turnover was with partners from the Global South.[38]

The economic decline occurred after 1975, primarily caused by low labour productivity, dependence on its socialist partners, little flexibility of the Czechoslovak government and insufficient technological innovation. On the other hand, the oil shocks had a minor impact on Czechoslovakia than on the neighbouring socialist countries, which were more economically linked with their Western European counterparts. Also, concerning fuels, Prague was in a relatively better position thanks to the domestic mining of brown coal and the still subsidized import of Soviet oil.[39] However, it did not mean that Czechoslovak government did not have to look for new strategies to overcome its economic decline. One of the solutions became to deepen the alliance with two new African states – Angola and Mozambique.

Czechoslovakia's contacts with Angola and Mozambique after their independence

The declaration of independence of Angola and Mozambique in 1975 served as a milestone in their relations with socialist Czechoslovakia. Until then, Prague's semi-legal military and humanitarian aid to the local liberation movements, in the Angolan case namely People's Movement for the Liberation of Angola (Movimento Popular de Libertação de Angola, the MPLA), in the Mozambiquan case Liberation Front of Mozambique (Frente de Libertação de Moçambique, FRELIMO), which began with the outbreak of the local wars of independence in the early 1960s, turned into an officially declared, large-scale Czechoslovak assistance programme. Also, Angola and Mozambique were eager to deepen their cooperation with the Soviet bloc, not only in the military but also in the economic area, which was strongly affected by the departure of most Portuguese and other skilled workers after 1974 and the reorientation to the socialist economic model.[40] The most requested assistance was in the renovation of their agriculture and industry. In the last one, Czechoslovakia, a traditionally industrial country with experience from other African states, could offer its help, including the dispatch of its experts in their companies and infrastructure.

Concerning the development of relations between Czechoslovakia and independent Lusophone African states, after 1975, cooperation with Angola, a geopolitically and economically more important country than Mozambique, developed faster. In May 1976, Prague sent an economic delegation there. In June 1976, the Czechoslovak embassy opened in the capital Luanda. It is already evident from the explanatory report for establishing the Czechoslovak diplomatic office there that Prague was also aware of Angola's economic potential. 'Further development of cooperation with the People's Republic of Angola will also benefit Czechoslovakia, especially in trade and economics.'[41] In the autumn of 1976, the first conception of Czechoslovak foreign policy towards Angola was adopted, specifying the further development of mutual contacts.[42] Since spring 1976, both states emphasized the development of economic cooperation.

Among the main motivations of the Angolan actors was the critical state of the country's economy after 1974. The reorientation to the socialist economic model and the departure of most skilled workers caused many factories and other workplaces to stop operating. In August 1976, the Angolan government officially asked Czechoslovakia to help revive the Angolan economy. It was interested not only in importing Czechoslovak goods to Angola, like Tatra trucks, but also the dispatch of its experts to local companies.[43] Czechoslovakia officially approved the Angolan request in October 1976.[44] In addition to political reasons, including the alliance with Moscow, Prague also pursued its economic interests with this step. It could secure scarce raw materials and agricultural products through closer cooperation with this country. In addition to Angolan oil, it was, for example, iron ore, granite, phosphates, coffee or tropical wood.[45] At the same time, thanks to its ties to the West, this country had hard currency, which was able to pay for Czechoslovak goods and services, including experts.[46]

In the case of Mozambique, the government there, like in Angola, was interested in accepting foreign workers in its enterprises and other institutions due to the departure of most of the skilled workforce from the country during decolonization. During his visit to the Soviet Union in May 1976, Mozambican President Samora Machel asked the socialist countries for help constructing heavy industry, modernization of agriculture, education and transport.[47] However, contacts with Czechoslovakia began to develop more intensively towards the end of the 1970s, as in the case of other Eastern countries. The reason for caution was the unstable Mozambican political and economic situation. In October 1978, three years after the declaration of Mozambican independence, the Czechoslovak embassy was opened in the capital Maputo, and the first Czechoslovak ambassador took office in 1980.[48]

Regarding economic relations, the first Czechoslovak delegation visited Mozambique in July 1977.[49] A year later, a trade agreement and an agreement on scientific and technical cooperation were signed by the Czechoslovak minister of foreign trade, Andrej Barčák, in Maputo.[50] From the first conception of the Czechoslovak foreign policy towards this country, approved in 1979, it was already evident that Prague attached increasing importance to the development of mutual relations in the area of trade cooperation and the dispatch of experts: 'It is necessary to take into account that the area of economic and scientific and technical cooperation will be of extraordinary importance, and therefore special emphasis will need to be placed on it.'[51] Further, it is stated that the economic cooperation between both states will be based on the 'perspectives of the

Mozambican economy and Czechoslovak needs and interests', and its goal is 'to develop mutually advantageous foreign trade'.[52]

From an economic point of view, Mozambique was considered promising due to its mineral wealth, agricultural production and developing industries such as mining and food processing. Beryl, bauxite and coal were mentioned as raw materials, and cotton, sisal, peanuts and cashews as agricultural products. Trade development was also promising due to its neighbourhood with the then economically prosperous Southern Rhodesia and South Africa.[53] From a political point of view, the political orientation of a new Mozambique government was crucial. According to the Czechoslovak authorities, it could inspire other African countries. The friendly attitude of the Mozambicans towards the Czechoslovak representatives and their willingness to establish close contacts were also mentioned.[54] Last but not least, the active stance of other socialist countries, such as the Soviet Union, Eastern Germany and Bulgaria, played its role.[55]

Main characteristics of the Czechoslovak expertise in Angola and Mozambique

With trade and military contacts, the essential cooperation between Czechoslovakia, Angola and Mozambique became the dispatch of Czechoslovak experts. Especially in the Angolan case, scientific-technical cooperation between both states, as this strategy was officially called, developed rapidly. The first Czechoslovak specialists paid by Angolan institutions came there in 1977. By the end of this year, more than fifty Czechoslovak experts were working there. In addition to the forty-three Czechoslovaks sent by the Polytechna, there were four technicians sent by Motokov,[56] two Czechoslovak doctors at Czechoslovak's expense and an unspecified number of geologists.[57] The number of Czechoslovak experts reached the highest number in this country in 1978, when sixty-one people worked there through the Polytechna alone.[58] On average, the number of experts in Angola ranged from fifty to sixty people per year between 1977 and 1983.[59] In March 1983, the largest Czechoslovak community was abducted by a rival movement of the MPLA, the National Union for the Total Independence of Angola (União Nacional para a Independência Total de Angola, UNITA) in the Angolan town of Alto Catumbela. After this serious incident, the cooperation declined. At the end of the Cold War, only few Czechoslovak experts worked in the country.

The first Czechoslovak experts were sent to Mozambique much later than to Angola. The first six geologists and three energy engineers arrived there in 1980 at Czechoslovak expense. It was not until a year later that the first specialists came commercially. It meant that the Mozambican side or another foreign actor completely covered their costs, including air tickets and salaries.[60] This delay was also in contrast to other Soviet bloc states. For example, the Soviet Union, East Germany and Bulgaria sent their specialists to Mozambican enterprises as early as 1977, a year after the Mozambican president requested help.[61] Similar to Angola, rapid development of this cooperation followed. At the beginning of 1982, the number of Czechoslovak specialists in Mozambique rose to fifty-five. Czechoslovak's expertise achieved the most outstanding development a year later when 110 Czechoslovaks worked there.[62] Even in Mozambique, however, this cooperation declined in the second half of the 1980s due to the escalating civil war there and the related economic crisis.[63] Compared to the numbers of Czechoslovak experts in the other states in the Global South, both Lusophone countries belonged to the destinations with their highest figures at that time.[64]

Regarding organizing the cooperation, most of the experts went to Angola and Mozambique through the foreign trade corporation Polytechna. Another Czechoslovak institution was the other foreign trade corporation Motokov, which sent its experts to these states with the Tatra deliveries. In Angola, they also repaired Zetor tractors.[65] The work and stay of technicians sent by Motokov were paid for through a bank loan as part of the export of Czechoslovak engineering products.[66] According to the respondents, the technicians sent by this institution to Mozambique were paid per diems that were allegedly much higher than the salaries from Mozambican employers. It was the same in the case of the ceramic industry there.[67]

In the case of Angola, there were only a few Czechoslovak experts sent at Czechoslovakia's expense.[68] Although even in the Mozambique case, the Czechoslovak authorities preferred sending experts commercially, the share of Czechoslovaks paid by Prague was much higher. It was characteristic of the beginning of this cooperation in 1980 and the second half of the decade. In 1986, almost a third of the thirty experts were sent at Czechoslovak's expense.[69] Three years later, it was nearly half of the eleven Czechoslovaks.[70] The commercial nature of this cooperation prevailed in Mozambique only in 1983.[71] The experts whose costs were covered by the Czechoslovak state included, for example, geologists, health professionals or experts in the ceramic industry. Most of them, especially at the beginning of the cooperation, were expected to prepare the conditions for sending their colleagues commercially, similar to Angola.

Another institution through which Czechoslovaks were dispatched to both Lusophone countries was the United Nations. In Angola, only one Czechoslovak expert was found who was sent through this organization for a longer time there. He worked between 1978 and 1983 as a teacher of general engineering in a development project at the National Vocational Training Center in Luanda. He was tasked with building a fully equipped workshop and classroom with colleagues from socialist countries.[72] Extant records from Mozambique testify to more Czechoslovaks sent by the United Nations, specifically through its Food and Agriculture Organization (FAO). These were, for example, university teachers at the veterinary faculty of the University of Maputo.[73]

Among the most frequently represented sectors in which Czechoslovaks worked in Angola and Mozambique were the wood technology and paper industry, energy, brewing and health care. In Mozambique, cooperation also thrived in geology and veterinary medicine. All these sectors were established in Czechoslovakia and had experience exporting abroad. In Angola, the essential Czechoslovak projects were implemented in the town of Alto Catumbela. In addition to the power substation and the health care centre, Czechoslovaks worked in the Cellulose and Paper Company (Companhia de Celulose e Papel de Angola, CCPA) between 1977 and 1983 there. This company was built during Portuguese rule in the 1950s and nationalized after independence. When the first thirty-one Czechoslovak experts arrived in 1977, it was in a state of disrepair and had to be repaired first, often in makeshift conditions. Its operation was restored two years later and became a model example of cooperation between the two countries. In addition to the financial benefits, Czechoslovakia attached considerable political weight to it and used it as evidence of the successful development of mutual relations and effective assistance to Angola.[74]

In the case of Mozambique, the most important Czechoslovak project was the wood technology company known as IFLOMA (from Portuguese Indústrias florestais de Manica) in the Mozambican town of Villa de Messica in the province of Manica. It was a large plant with a sawmill, line for plywood production, joinery and other facilities. It was built, including accommodation, in 1982 by a Swedish company supported by the Swedish government agency SIDA as part of its development cooperation with Mozambique. The Swedes also covered the costs associated with this project throughout, including the salaries of Czechoslovak experts.[75] The first group of twenty-four Czechoslovaks arrived at IFLOMA in 1983, and a year later they managed to get the whole plant up and running. Still, by 1985, due to the deterioration of the overall situation in the country, it was operating at only a quarter of its capacity. The official records show that the project fulfilled not only the economic but also the political objectives of both countries: 'Today (in 1985, note) Mozambique is unable to keep the plant running without the help of foreign experts. The presence of Czechoslovak experts is therefore not only of economic but also of political importance.'[76] The last Czechoslovaks left IFLOMA in 1988, despite Czechoslovakia's interest in continued cooperation.[77]

Economic roles of Czechoslovak experts in Angola and Mozambique

The objectives pursued by Czechoslovakia in sending its experts to Angola and Mozambique can be divided into economic, political and development cooperation, with the emphasis on the economic dimension of this strategy dominating the Czechoslovak official record. This is confirmed, for example, in the abovementioned first conception of Czechoslovak policy towards Mozambique in 1979[78] or in official documents concerning Angola.[79] It is also evidenced by the inclusion of this strategy and trade exchange in the area of economic relations in Czechoslovak foreign policy conceptions towards these countries.

Prague pursued its several economic interests through this strategy in both countries. One of them was to secure the scarce hard currency for the Czechoslovak state budget. It concerned mainly Czechoslovaks sent by the Polytechna, with most of them working in Angola through this institution and at least two-thirds of them in Mozambique at the time of the most outstanding development of this cooperation. These specialists were obliged to contribute hard currency from their salaries to the Polytechna account in Czechoslovakia. It was 40 percent to two-thirds of the foreign exchange portion of their monthly salary, depending on the type of contract. Documents from Mozambique show that these contributions varied considerably according to educational attainment and job position. In the case of a direct agreement for a secondary school position in a Mozambican brewery with a monthly salary of around 820 USD, the expert deducted 123 USD per month.[80] The annual contribution was around 1,500 USD. For a two-year stay in Mozambique, the amount was equivalent to the price of a new Škoda car.[81] However, the monthly salary of a project manager with a university degree in the Mozambican woodworking industry, also on a direct contract, was already around 2,870 USD and Polytechna's dues were 650

USD per month.[82] He thus paid 7,800 USD annually. In the case of the indirect contract at IFLOMA, the manager's salary per month was also around 2,870 USD.[83] However, the documents do not indicate the levies on this amount.

Due to the unavailability of most of the documents from the Polytechna, it is difficult to reach any general conclusions about the number of annual contributions from the salary of individual experts and their actual contribution to the Czechoslovak state budget. Although the respondents agreed that the compulsory contributions to the Polytechna were a valuable source of foreign exchange for the state budget,[84] it is impossible to verify whether this was the case. One of the few available data dates from 1983, when a record number of Czechoslovaks were working in the country. According to the data, the average payment of individual experts on direct contracts to the Polytechna was 126 USD per month,[85] equivalent to the aforementioned high school position in a Mozambican brewery. At that time, fifty Czechoslovaks worked in the country on direct contracts, which meant Czechoslovakia would have received 75,600 USD a year from their salaries. Compared to the amount of trade between the two countries, which a year later exceeded five million USD,[86] this would be a negligible amount. However, as already mentioned, in the case of indirect contracts, the levies were higher, and even the wage levels for individual direct contracts varied. The trade between the two countries was also, in most cases, on credit, unlike the levies, which was more or less a sure and regular income for the Czechoslovak state. Also wholly missing is a comparison of the salaries and dues of Czechoslovaks working in Angola. However, according to the respondents, Czechoslovaks' wages in the Angolan timber industry were higher than in Mozambique.[87] What is certain is that the Czechoslovak authorities preferred in both cases to send experts on indirect contracts, which, as they stated, were 'more commercially interesting for them'.[88] In Angola, these were almost all projects, including the CCPA in Alto Catumbela, while in Mozambique, they were only a few, including the sock factory in Maputo and the IFLOMA company.

Another 'economic role' of Czechoslovak experts in both countries was to broker new business opportunities. This is evidenced by the surviving records on Angola, where the Czechoslovak authorities repeatedly requested an increase in specialists because they influenced the decision-making of local economic actors.[89] The experts were instrumental in securing the export of Czechoslovak malt to Mozambique between 1984 and 1985, which was preferred to the existing French suppliers. A total of four deliveries of these goods were made. However, the testimonies also point to the negative aspects of this trade, caused by the low quality of Czechoslovak malt, when mould appeared in the last deliveries. As one expert explains in his report, 'It was only thanks to the good position of comrade Mrázek and myself at SOGERE (Sociedade geral de cervejas e refrigerantes de Moçambique) that even these deliveries could be processed without customer complaints.'[90] The Czechoslovak brewers also tried to negotiate the participation of domestic companies in the reconstruction of local breweries and the purchase of machinery from Czechoslovakia. However, as the respondent points out, competition from the West was also evident in this sector, with Portugal and Belgium being the main rivals of Czechoslovakia. They did provide Mozambique with the necessary loans in capitalist currency, but they were tied to purchasing their goods and services. In some cases, there was interest on their part to cooperate, but no concrete projects in this sector were implemented.[91] Czechoslovak malt was also imported to Angolan breweries.

Another example was the so-called complex contracts, where Prague supplied not only its experts but also equipment and technology. It was the case, for example, with the sock factory in Maputo, where, in addition to its experts, it also provided machinery in the form of twelve knitting machines of its manufacture, worth over two million USD.[92] Another project was expanding a ceramic tile factory in Umbeluzi, near Maputo. It also included the export of glaze, cement and pressing materials from Czechoslovakia worth five million USD.[93] Both projects were financed by an interbank loan granted to Mozambique by the Czechoslovak state.[94] In Angola, the project involved the modernization of a hospital in the town of Ganda, where Prague was to supply the necessary equipment, including, for example, aggregates, a kitchen and laundry, worth five million USD, paid for by the Angolan side.[95]

Czechoslovak experts were also included in the negotiations about importing raw materials from both Lusophone countries to Czechoslovakia. Prague had great expectations, especially from Czechoslovak geologists who explored iron ore and apatite deposits in the north of Mozambique between 1982 and 1983. Czechoslovakia even became the primary coordinator of geological exploration there, together with the GDR, which focused on coal mining.[96] In the case of Angola, Czechoslovak experts were supposed to help secure the importation of its oil, but due to the West's monopoly on this sector in the country, this failed. The possibility of importing tropical wood was more promising, and establishing a Czechoslovak-Angola company for extracting, processing and exporting tropical timber in the Angolan enclave of Cabinda was also considered.[97] However, in both countries, a similar scenario was repeated in most cases. The Czechoslovak authorities first sent experts at their own expense to prepare projects. Their costs should be repaid by importing raw materials and other products into Czechoslovakia. In Mozambique, the Czechoslovak state paid five million USD for geological surveys.[98] The return on the money spent was to be ensured by the preferential purchase of Mozambican raw materials for the needs of the Czechoslovak economy.[99] However, the original expectations were not met due to the rapidly deteriorating security situation in both countries. In Mozambique, geological exploration was halted due to the control of the area by the opposition movement. The same development occurred in Angola, where the forest inventory in the northern provinces could not be completed.[100]

Conclusion

This chapter discussed varieties of economic nationalism of smaller socialist states in the late Cold War on the example of the dispatch of Czechoslovak experts in Angola and Mozambique. In particular, it focused on one of its variants: the aims and outcomes of this strategy, the Czechoslovak government's motivations and the Cold War's role in its implementation.

As was analysed in the previous sections, Prague pursued several economic goals with this strategy. Probably the most significant benefit was the acquisition of hard currency through compulsory deductions from the experts' salaries. According to extant examples, these levies on direct contracts in Mozambique ranged from 1,500 to 7,800 USD per year per expert in the first half of the 1980s.[101] Unfortunately, it was not found how high they were in the case of Angola, which was the economically stronger of the two countries and where indirect contracts prevailed. On the other hand, according to the available data, the amounts received were far from the annual trade between Czechoslovakia and these countries, even in the case of the poorer Mozambique. Therefore, the question remains whether these revenues can be considered a significant enrichment of the Czechoslovak state budget.

Another economic motivation was accessing local raw materials, iron ore, phosphates in Mozambique and tropical timber in the case of Angola. However, even here, the original expectations were not met, as the escalating civil conflicts and the deteriorating economic situation forced the suspension of the projects in both cases. The last identified economic role was to broker new business opportunities, with Czechoslovak experts succeeding, for example, in securing the export of Czechoslovak malt to breweries in both countries. Other contracts included supplying machinery to a Mozambican textile factory or a ceramic factory. In all cases, however, the profits did not cover the costs incurred, as evidenced by the complaints of the Czechoslovak authorities.

Despite poor outcomes of this strategy, where failure was also caused by the escalating civil wars in both countries in the 1980s, beyond the control of Czechoslovak actors, the archival materials show that developing mutual economic relations was a priority. Other motivations, such as solidarity with new allies and the development of political cooperation, were mentioned in these documents but only in second place. This rhetoric also corresponded to practice when sending Czechoslovak experts together with trade exchange and military contacts, often associated with purchasing Czechoslovak military equipment, which became the most significant areas of cooperation. Another feature that supports the argument of prioritizing national economic interests over other motivations is the emphasis on the mutual advantage of this strategy. It confirms the opinion of other researchers dealing with the approach of the state socialist countries towards the Global South in the late Cold War, who point out that it was characterized primarily by economic pragmatism.[102]

On the contrary, the research does not show that the size of Czechoslovakia would play a crucial role in developing economic contacts with these states. For example, they would prefer it over the most powerful Soviet Union. The previous experience with cooperation and Prague's willingness to engage in both states immediately after gaining their independence in other forms than the development of economically beneficial relations was more important. The local governments compared the Czechoslovak willingness to the involvement of other members of the Soviet bloc, and Prague was rather criticized for its emphasis on economic pragmatism. In practice, however, it was noticeable that there were competitive struggles between actors from the East and the West when the socialist states, due to their technological backwardness and inflexible approach, failed to establish themselves in the most lucrative sectors, such as the Angolan oil industry. The disadvantage of the socialist countries was also evident in Angola's wood technology and energy industry, where Czechoslovakia supplied the workforce and the West, in particular Sweden, supplied technological equipment.

Finally, in the broader context of the academic discussion on varieties of economic nationalism, it is possible to identify the Czechoslovak dispatch of its experts in both Lusophone African states as liberal/outward-looking, which is characterized by deepening cooperation with external actors, in this case with the Global South, to protect Prague's economic interests. As mentioned at the beginning of the chapter, this was not an unusual approach in its case. For most of the twentieth century, Czechoslovak export-oriented economy was based, with short exceptions, on deepening cooperation with abroad.

Notes

1 Judt, *Poválečná Evropa*, 490.
2 Ibid.
3 For more on the Czechoslovak foreign trade in the interwar period see Lacina, *Formování československé ekonomiky*, 132–68.
4 For more on the academic discussion about varieties of economic nationalism see the Preface of this volume, page 12, and the chapter of Adrian Brisku.
5 For more on the conservative economic policy of Czechoslovakia in the first half of the 1970s see Szobi, Czechoslovakia's Pan-European Relations During the 'Long 1970s', in Romano and Romero, *European Socialist Regimes,* 134–58.
6 Preface of this volume and the chapter of Adrian Brisku.
7 See Romano and Romero, *European Socialist Regimes.* Or Lorenzini, 'The Socialist Camp and the Challenge of Economic Modernization in the Third World'. Or Trecker, *Red Money for the Global South.* Or Mark, Kalinovsky and Marung, *Alternative Globalizations.*
8 Ibid., 136–8.
9 Průcha, *Hospodářské dějiny Československa*, 671 and 690.
10 Buzássyová, *Socialist Internationalism in Practice*, 113 and 119.
11 Trecker, *Red Money for the Global South*, 121–2.
12 Menclová, *Mezi globálními ambicemi a ekonomickým pragmatismem*, 69.
13 See, for example, Lorenzini, 'The Socialist Camp and the Challenge of Economic Modernization in the Third World', or Trecker, *Red Money for the Global South*, or Mark, Kalinovsky and Marung, *Alternative Globalizations.*
14 For more on the definition of the small state see Kruizinga, *The Politics of Smallness in Modern Europe*, 6–7.
15 Romano and Romero, *European Socialist Regimes.*
16 In the case of Czechoslovakia see Szobi, 'Czechoslovak Economic Interests in Angola in the 1970s and 1980s', in Calori, *Between East and South*, 165–96.
17 Průcha, *Hospodářské dějiny Československa.*
18 See, for example, Hatzky, 'Os Bons Colonizadores', Harisch, '10 East German Friendship Brigades and Specialists in Angola', in *Transregional Connections in the History of East-Central Europe*, Castryck-Naumann.
19 Buzássyová, *Socialist Internationalism in Practice.*

20 For more on the memories of Czechoslovak forest experts in Angola see Menclová, 'Czechoslovak forest experts in Cold War Angola', in Pešta, *Prague Papers on the History of International Relations*, 1–2.
21 Trecker, *Red Money for the Global South*, 121.
22 Burton, 'From Convergence to Divergence', 8.
23 Trecker, *Red Money for the Global South*, 155 and 157.
24 Lorenzini, 'The Socialist Camp and the Challenge of Economic Modernization in the Third World', 355.
25 Ibid., 359.
26 Trecker, *Red Money for the Global South*, 69–70.
27 Ibid., 65.
28 Lorenzini, 'The Socialist Camp and the Challenge of Economic Modernization in the Third World', 352.
29 Trecker, *Red Money for the Global South*, 112.
30 Ibid., 176.
31 Lorenzini, 'The Socialist Camp and the Challenge of Economic Modernization in the Third World', 357.
32 Trecker, *Red Money for the Global South*, 168, 196.
33 For more on the role of the Polytechna see Buzássyová, *Socialist Internationalism in Practice*, 37.
34 Ibid., 93 and 193.
35 Buzássyová, *Socialist Internationalism in Practice*, 103, Koura and Pešta, 'Československo a studená válka v Africe', 7.
36 Buzássyová, *Socialist Internationalism in Practice*, 106 and 188.
37 Ibid., 113 and 119.
38 Průcha, *Hospodářské dějiny Československa*, 661.
39 Ibid., 674, 688–9.
40 Between 1974 and 1976, between 500,000 and 700,000 people came to Portugal from its former colonies, mainly Angola and Mozambique. See Rosas, *História a História, África*, 185.
41 AMZV ČR. TO-T 1975–9. Angola, Karton 1. Angolská lidová republika – zřízení čs. ZÚ v Luandě. Důvodová zpráva. 9. 8. 1976.
42 AMZV TO-T Angola 1975–79 Karton 1, Zaměření a hlavní úkoly československé zahraniční politiky vůči ALR, 12 October 1976.
43 AMZV TO-T Angola 1975–9 Karton 1, Zaměření a hlavní úkoly čs. zahr. politiky vůči ALR, 13 November 1976.
44 NA ČR, Fond Federální ministerstvo zahraničního obchodu, Karton 1652 Angola, Současný stav rozpracovaných případů. 21 October 1976.
45 AMZV TO-T Angola 1975–9 Karton 1, Zaměření a hlavní úkoly čs. zahr. politiky vůči ALR, 12 October 1976.

46 AMZV TO-T Angola 1975–9. Karton 2, Přehled o hodnocení technické pomoci a vědecko-technickém stavu spolupráce mezi ČSSR a ALR za 1. pololetí 1979 a porovnání s vývojem spolupráce ostatních ZSS, 21 August 1979.
47 AMZV ČR, Fond TO-T, Mosambik 1975–9, Karton 1, Informace o návštěvě mosambického prezidenta v SSSR, Mosambik – vyhlášení nezávislosti, 8 June 1976.
48 AMZV ČR, Fond dokumentace teritoriálních odborů 1945–89, Návštěva ministra zahraničních věcí MsLR Joaquima Alberta Chissana v ČSSR ve dnech 31 January–5 February 1981, II. informační část, 6. Základní informace a Historicko-politický přehled.
49 AMZV ČR, Fond TO-T, Mosambik 1975–9, Karton 1, Materiál pro schůzi P ÚV KSČ – Zřízení čs. ZÚ v Mosambické lidové republice, 17 August 1977.
50 AMZV ČR, Fond dokumentace teritoriálních odborů 1945–89, Nezpracovaná část – Čs.-mosambické vztahy 1981–3, Vztahy MsLR k ostatním státům a skupinám států 1983, Vývoj čs.-mosambické ekonomické spolupráce, 31 January 1983.
51 AMZV ČR, Fond TO-T, Mosambik 1975–9, Karton 1, Zaměření a hlavní úkoly čs. zahraniční politiky vůči Mosambické lidové republice, 29 August 1979.
52 Ibid.
53 AMZV ČR, Fond TO-T, Mosambik 1975–9, Karton 1, Návrh na zřízení zastupitelského úřadu v Mosambiku, 29 October 1975; AMZV ČR, Fond TO-T, Mosambik 1975–9, Karton 1, Návrh na uznání Mosambiku a navázání diplomatických styků, 27 May 1975.
54 AMZV ČR, Fond TO-T, Mosambik 1975–9, Karton 1, Materiál pro schůzi P ÚV KSČ – Zřízení čs. ZÚ v Mosambické lidové republice, 17 August 1977; AMZV ČR, Fond TO-T, Mosambik 1975–9, Karton 1, Zřízení ZÚ v Mosambické lidové republice – návrh do vlády ČSSR, 1977.
55 Zídek, Sieber, *Československo a subsaharská Afrika*, 154.
56 AMZV TO-T Angola 1975–9 Karton 2, Zpráva o stycích s čs. experty za rok 1977, 12 January 1978.
57 AMZV TO-T Angola 1975–9, Karton 2, Zpráva o stavu spolupráce ALR se státy RVHP v oblasti VTS, 14 November 1977.
58 NA ČR, Fond Federální ministerstvo zahraničního obchodu, Karton 1651 Angola, Přednes do vlády – zpráva o výsledcích obchodně politických jednání s ALR, 6 May 1978.
59 AMZV, TO-T Angola 1980–9, Karton 4, Vyhodnocení plnění Protokolu z I. a II. zasedání smíšené mezivládní komise pro vědeckotechnickou spolupráci mezi ALR a ČSSR, 28 May 1981; AMZV TO-T Angola 1980–9, Karton 2, Záznam o rozhovoru ekonomického rady ČSSR s ekonomickým radou NDR, 6 January 1983. For further information on the number of experts from Czechoslovakia and other socialist countries, see Szobi, '7. Czechoslovak Economic Interests in Angola', 174.

60 NA ČR, Fond KSČ ÚV 1945–89, Praha – Gustáv Husák, Oficiální přátelská návštěva předsedy FRELIMO a prezidenta Mosambiku S. M. Machela v ČSSR ve dnech 19–23 October 1981, Dopis čs. ministra zahraničního obchodu čs. ministru financí, 14 October 1981.

61 AMZV ČR, Fond TO-T, Mosambik 1975–9, Karton 1, Mosambická lidová republika – Návrh pro P ÚV KSČ na zřízení čs. zastupitelského úřadu v Maputo, 8 May 1977.

62 AMZV ČR, Fond TO-T, Mosambik 1980–9, Karton 3, Plnění smluvních dokumentů uzavřených mezi ČSSR a MsLR, 5 March 1984.

63 Menclová, *Mezi globálními ambicemi a ekonomickým pragmatismem*, 11.

64 Ibid., 69.

65 AMZV TO-T Angola 1975–9 Karton 2, Zpráva o stycích s čs. experty za rok 1977, 12 January 1978.

66 AMZV ČR, Fond TO-T, Mosambik 1980–9, Karton 1, Záznam o rozhovoru čs. 1. tajemníka J. Suttnera s chargé d'affaires a. i. Rumunska N. Vulpascinem, 11 November 1983.

67 ABS ČR, Svazek Sahara-Afrika, č. sv. 22907, OBZ_19715_MV, Zpráva: O vytěžení po návratu ze zahraničí (Mosambik) – TS Král; Interview 10, Praha, 26 November 2021.

68 AMZV, Angola 1976 – I. díl, Dokumentace 8.t.o. od vyhlášení nezávislosti Angoly 11 November 1975 do 31 December 1976, Zpráva ZÚ Luanda ze dne 16 September 1976. Tisková konference s čs. lékaři v Lobito. č. j. 111.081/76–8.

69 AMZV ČR, Fond TO-T, Mosambik 1980–9, Karton 3, Zpráva o plnění zaměření a hlavních úkolů čs. zahraniční politiky vůči MsLR, 24 April 1986.

70 AMZV ČR, Fond TO-T, Mosambik 1980–9, Karton 1, Hodnocení plnění Zaměření a hlavních úkolů čs. zahraniční politiky vůči Mosambické lidové republice a Království Lesotho, 12 June 1989.

71 AMZV ČR, Fond TO-T, Mosambik 1980–9, Karton 1, Zpráva o služební cestě do provincie Manica – závod IFLOMA, 24 January 1986. Více viz kapitola Hlavní projekty československé expertizy v Mosambiku.

72 AMZV ČR, Fond TO-T, Angola 1980–9, Karton 4, Vyhodnocení plnění Protokolu z I. a II. zasedání smíšené mezivládní komise pro VTS mezi ALR a ČSSR, 28 May 1981.

73 AMZV ČR, Fond TO-T, Mosambik 1980–9, Karton 3, Hodnocení činnosti a plnění plánu ZÚ Maputo v roce 1984, 8 February 1985.

74 NA ČR, Fond Polytechna, Svazek Angola, CCPA Alto Catumbela, Dopis Výboru ZO ROH Alto Catumbela předsedovi Výboru ZO Luanda, 19 July 1982.

75 Interview 1. The Swedish Government Agency SIDA still exists today. More to its activities https://www.sida.se/en (accessed 12 January 2023).

76 AMZV ČR, Fond TO-T, Mosambik 1980–9, Karton 3, Zpráva o služební cestě do provincie Manica a prověrce bezpečnosti na závodě IFLOMA, 14 June 1985.

77 NA ČR, Fond Polytechna, Karton 1198, Mosambik, Zpráva z cesty M. Petruse na veletrh FACIM 88 v Maputu, 27 August–7 September 1988.

78 AMZV ČR, Fond TO-T, Mosambik 1975–9, Karton 1, Zaměření a hlavní úkoly čs. zahraniční politiky vůči Mosambické lidové republice, 29 August 1979.

79 Ibid., AMZV ČR, Fond TO-T, Angola 1975–9, Karton 2. Přehled o hodnocení technické pomoci a vědecko-technickém stavu spolupráce mezi ČSSR a ALR za 1. pololetí 1979 a porovnání s vývojem spolupráce ostatních ZSS, 21 August 1979.

80 Dodatek ke smlouvě mezi Polytechnou a panem X ze dne 5 June 1981, Personal archiv Mr. X.

81 Závěrečné vyúčtování mezi Polytechnou a panem X (for reasons of privacy, the name has been omitted) ze dne 9 July 1985; Interview 2; Lískovec, 16.

82 Smlouva mezi Polytechnou a panem Y (for reasons of privacy, the name has been omitted) ze dne 29 February 1984, Personal archiv Mr. Y; NA ČR, Fond Polytechna, Karton 1198, Mosambik, Zpráva z cesty Karla Hanáka, ředitele obchodní skupiny 23 – Polytechna, do Mosambiku, 16 March–25 March 1986.

83 NA ČR, Fond Polytechna, Karton 1198, Mosambik, Zpráva z cesty Karla Hanáka, ředitele obchodní skupiny 23 – Polytechna, do Mosambiku, 16 March–25 March 1986.

84 Interviews 1–12.

85 NA ČR, Fond Polytechna, Karton 1198, Mosambik, Zpráva z cesty Karla Hanáka, obchodního ředitele PZO Polytechny, do Mosambiku a Angoly ve dnech 7.–24 February 1983.

86 AMZV ČR, Fond TO-T, Mosambik 1980–9, Karton 1, Mosambik – návrh na vyslání čs. delegace na oslavy 10. výročí nezávislosti, 7 June 1985.

87 Interview 10, Praha, 26 November 2021.

88 NA ČR, Fond Polytechna, Karton 1198, Mosambik, Zpráva z cesty L. Greé do Mosambiku, 29 May–11 June 1988; Závěrečné vyúčtování mezi Polytechnou a panem X ze dne 9 July 1985; Rozhovor 2; Smlouva mezi Polytechnou a panem Y ze dne 29 February 1984.

89 AMZV ČR, Fond TO-T, Angola 1975–9, Karton 2, Zpráva o stavu spolupráce ALR se státy RVHP v oblasti VTS. 14 November 1977; AMZV ČR, Fond TO-T, Angola 1980–9, Karton 4, O pobytu ministra zahraničního obchodu ČSSR s. A. Barčáka v ALR při příležitosti 2. zasedání 'smíšené angolsko-československé komise pro hospodářskou a technickou pomoc', 28 January 1981.

90 Michal Pomahač, Závěrečná zpráva z dlouhodobé expertizy, srpen 1985, Personal archive M. Pomahače.

91 Ibid.

92 AMZV ČR, Fond dokumentace teritoriálních odborů 1945–89, Čs.-mosambické vztahy 1981–3, Vztahy MsLR k ostatním státům a skupinám států 1983, Čs.-mosambická spolupráce – otevření závodu na výrobu ponožek, 7 January 1983.

93 AMZV ČR, Fond TO-T, Mosambik 1980–9, Karton 1, Vztahy ČSSR s Mosambikem, 11 January 1988.

94 AMZV ČR, Fond TO-T, Mosambik 1980–9, Karton 1, Mosambik (pro schůzi vlády), Zpráva o průběhu a výsledcích oficiální přátelské návštěvy předsedy Strany FRELIMO a prezidenta MsLR S. M. Machela v ČSSR ve dnech 19.–23. října 1981.

95 NA ČR, Fond Federální ministerstvo zahraničního obchodu, Karton 1651, Angola, Podklady pro jednání s. náměstka Ing. J. Jakubce se subjekty zahraničního obchodu SSSR, nedatováno (okolo 1980, pozn. aut.).

96 AMZV ČR, Fond dokumentace teritoriálních odborů 1945–89, Čs.-mosambické vztahy 1981–3, Vztahy MsLR k ostatním státům a skupinám států 1983, Vývoj čs.-mosambické ekonomické spolupráce, 31 January 1983; AMZV ČR, Fond dokumentace teritoriálních odborů 1945–89, Čs.-mosambické vztahy 1981–3, Vztahy MsLR k ostatním státům a skupinám států 1983, Hospodářská a vědecko-technická spolupráce (FMZO, září 1981).

97 NA ČR, Fond Federální ministerstvo zahraničního obchodu, Karton 1651, Angola, Zpráva o poskytování pomoci a o spolupráci ČSSR s ALR v různých odvětvích národního hospodářství, 1980.

98 AMZV ČR, Fond TO-T, Mosambik 1980–9, Karton 3, Hodnocení činnosti a plnění plánu ZÚ Maputo v roce 1983, 31 January 1984; AMZV ČR, Fond TO-T, Mosambik 1980–9, Karton 3, Zpráva o plnění zaměření a hlavních úkolů čs. zahraniční politiky vůči MsLR, 24 April 1986.

99 AMZV ČR, Fond TO-T, Mosambik 1980–9, Karton 1, Mosambik (pro schůzi vlády), Zpráva o průběhu a výsledcích oficiální přátelské návštěvy předsedy Strany FRELIMO a prezidenta MsLR S. M. Machela v ČSSR ve dnech 19.–23. října 1981.

100 Interview 1, Brandýs and Labem, 24 September 2019 and 24 June 2022.

101 NA ČR, Fond Polytechna, Karton 1198, Mosambik, Zpráva z cesty L. Greé do Mosambiku, 29 May – 11 June 1988; Závěrečné vyúčtování mezi Polytechnou a panem X ze dne 9 July 1985; Rozhovor 2; Smlouva mezi Polytechnou a panem Y ze dne 29 February 1984, osobní archiv pana Y.

102 Lorenzini, 'The Socialist Camp and the Challenge of Economic Modernization in the Third World', 351.

Part III

Détente through Foreign Trade

5

'Doing business with the colonels': Greece's financial relations with Austria and the German Democratic Republic during the Greek military dictatorship, 1967–74

Ioannis Brigkos

Introduction

The late 1960s and early 1970s marked a significant historical rupture in Greece's contemporary history. Greece ultimately acquired the desirable post-war stability after a devastating tripartite occupation during the Second World War and a sanguineous and almost equally destructive civil war. Notwithstanding that the level of democratization may not have been to the highest standards, the country had achieved multiple positive apparent results in the socio-economic and foreign relations field.[1] Yet on 21 April 1967, after two years of severe political unrest and multiple parliamentary crises,[2] a group of low- to mid-ranking military officers usurped power abruptly after their successful coup and established a seven-year dictatorship.[3] This would test the strength primarily of the domestic pylons of the society and would also affect the function of the economic and foreign relations policy of the country.

The ascension to power of the military rulers in Greece caused sheer abhorrence to many Western countries, especially when the global human rights movement was growing stronger day by day. Public opinion expressed its ire and concerns about the (mis)happenings in Greece. Major transnational institutions decided to put aside the typical Cold War realpolitik and the wait-and-see approach of many foreign governments. They adopted a firmer stance against the dictatorship.[4] The most prominent and tangible example of international opposition against the junta[5] stemmed from the Council of Europe.[6] After two and a half long years of parliamentary meetings, hearings, testimonies and thousands of pages dedicated to the abuse and violation of human rights in Greece, the Greek Minister of Foreign Affairs Panagiotis Pipinelis announced on 12 December 1969 his country's voluntary withdrawal from the Council, before its imminent expulsion from it.[7]

While undoubtedly though, the public condemnation of the dictatorship in the West may have been one side of the coin, there was also the aspect of foreign policy drawing and implementation, which had, to some extent, borne fruits for the military regime. The military rulers had realized, up to a point, their inability to undertake the formal diplomatic representation of the country and abide by specific rules of international relations, including external commerce and its interconnection with interstate diplomacy. Therefore, they wittingly placed former experienced diplomats in crucial positions who could aid them in their endeavour to elevate the international status of the regime, aiming to make Greece an adroit intermediary, at least in the Mediterranean periphery.[8]

However, the acute problem faced by the dictatorship was its recognition by foreign governments. This problem was exacerbated by the unsuccessful royal counter-coup on 13 December 1967, which led to the exile of King Constantine. This created fear among the ringleaders that foreign states would declare their support for the exiled king, and consequently, any attempt to legitimize the military regime would be in vain. Therefore, the colonels tried to cultivate the image of a more autonomous 'regional power' whose legitimacy did not depend on the king's approval. In other words, the regime could develop its own diplomatic mechanism and garner support not only from the major powers of the time, which, as it turned out later, showed tolerance almost from the beginning, but also from smaller countries, diametrically opposed to the dictatorial regime, both politically and ideologically. Nonetheless, the dictatorship employed a certain nationalist rhetoric that aimed to justify its financial policy. According to Georgios Papadopoulos, the leader of the coup, one of the regime's objectives was to address economic underdevelopment, the absence of essential prerequisites for swift economic and social progress, and the overall inefficiency of the state administration.[9] The military rulers were a sui generis category of economic nationalists who preferred free trade, as their survival hinged, among other things, on exchanges with international markets.[10] This, they thought, could elevate their prestige and Greece's international status and financial flexibility.

The economic policies of the Greek dictatorship were influenced by its lack of political and moral legitimacy, as the regime sought to bolster public acceptance by prioritizing economic growth. Despite this aim, the dictatorship ultimately aimed to align its policies with those of previous democratic governments, demonstrating a continuation of pre-dictatorial economic strategies.[11] Industrial growth remained a central focus, with an increased emphasis on sectors like tourism and construction. The regime aimed to adhere to established economic principles such as maintaining a stable exchange rate, enforcing fiscal discipline and ensuring nominal wage growth in line with or below productivity growth. In the short term, the dictatorship managed to boost productivity and investment by largely following the economic policies of previous governments, which emphasized outward-facing strategies, industrialization and attracting foreign investment.[12] However, despite initial successes, the regime's policies ultimately led to economic difficulties and challenges that were difficult to manage in the long run. These shortcomings became increasingly evident, particularly following the events of 1973, including Colonel Dimitrios Ioannidis' coup and international economic shocks.[13]

On the one hand, this chapter will examine how Austria decided to put aside its neutrality policy and even expand the 'active neutrality policy' of the Kreisky government.[14] To achieve that, Vienna signed one of the most significant foreign industrial investments of the post-war Austrian state with dictatorial Greece in 1972, that of Steyr-Hellas. This investment demonstrated Vienna's need to internationalize parts of its state industry, such as the automobile company Steyr-Daimler-Puch AG (SDPAG), and 'open' new markets and financial opportunities for its products.[15] On the other hand, GDR's *Westpolitik* will be considered by focusing on its financial relations with Greece under the colonels. The attempts of both states to overcome international isolation and develop cordial financial relations will be analysed,[16] having at their epicentre the construction and installation in Greece of six electric power plants from the East German state-owned company 'Elektrotechnik Export-Import'.

The case studies under discussion showcased signs of financial dependence on the other two countries. Yet, these two countries decided to overcome their ideological barriers against an autocratic, dictatorial regime and establish genial economic relations. For the dictators, closer cooperation with the other two states meant strengthening national economy-building, primarily for domestic consolidation and international acceptance.[17] For Austria and the GDR, it was a tangible example of bolstering their national economies through increased exports and generous investment in the dictatorial regime.

This chapter is also an attempt to enrich the small state literature and indicate that through these two paradigms under discussion, the regional possibilities of Cold War relations can be expanded and supplemented with novel studies.[18] All three small states under discussion were mainly 'rule-takers' rather than 'rule-makers' during the Cold War era. Yet their 'smallness' was much more flexible than one can imagine.[19] It is important to underline that there can be no overstatement to assert that there was an economic breakthrough or a financial miracle between Greece and the two other states under analysis. It will be argued that all three peripheral[20] countries employed a certain amount of their foreign policymaking mechanisms, to create a viable interstate communication and accommodate their national financial interests. Furthermore, certain aspects of the subject under discussion will be examined under the scope of the New Diplomatic History.[21] It will be demonstrated that the meticulous examination of first-hand diplomatic narratives and the disclosure of the accounts of the (financial and political alike) diplomats' agencies defined and influenced mutatis mutandis the implementation of national foreign policy.

Finally, this chapter seeks to illustrate that through state intervention, whether from lobbying or a centrally planned economy, Austria and the GDR made impressive economic approaches to Greece. This had at its core the notion that 'through the success of a nation's core firms, the well-being of the nation's citizens is assured'.[22] Towards this logic and attempting an expansion of a definition of economic nationalism, according to Andreas Pickel, 'the extension of economic activity beyond national boundaries does not equal the end of national economy; the latter, qua political, social, and cultural economy, continues to be the basis for the former'.[23]

All three countries in question had as their principal focus the stimulation of their national economies to one extent or the other.[24] For the colonels, for reasons of regime stabilization and because of the size of the country, they decided to adopt more liberal and progressive economic policies.[25] Yet they did not omit to accentuate their nationalistic discourse in an attempt to legitimize their financial policies. The correlation between ideology, nationalism and economic development appeared not only in the speeches of the highest military leaders of the country but also in the appointed ideologists or propagandists of the military regime. One of the main texts elucidating the ideology of the dictatorship, written by Georgios Georgalas, mentioned that among the primary aims of the 'Revolution' was to economically integrate Greece into the twentieth century, aligning it with the community of technically and economically advanced nations.[26] This would elevate Greece's financial autonomy and subsequently improve the national living standards.

To achieve this goal, the colonels relied on the agency of state and non-state actors, both from their side and that of the other two states involved, to create novel national-economic spaces, allowing them room for manoeuvre, domestically and internationally. They succeeded in this contending – up to a point – that they were able to attract foreign investment, which served as a method for enhancing the development of the domestic economy, achieving the goal of generating employment, catalysing economic expansion and facilitating the transfer of technology and expertise to the nation. Austria and East Germany, on their behalf, managed to employ their own version of 'extreme' economic nationalism. These acts significantly ameliorated relations between Greece under the junta and two countries with dissimilar political backgrounds. They also demonstrated how countries with disparate conceptions of economy or economy-building manifest the pluralism and the varieties of economic nationalism.[27]

The economics of the dictatorship: Commercializing the foreign relations

The first signs of the economy under the military rulers did not offer a strong case for comparison with the previous democratic governments, as the fundamental economic trends and the financial policymakers remained practically the same.[28] Economists within post-war Greece originated from financial and academic institutions and government agencies. The colonels' rule did not disrupt this structuring significantly. Due to the absence of their group of technocrats and financial experts, the regime heavily relied on pre-existing economic establishments and their personnel. While some high-ranking figures resigned or were replaced, they were swiftly succeeded by their subordinates, with the explicit aim of preserving the stability of institutions and continuity in policy matters. Consequently, most individuals labelled as the regime's 'new' experts were not newcomers at all. Many had occupied various positions and cultivated relationships with professional organizations and the business community for the post-war era. The dictatorship's financial plans to bolster the national economy bore astonishing similarities to documents covering the pre-junta period. These had been commissioned during the tenure of the centrist government led by George Papandreou.[29]

The annual growth rate in 1967, the year of the coup, may have declined from 6.5 per cent to 5.7 per cent (in 1966), yet that was only temporary, as from

1968 until 1973, it would continue to have upward trends.[30] Since the beginning, dictatorial governments have tried to maintain the economic push from the previous years and the high development rates to similar or even higher levels. It is also essential to notice that the Greek dictators never tried to monopolize or nationalize sectors of the economy, as did, for instance, Nasser's regime in Egypt.[31] It had adopted a loosely defined laissez-faire tactic, which would accommodate private entrepreneurship and attract the much-needed foreign capital.[32] Of great significance and a piece of corroborative evidence here are two compulsory laws that were passed in 1967 and 1968 by the dictatorship, which were institutionalized and also secured by the new constitution of the junta, concerning the prevention of amendments to the legislation on the rights of foreign companies in Greece.[33]

In February 1968, the Greek minister of coordination and one of the three leading figures of the dictatorship, Nikolaos Makarezos, announced the Five-Year plan that the junta had sketched for the Greek economy.[34] Regarding foreign capitals, he mentioned:

> The program places particular emphasis on attracting foreign capital due to its multiple contributions to the country's economic development … The main role of foreign capital in the coming five years will consist of financing the required increased imports, introducing modern methods of organizing and managing businesses, and creating conditions for the infiltration of Greek products into foreign markets.[35]

One considerable implication that the junta had to deal with was the freezing of association with the European Economic Community (EEC). In 1962, Greece became the first member outside the six to have signed the association agreement, which aimed at Greece's full membership in the years to come.[36] The financial benefits Greece would enjoy were the tariff cutbacks on behalf of the EEC against Greece and vice versa, as well as a series of development loans. The usurpation of power by the military prompted not only the freezing of the association but also a political imbroglio that severely affected Greece's international reputation that the rulers were so eager to elevate.[37] However, it should be noted that the trade balance between Greece and the EEC remained practically intact during the dictatorship. It caused, though, the loss of almost $200 million in loans and undoubtedly sparked a major international political outcry between the Western states and their respective public opinion while also raising the issue of Greece's definite exclusion from the EEC.[38] Yet for European states such as the FRG, Great Britain and France, breach of financial relations was not easy to implement due to their heavy export policies that had been adopted towards Greece during the past years.

In the mindset of the military rulers, there was never any thought regarding abandoning the economic system of capitalism that had been strongly established after the Second World War and the civil war, which included heavy dependence on foreign loans and investments. Yet, on behalf of the Europeans, there was a growing fear that in case the dictatorship was to be left alone, there was a serious possibility that it could adopt an Eastern-oriented policy, which could have severe implications for the West, on a political, diplomatic and financial level as well.[39] Tangible examples of financial realpolitik were the junta's relations with West Germany, the largest trading partner of Greece during most of the Cold War era, including that of the dictatorship.[40] The FRG was not only a major creditor to Greece but also provided Athens with arms privately and within the framework of NATO.[41] A similar policy, especially regarding armaments sales, was also followed by Great Britain primarily under the Heath cabinet (1970–4)[42] and the French with the high-profile visit of the Secretary General of the French Ministry of Foreign Affairs in 1972 and the subsequent commercial deals that were signed.[43]

Yet for the colonels to set a strong foothold within the country, provide a sense of stability and avoid countercoups and anti-dictatorial acts, such as the failed royal coup of December 1967, they needed to demonstrate the ability for a multidimensional foreign end economic policy.[44] To achieve this, it was imperative to strengthen their ties with smaller states, even if this meant perforating the Iron Curtain.[45] Both the diplomatic mandates and the financial necessities of the Cold War dictated the shift of foreign policy towards every country willing to break the international isolation against the dictators and ameliorate its interstate communication with them.[46] In this context of particular interest are the junta's approach to a neutral but Western-oriented country such as Austria, and to a Warsaw pact-bound country which, though, attempted to escape the Soviet Union's shadow and, up to a point, define its concept of foreign policy, primarily through the edicts of financial exigencies.

Between neutrality and pragmatism: The case of the Austrian enterprise Steyr-Hellas

The military coup in Greece did not come as a total surprise to Vienna. Rumours had been circulating already since 1966 that military intervention in domestic politics could happen anytime due to the political crisis that the country faced for at least two years.[47] Yet after the coup did take place, the Austrian government did not hasten to condemn it. Although the Austrian ambassador in Greece and Cyprus, Ludwig Steiner, initially favoured a policy of political pressure from Austria and other Western states, he also acknowledged the significance of Austrian financial interests in Greece.[48] In his report on 3 January 1968 towards the Austrian MFA he mentions:

> Considerations about Greek-Austrian relations must not, of course, leave out of sight the economic aspects. Austria exports four to five times as much to Greece as it imports from Greece. Trade sanctions from Greece against Austria would therefore undoubtedly affect us.[49]

Steiner's rationale cannot be considered trivial. Until then, Austria exported significant quantities of chemical products (such as fertilizers), timber, processed paper and textiles to Greece. In 1967 Vienna's exports to Athens amounted to more than $21 million. And by 1970, these had increased to almost $28 million.[50] Steiner, having these figures in mind and despite his stark democratic sentiments, could not help but realize the cynical aspect of Vienna's financial interests and their predominance in the interstate communication with Athens, mentioning further: 'Even if the ideological values that are currently at stake in Greece are much more important, it is clear that they cannot outweigh other considerations when it comes to realpolitik.'[51]

Even though the Austrian diplomatic machinery had acted primarily – under the table – up until this point, the Greek diplomatic authorities had also acknowledged that Vienna was moderately friendly towards the military regime, as previously demonstrated in the Council of Europe.[52] Towards this direction, they sought to capitalize on this positive stance on a financial level as well, as a means to legitimize their rule. This rapprochement seems more plausible to have been adopted by the right-wing government of Josef Klaus and the People's Party (ÖVP one-party government, from 1966 to 1970). However, it was the social democratic Kreisky cabinet that elevated the financial relations between the two countries to a newer and unprecedented level up to this point. This materialized with the investment of the automobile company Steyr-Daimler-Puch AG in 1972, which had already been planned since 1970. On 9 July 1970, the Austrian Minister of Commerce Josef Staribacher[53] wrote in his diary:

> We strive all the more to make the motto 'Service for the economy' a breakthrough in individual cases. This is how it was possible that gen.(eral) dir.(ector) Rabus[54] from Steyr-Daimler-Puch AG … was immediately promised my

> support. Steyr-Daimler-Puch AG wants to set up a joint venture in Greece with Italian companies.[55]

The lobbying of SDPAG's director Rabus had been of considerable importance, as before the signing of the contract he had persuaded Staribacher to invite personally the Greek Deputy Minister of National Economy Antonis Choriatopoulos to Vienna at the beginning of May 1972. Therefore, Rabus hoped the deal would be ultimately signed, and this visit would be considered a gesture of goodwill towards the junta on behalf of the Austrian government.[56]

All in all, the investment of Steyr in Greece foresaw the construction of 70,000 square metres of industrial facilities, which would employ four thousand workers and include the production of thousands of tractors, trucks, mopeds, motorcycles and bicycles, including in later stages military trucks.[57] The significance of this project can be summarized in two fundamentals. Firstly, one of the essential clauses established as part of the deal between the Greek government and the Austrian enterprise was that the whole Greek market would introduce a ban on truck imports for SDPAG to monopolize it through local production.[58] Secondly, concerning the economic terms of the deal, SDPAG owned 67 per cent of the project, the Greek state 30 per cent and the remaining 3 per cent consisted of private shareholders, whereas the aggregate sum of the investment amounted to $78 million.[59] On the day of the signing, SDPAG's director Karl Rabus underlined that the Austrian government had shown great interest in the project. The signed contract is a major achievement in economic relations between the two countries and promised better prospects for the future. Finally, the Greek Minister of Coordination Nikolaos Makarezos concluded that 'through the signing of this contract, new horizons in the traditionally friendly relations between the two states will be opened', and he hoped that the Greek exports to Austria would be increased in the years to come, just as the respective imports have.[60]

Even though Austria tried to maintain a low profile and keep this investment relatively secret or minimize its significance, the Greek press attributed it great value as Ambassador Steiner underlined in a report a few days later:

> Last week's finalization of the Steyr-Daimler-Puch-AG project in Greece was extensively covered by the Greek daily press … a political commentary appeared in the Junta-friendly newspaper 'Eleftheros Kosmos' … It says that the investment … by Steyr also demonstrates confidence in (Greece's) political stability. No foreign company would risk such an investment in a country with internal instability and ambiguous foreign policy orientation.[61]

The Greek dictatorship had accomplished what since its establishment desired, namely, the attraction of foreign capital and the skilful development of financial diplomacy. While the SDPAG investment alone may not have been the 'financial cradle' of the foreign investments in Greece, it certainly was one of the most significant ones, which provided it with the opportunity to demonstrate both domestically and on an international level that the military rulers were able to conduct business regardless of the regime's character, while also securing a 'cloak of legitimacy' to the junta. Even under the leadership of Bruno Kreisky and his multifaceted humanitarian-oriented foreign policy, the Austrian side would once again seek to collaborate financially with dictatorships, as demonstrated by the armaments sales towards Chile in 1980, which though was ultimately cancelled.[62] Vienna, entangled in Cold War politics and foreign policy directives, eventually decided to implement its own realpolitik and demonstrate how flexible the proclaimed Austrian neutrality was.

The 'fascists' and the communists: Financial *Ostpolitik* lessons from the junta

The relations between the junta and the GDR are one of a unique nature, as until May 1973, there was no official recognition between Greece and the GDR.[63] Both countries faced international isolation in the maelstrom of Cold War developments, each for its own reasons. The GDR, after all, was at the centre of international Cold War confrontation from the very first moment of the division of Europe after the Second World War. Nowhere was this confrontation more vividly expressed than in the efforts of Eastern Germany to gain international recognition and elevate its status in the global community. These efforts encountered certain obstacles, such as the policy of isolation and non-recognition, the so-called Hallstein doctrine, as had been adopted by the FRG and, subsequently, its allies.[64] The fact, though, that eventually the two countries recognized each other amidst a regime that abhorred communism and its ideals,[65] while it was characterized by the GDR as 'fascist',[66] proves that the mutual approach tactic became gradually a priority in their political and diplomatic agenda, as they were equally trying to break the international isolation they were facing.[67] For the GDR, Greece's membership in NATO was also a critical factor in seeking a more significant development of their interstate relations. The East Germans already considered Greece a weak link within the military coalition. Namely, not only would it be beneficial for securing lucrative financial deals, but simultaneously, they could also 'penetrate' and disrupt the cohesion of the southeastern flank of the alliance.[68]

The colonels' coup had not initially convinced the Eastern Bloc states that the military would be able to remain in power for a long time. Due to this conviction, Moscow urged its allies to reduce relations with the Greek junta to a minimum. Therefore, the Western orientation of the junta and its close ties with the FRG were considered imperative concerning the regime's external diplomatic and financial relations. After 1969 though, and the solid internal stabilization of the regime, the Greek trade deficit had increased substantially. Thus, disregarding its loudly proclaimed anti-communist ideological principles, the military dictatorship made new and innovative attempts for a gradual rapprochement with the socialist states. A tangible example was the European Athletics Championships held in Athens in 1969. On the one hand, they served as the political propaganda of the military regime. On the other hand, the socialist states sent large delegations to Athens, inaugurating a period of closer relations between Greece and many communist states. The GDR was, in fact, the most successful national team in the tournament, celebrating twenty-five medals in total.[69] The end of the isolation period between the Eastern countries and the Greek dictatorship after 1969 could not leave the financial aspect out of the question. Already since 18 December 1968, a classified document from the Ministry of Foreign Affairs to the Ministry of External Commerce of the GDR mentioned the need to revise the anti-dictatorial measures:

> The aim of foreign policy and foreign economic measures toward Greece in the near future should be to … consolidate the position of the GDR and thus, at the same time, counter West Germany's exclusive mandate of recognition (Alleinvetretungsanspruch, writer's note) in this framework.[70]

This view was further corroborated a few months later, in April 1969, when the Council of Ministers of the GDR issued a new assessment of the military regime. It was mentioned inter alia that the goal of the socialist states to isolate the Greek military regime in terms of foreign policy and external trade directives, as had been planned initially, could not be ultimately achieved. Thus, it would be advisable or rather necessary for the Comecon member states to normalize their relations with Greece from that time onwards gradually.[71]

The growing political pressure from the Western countries, due to the pressure from their domestic public opinion towards the Greek dictatorship, led the military rulers to seek an expansion of their foreign policy edicts. So, they could prove that isolation from the West did not necessarily mean a full-scale disengagement from the international community. That was also known to Western and Eastern European diplomats serving in Greece. In turn, they acknowledged that the socialist states were always an alternative, specifically to the economic needs of the military regime.[72] Regarding the GDR-Greek financial relations after 1970, prominent examples of this attitude were the doubling of the volume of imports (1970: $12 million to 1975: $24 million) and the five times increase of the exports' volume (1970: $7 million to 1975: $39 million).[73]

Unquestionably, the pinnacle of financial cooperation between the two states was reached in the public sector. In May 1970, East Berlin managed to secure the signing of a bilateral agreement, which allowed the state-owned electrical company 'VEB Elektrotechnik Export-Import' to deliver and install three high-voltage electrical plants for DEI (Public Power Corporation) in the region of Attica, with a delivery capacity of 400,000 volts. The aggregate sum of this investment amounted to $15 million.[74] Simultaneously, Greek diplomacy expressed its wish to the Eastern Germans to establish a chamber of commerce, dispatch a diplomatic envoy to East Berlin and ameliorate the financial relations between Greece and the GDR.[75] This would primarily accommodate financial deals and contracts but also favour foreign policy directives through economic mandates, as the official diplomatic relations between the two countries were practically non-existent.[76] One year later, in May 1971, after new consultations between the financial authorities of the two states took place, a new contract was signed. This foresaw the construction of three more transformer power plants, this time in Northern Greece, and their delivery was estimated towards 1974 and 1975. The sum of this investment reached the amount of $14 million. Both deals were clearing transactions in which the GDR would set up and initiate the function of the facilities, and Greece would repay the owed amount with agricultural products.[77]

These deals gave the impetus to both states to enhance the financial interplay between them in the forthcoming years. After completing the power plant investments, both governments sought to expand their cooperation. During a meeting between Greek Minister of Coordination Nikolaos Makarezos and the head of the GDR's chamber of commerce in Greece, Karl Heinz Jelen,[78] the first expressed Greece's 'great interest in the further development of economic relations' between Athens and East Berlin. Towards this direction, and after consultation with the representative of the USSR's Ministry of External Commerce, Valerian Sorin, it was decided that it would be favourable for the GDR to pursue the signing of further financial deals with the Greek military regime.[79] The result of these efforts to strengthen economic relations with Greece included a lignite mining project in the region of Ptolemaida in the northern part of the country. Although the commissioning of this project was finalized in 1976 and was undertaken as a joint venture between the East German state-owned company AHB-Maschinen Export and the West German company Krupp, it is worth noting that the talks had been initiated in 1972 during the rule of the dictatorship.[80]

While Greece's financial *Ostpolitik* was not considered a complete breakthrough or a model of comparison among other Western countries such as the FRG, the fact that a military anti-communist regime developed a multifaceted bilateral economic cooperation with the GDR, especially when during the junta's early establishment East Berlin led the denunciation of the dictatorship among the socialist world, demonstrates that realpolitik sooner than later surpassed ideology to serve the primary foreign policy mandates and secure each state's survival and consolidation. Having acknowledged the potential of specific openings in the Greek market and vice versa, the GDR attempted to achieve a twofold goal. Firstly, to cover its financial needs by extending its trade network and industrial exports to the West, even at the expense of its ideological background. Secondly, it managed to break the monopole of West German financial interests in a country where the latter had been omnipresent since the dawn of the Cold War era.

Conclusion

The economic policy of rapid development through stability and investment had been a cornerstone of Greece's approach throughout the 1950s and 1960s. The advent of the junta in 1967 did not alter this fundamental strategy. Despite its fervent nationalism and revolutionary rhetoric, the regime lacked a coherent ideological framework. Its main promise for the national economy was to deliver the benefits of development by rooting out corruption from previous governments. Emphasizing the importance of foreign capital inflows, the dictatorship sought investment not only from traditional post-war allies but also from other countries, which would be willing to exhibit a pragmatic approach to economic cooperation. As demonstrated in this chapter, the junta effectively leveraged unconventional partners attempting to stimulate the Greek economy and bolster its own image.

While the final account of the influx of foreign capital may not have reached the intended level as estimated at the outset of the dictatorship era, it became an essential asset to the junta's financial strategy. The strong political pressure against the military regime globally created an inherent fear in the military rulers that Greece's international isolation was *ante portas*. This prompted the regime to adopt more flexible liberal policies that accommodated further foreign investments, fitting the pattern of progressive economic nationalism.[81] Economics became thus a practical tool for diplomacy and an outward laissez-faire foreign policy implementation for the dictatorship. This often constituted the apple of discord for many states, which sought the most advantageous agreements in their efforts to strengthen their economies through foreign investment and exports. Small countries such as Austria and the GDR found eager potential openings in colonels' Greece, demonstrating how closely varieties of economic nationalisms interrelate.

On the one hand, towards this direction and despite the dissimilar structure of the polity, Vienna decided to move beyond the ideological constraints of social democratic principles. Even though the Austrian government intervened multiple times in cases of Greek political prisoners during the junta's seven-year rule, that never became a barrier to accommodating its financial interests, despite occasional humanitarian diplomatic confrontations.[82] On the other hand, the relations between the GDR and the Greek junta were undoubtedly ambivalent and characterized simultaneously by a profound aversion and cynic realism. Yet, during these seven years and despite mutual polemic rhetoric, political and economic deals were concluded, which could have never been achieved under normal circumstances. By slowly but steadily putting aside ideological inhibitions, the GDR achieved a long-sought financial partnership with a regime that stood on the opposite ideological corner. This proved that smaller states, amidst the Cold War era, decided to overcome some of their fundamental differences. They did so by exerting their 'individual' agency on diplomatic affairs to achieve a novel and unprecedented interstate communication both on a financial level and on foreign relations, two fields oftentimes inseparably interrelated.

Notes

1 For Greece's post-war socio-economic transformation, see Mazower (ed.), *After the War Was Over*; see also Close, *Greece since 1945*.

2 On the political crises of the 1960s in Greece see parts 4 and 5 in Vasilakis (ed.), *Από τον Ανένδοτο στη Δικτατορία (From the Unrelentless Struggle to Dictatorship)*.

3 The military coups were not a novel phenomenon in Greek politics. Yet it was the first and only time that a military group had seized the power and overthrown a democratic regime in order to keep it for itself, and on top of that, its origins stemmed from the lowest rankings in the military hierarchy. For the history of military interventions in Greece see Veremis, *Ο Στρατός στην Ελληνική Πολιτική (Military in Greek Politics)* & Papadiamantis, *Στρατός και Πολιτική Εξουσία (Army and Political Power)*.

4 See Amnesty International's campaign and reports on the situation in Greece, Amnesty International, *Report on Torture*; Amnesty International, *Torture in Greece*.

5 In this essay the term 'junta' is used interchangeably with the word 'dictatorship'. The dictatorship of the colonels in the period under discussion has been established in historiography as the 'colonels' junta'. See Kallivretakis, *Δικτατορία και Μεταπολίτευση (Dictatorship and Metapolitefsi)*, 13–65.

6 Konstas, *Η Ελληνική Υπόθεση Στο Συμβούλιο Της Ευρώπης (The Greek Case in the Council of Europe)*.

7 The literature on the events that led to Greece's withdrawal from the Council of Europe is constantly enriched with noteworthy essays and publications. See indicatively Kjærsgaard, 'Confronting the Greek military junta', 51–69; Fernández Soriano, 'Facing the Greek Junta', 358–76.

8 On the experienced diplomats that served as ministers and vice-ministers of foreign affairs during the Greek dictatorship see Makrydimitris, *Οι Υπουργοί των Εξωτερικών της Ελλάδας 1829–2000 (The Foreign Ministers of Greece 1829–2000)*, 98, 102–3, 113.

9 Clogg, 'The Ideology of the Revolution', 36–58.

10 Nakano, 'Theorizing Economic Nationalism', 211–29.

11 Kazakos, 'Πολιτικοί Θεσμοί και Οικονομική Ανάπτυξη (Political Institutions and Economic Development)', 136–67.

12 Iordanoglou, *Η Ελληνική Οικονομία μετά το 1950 (The Greek Economy after 1950)* 143–4.

13 The year 1973 was a turning point in the Greek economy due to both internal and external shocks in the Greek and global economy. This period of growth was followed by a significant economic slowdown. Ibid. and Alogoskoufis, 'Historical Cycles', 10.

14 Höll, 'The Foreign Policy', 32–77.

15 On SDPAG's history see Pfoertner, 'Die Steyr-Daimler-Puch AG (SDPAG)', 311–35.

16 On an overall approach to Greece's 'Ostpolitik' during the Cold War see Stergiou, *Greece's Ostpolitik*.

17 On national economy-building see the chapter of Adrian Brisku in this edited volume, 'Varieties of Economic Nationalism'.

18 The theory, typology and literature on small states are elaborate, and this detailed analysis has offered various definitions of 'smallness'. This study concurs with the notion of Neal G. Jesse and John R. Dreyer that a 'small state is a state that is

always weak at global and regional levels, but strong at sub-regional level', Jesse, and Dreyer, *Small States in the International System*, 10.

19 See the introductory segment in Kruizinga (ed.), *The Politics of Smallness*, 2.

20 Here the term 'peripheral' does not denote the geographic aspect of the periphery such as regional countries, it rather refers to the significance of smaller states in the historiography and decision-making process of the Cold War.

21 On the New Diplomatic History see Alloul, and Auwers, 'What Is (New in) New Diplomatic History', 112–22; Weisbrode, 'The New Diplomatic History'.

22 Baughn, and Yaprak, 'Economic Nationalism', 759–78.

23 Helleiner, and Pickel (eds), *Economic Nationalism*, 6.

24 Brisku, 'Varieties of Economic Nationalism'.

25 Ibid.

26 Georgalas, *Η Ιδεολογία της Επαναστάσεως: όχι δόγματα, αλλά ιδεώδη (The Ideology of the Revolution: Not Dogmas, but Ideals)*, 8.

27 On the diversity of economic nationalism and a more recent approach see also Helleiner 'The Diversity of Economic Nationalism', 229–38.

28 Kazakos, 'Πολιτικοί Θεσμοί και Οικονομική Ανάπτυξη (Political Institutions and Economic Development)', 136–67.

29 Kakridis, 'Economic Policy', 73–102.

30 In the first years growth slowdown was triggered by the decline in investments in general and in particular by the reduction in capital spending in the construction sector and manufacturing. In 1968 the growth rate of the GDP was 7.2 per cent, in 1969 11.6 per cent, in 1970 8.9 per cent, in 1971 7.8 per cent, in 1972 10.2 per cent, and 1973 8.1 per cent. See Kazakos, *Ανάμεσα σε Κράτος και Αγορά (Between State and Market)*, 267–8.

31 See Osman, *Egypt on the Brink*, 50–85.

32 The dictatorial government declared on 16 December 1968 that: 'The philosophy of the economic policy of the National Government is: Individual initiative. All the measures taken by the National Government … aim … to encourage private initiative.' Grigoriadis, *Ιστορία της Σύγχρονης Ελλάδας (History of Modern Greece)*, 349.

33 Ibid., 1012–13.

34 Meletopoulos, *Η Δικτατορία των Συνταγματαρχών (The Dictatorship of the Colonels)*, 404–5.

35 Grigoriadis, *Ιστορία της Σύγχρονης Ελλάδας (History of Modern Greece)*, 351–2.

36 For a general overview of Greece's relations with the EEC see Yannopoulos (ed.), *Greece and the EEC*; see also Minotou, *Η Ελλάδα στο Σταυροδρόμι των Ευρωπαϊκών Επιλογών (Greece at the Crossroads of European Choices)*.

37 On the political repercussions of the freezing of association with the EEC see Coufoudakis, 'The European Economic Community', 114–31.

38 See indicatively Karamouzi, 'Taking a Stance' 110–23; Kakridis, 'Economic Policy', 73–102.

39 The Austrian ambassador also shared this fear in Athens towards a report to the Austrian Ministry of Foreign Affairs on 2 May 1967. Ambassador Ludwig Steiner writes:

> However, a difficult balancing act begins here for the West. If it does not succeed in democratizing the regime through kind words and cautious restraint in the delivery of aid, it will be necessary at best, to completely cut off deliveries. However, this could very easily lead to a shift of the regime toward Nasserism in the truest sense of the term.

See ÖStA/AdR, BMfAA, GZ. 21.117-19-POL/67, 'Militärputsch in Griechenland'.

40 For a detailed analysis of the post-war financial relations between the FRG and Greece, including the period of the dictatorship see Tsakas, *Post-war Greco-German Relations*.

41 For an overview of the FRG's financial and armament policy towards the military dictatorship in Greece see Pelt, 'West Germany's Policy toward Greece', 295–319.

42 For an accurate reappraisal of the Anglo-Greek relations during the junta see Nafpliotis, *Britain and the Greek Colonels*; see also Maragkou, *Britain, Greece and the Colonels*.

43 On Franco-Greek relations at the same period see Vaïsse, 'France and the Greek Colonels', 39–47.

44 Xydis, 'Coups and Countercoups in Greece, 1967–1973', 507–38; Botsiou, 'Οι σχέσεις του στέμματος (Crown's Relations)', 113–35.

45 On the interconnection of foreign policy and small state theory, see Jesse, and Dreyer, *Small States in the International System*, 3–55.

46 To a greater or lesser extent there were plenty of countries which not only tolerated the junta but, in some cases, developed cordial relations with it. Different case studies, each one unique in its own right, can be found for instance regarding the Romanian-Greek relations in Pechlivanis, 'An Uneasy Triangle', or the relations of the dictatorship with certain African countries in Panoutsopoulos, 'Η Αφρικανική διάσταση (The African Dimension)', 408–30.

47 Although the Austrian ambassador in Athens, Steiner, did not anticipate a military dictatorship in the near future, he had oftentimes informed the Austrian Ministry of Foreign Affairs with multiple reports that those rumors were widespread in Greece. See, for example, his report on 2 March 1966 with the title 'Rumors of a possible military dictatorship in Greece' in ÖStA/AdR, BmfAA, GZ. 46.934-11-POL/66, 'Gerüchte über eine mögliche Militärdiktatur'.

48 On the political and diplomatic deeds of Ludwig Steiner including his capacity as the Austrian ambassador in Greece and Cyprus, see Steiner, *Der Botschafter*; from Steiner also, *Diplomatie – Politik*.

49 ÖStA/AdR, BMfAA, GZ. 110.571-1-POL/68, 'Die Beziehungen zur griechischen Militärjunta'.

50 These statistics, as well as the exact products that were imported and exported from Austria to Greece and vice versa can be found in the statistical yearbooks of the Hellenic Statistical Authority. See ELSTAT, *Εξωτερικό Εμπόριον (External Commerce).*

51 ÖStA/AdR, BMfAA, GZ. 110.571-1-POL/68, 'Die Beziehungen zur griechischen Militärjunta'.

52 See the chapter by Adamantios Skordos on Austrian-Greek relations during the era of the dictatorship in Greece 'Die Beziehungen Österreichs zur griechischen Junta', 266–74.

53 On Josef Staribacher see https://www.wienerzeitung.at/nachrichten/chronik/wien-chronik/2097394-Zum-100.-Geburtstag-gibt-es-in-Wien-einen-Strassennamen-fuer-den-Happy-Pepi.html; and the website of the Austrian parliament https://www.parlament.gv.at/person/1829, accessed 19 January 2023.

54 Karl Rabus was the general director of SDPAG from 1966 to 1976. See Pfundner, *Die Auto – Österreicher*; https://steyrerpioniere.wordpress.com/2011/10/26/karl-rabus/, accessed 19 January 2023.

55 Josef Staribacher kept a detailed diary with his personal notes and meetings throughout his entire term in office under the Kreisky governments. The entire diary comprises approx. twenty thousand typewritten manuscript pages and is available online in digitized form. See Tagebücher Josef Staribacher. Digital Edition. Ed. from Kreisky-Archiv and ACDH. p. 02-0344. https://staribacher.acdh.oeaw.ac.at/get/staribacher.99_1, accessed 19 January 2023.

56 Der Spiegel, Österreich: Gar vielerlei, 18 June 1972.

57 Ibid.

58 Mayrhofer, *Steyr-Daimler-Puch AG*, 53.

59 Der Spiegel, Österreich: Gar vielerlei, 18 June 1972.

60 See the article in the Greek newspaper *Makedonia*, 'Επένδυσις 34.000.000 Δολλαρίων (Investment of 34.000.000 dollars), 14 April 1972.

61 ÖStA/AdR, BMfAA, E.B.Z.: 21234, Austroamb Athen An Außenamt Wien, 18 April 1972.

62 In 1980 the export of weaponry between an Austrian enterprise and the Chilean government amounted to an aggregate sum of $162 million. Yet after intense domestic debates and the condemnation by the Austrian public opinion the deal was called off. See Graf, 'Beyond Victims of Communism', 178–95.

63 On the commencement of the Greek-East German relations, see the official report of GDR's ambassador in Belgrade, where the official discussions between Greece and the GDR took place, culminating in the signing of bilateral official recognition on 25 May 1973. PA, AA/M1-C/423-78, 'Über ein Gespräch', 29 January 1973.

64 Gray, *Germany's Cold War*; Kilian, *Die Hallstein-Doktrin*.

65 The anti-communist orientation of the regime was ubiquitous since its inception and was also constantly expressed in officials' speeches and press articles. Clogg, 'The Ideology of the Revolution', 36–58.

66 From the outset of the dictatorship the GDR rushed to condemn the military coup, which was characterized as 'monarcho-fascist'. BArch/SAPMO/DY 30/97763, 'Information über die Ereignisse in Griechenland', 28 April 1967.

67 On the difficulties of the Greek military regime to gain international recognition, specifically during the first years after the coup see Grigoriadis, *Ιστορία της Σύγχρονης Ελλάδας (History of Modern Greece)*, 325–46.

68 Stergiou, 'Ελληνική Χούντα και Ανατολική Γερμανία (Greek Junta and East-Germany), 123–44.

69 On the media coverage of the GDR's success in the European games see the article 'DDR-Leichtathleten am erflogreichsten' in the official newspaper of the ruling party in the GDR 'Neues Deutschland' on 21 September 1969, https://dfg-viewer.de/show/?set%5Bmets%5D=https://content.staatsbibliothek-berlin.de/zefys/SNP2532889X-19690921-0-0-0-0.xml, accessed 3 April 2023.

70 PA/AA/M1-C/413-78, 'Konzeption zur Gestaltung', March 1968.

71 BArch/DY 30/50037, 'Beschluß zur Konzeption', 16 June 1969.

72 According to the memoirs of the Dutch ambassador in Athens, Carl Barkman, in 1969,

> Some of my East European colleagues are praising the stability of the Greek regime. According to them most governments now consider that the Papadopoulos regime which has remained in power undisturbedly for four years must be accepted as a more or less permanent political factor in Europe …The communist countries seem to be rather satisfied with the present state of affairs. They are able to improve their relations with Greece … and they are nor unhappy about the existing dissensions in NATO. (Barkman, *Ambassador*, 49)

73 Kuppe, 'Die Beziehungen zwischen der DDR und Griechenland', 337.

74 BArch/DII 1/ 22817, 'Export Griechenland', 8 September 1970.

75 BArch/DL 2/16742, 'Status der Handelsvertretung', 23 January 1970.

76 Walden, *Παράταιροι εταίροι (Unseemly Partners)*, 132–3.

77 Stergiou, *Im Spagat*, 134.

78 On the personnel of the GDR's diplomatic/commercial delegation in Greece see Radde, *Der Diplomatische Dienst der DDR*, 201–2.

79 BArch/DY 30/16531, 'Unserer Stellungnahme zur Vorlage', 13 January 1972.

80 BArch/DY 30/17793, 'Information über die derzeitige Situation', 1 March 1976.

81 Brisku, 'Varieties of Economic Nationalism'.

82 Skordos, 'Die Beziehungen Österreichs zur griechischen Junta', 300–17.

6

Austrian *Osthandel* as economic nationalism? Reassessing the role of foreign trade in Austro-Keynesianism

Maximilian Graf

Introduction

In the 1970s, economic relations between the East and West were decisively shaped by incipient globalization and the changes in the international economic and financial order. The end of Bretton Woods and the two oil price shocks of 1973 and 1979 were drastic events that initially hit the West, but in the long-term the East all the harder. Sharply rising interest rates from the late 1970s onwards quickly caused a debt crisis of the socialist countries, which hit Romania, Poland, Hungary, the German Democratic Republic (GDR) and Yugoslavia particularly hard in the early 1980s. In 1981, Poland, Romania, Bulgaria and Yugoslavia became practically insolvent and requested their debts in the West to be rescheduled.[1] For neutral Austria this constituted a severe challenge. Second to Finland, the country had the highest share of trade with Eastern Europe in its overall foreign trade. Given the loan-financed development of trade with Eastern Europe in the 1970s, this resulted in Austria being the per capita most exposed Western creditor. This striking outcome has its roots in the politics of 'Austro-Keynesianism' aiming at preserving full employment in a decade of economic crises.

Austria had been one of the small states that managed to 'remain neutral and independent' during the Cold War.[2] After the conclusion of the Austrian State Treaty through which the country regained its full sovereignty and the adoption of the neutrality law in 1955,[3] the Soviet Union aimed at shaping its relations to neutral Austria as a masterpiece of its foreign policy concept 'peaceful coexistence'. Without a doubt, Moscow thereby primarily aimed at shaping Austrian neutrality alongside Soviet ideas and beliefs. One of them was to encourage Austria to develop relations with the socialist states.[4] This enabled Austria to pursue its own *Ostpolitik* quite successfully, although not necessarily in the way intended by Moscow. One of the characteristics of Austrian *Ostpolitik* was a strictly bilateral approach, pronouncing the diversity of the Socialist bloc, and the promotion of trade with Eastern Europe. Within the geopolitical limits of the East-West divide, small Austria gradually (under the surface and in day-to-day interactions) started to behave as regional power in the area of the former Habsburg Empire. As a Western actor in neutral clothes Vienna maintained good relations with the Soviet Union and especially under foreign minister Bruno Kreisky (1959–66) and Chancellor Josef Klaus (1964–70) managed to make first striking progress in improving relations with almost all the Socialist bloc's countries throughout the 1960s and thus before the heyday of international détente.[5]

Given its international positioning, Austria became a meeting place for East and West and aimed at being a mediator between the blocs. Despite the special relationship with the Soviet Union and intensifying relations with the other Warsaw Pact member states, Austria's neutrality was only a military and not a political one. Ideally but not institutionally, the country was fully anchored in the West. This resulted in several political and economic specifics. In the economic field the existence of a large nationalized sector (which was a result of developments during the period of quadripartite Allied occupation from 1945 to 1955) and membership in the European Free Trade Association (EFTA) are noteworthy characteristics.[6] Regarding government it is remarkable that from 1947 to 1966 Austria was ruled by a so-called Grand Coalition of the conservative People's Party (Österreichische Volkspartei, ÖVP) and the Socialist Party (Sozialistische Partei Österreichs, SPÖ) representing more than 90 per cent of the Austrian voters and aiming at a consensual post-war reconstruction and re-establishment of the country in the international arena. The post-war tradition of the grand coalition ended in 1966 and was followed by single-party governments of the Conservatives (1966–70) and the Socialists (1970–83) – the 'Kreisky era' which is the main focus of this chapter. Kreisky's reign is usually associated with important legal and educational reforms, an active foreign policy, the developing of the welfare state and deficit spending. During the electoral campaign of 1979, he made one of the most famous statements of his chancellorship: 'And when someone asks me how it is with the debt, I tell them what I always say: that a few billion more in debt gives me fewer sleepless nights than a few hundred thousand unemployed give me.'[7]

During the *trente glorieuse* Austria developed as a Western democracy and prospered economically. The politics of 'Austro-Keynesianism', as Kreisky's approach has been labelled, had secured full employment until the late 1970s but also caused delays in structural change of Austria's nationalized industries which finally proved to be inevitable by the mid-1980s.[8] In comparison with other Western countries, neutral Austria had a large nationalized industrial sector. As elsewhere in Western Europe, the heavy industries came under pressure in the 1970s. Unprofitable branches were financed by the profits of those who were competitive; consequently, restructuring was delayed. One of the reasons why this strategy seemingly worked was *Osthandel*; however, it was also one of the main reasons why the largest enterprise of the nationalized industries, United Austrian Iron and Steelworks (*Vereinigte Österreichische Eisen- und Stahlwerke*, VÖEST), collapsed in 1985.

This chapter reassesses the internal motivations for the foreign trade strategy chosen and its development in the international context. After a brief introduction to the history of Austrian *Osthandel* in Cold War Europe, the analysis proceeds with case studies addressing Austria's economic and financial dealings with Poland and East Germany. It addresses the crucial decade from 1975 to 1985 by reviewing internal discussions and the implementation of foreign trade strategies. By doing so, it sheds some fresh light on the Western responses to the global economic challenges of the time. Furthermore, it provides insight to the Western perspective of how the Eastern red river of ink was accumulated in the 1970s and how a heavily involved small state acted during the crucial years of the acute debt crisis. The analysis of these overlapping developments is guided by the question whether they can be assessed as economic nationalism and, if so, what kind of economic nationalism it was?

Austrian *Osthandel* in Cold War Europe

The common economic space of the Habsburg Empire ceased to exist with the end of the First World War and the collapse of the monarchy. This was already evident in the interwar period, especially after the onset of the Great Depression (shaped by protectionism in the sense of 'conservative/defensive' economic nationalism with fatal consequences). After 1945, as a consequence of the East-West division of the European continent, the share of the successor states in Austrian foreign trade declined even further. Nevertheless, until 1955, the Council for Mutual Economic Assistance (CMEA) area remained an important economic space for Austria, but its importance was steadily declining. The trade balance was always passive. After successful post-war reconstruction decisively facilitated by the European Recovery Programme, Austria embarked on its somewhat delayed 'economic miracle'. From 1956 to 1971 the share of the socialist countries in Austrian foreign trade fluctuated between 10 and 15 per cent. During this period, the Austrian trade balance with the entire CMEA area became active. While Austria primarily exported semi-finished and finished goods, machines and means of transportation, it mostly imported fuel, food and raw materials from the CMEA member states. Ever since the Austrian State Treaty and until the end of the Cold War the Soviet Union was Austria's most important economic partner in the East.[9] The USSR became Austria's main supplier of energy – the origins of today's dependency on Russia. In 1968, Austria was the first Western country to conclude a long-term deal on gas supplies. Vienna provided a 110 million USD loan necessary for financing the pipes delivered by Austrian enterprises. Unswayed by the Warsaw Pact intervention in Czechoslovakia that ended 'Prague Spring' gas deliveries commenced as planned.[10] Despite the growing importance of energy supplies in East-West trade, this chapter does not detail economic relations with the USSR.

By the mid-1970s, trade with Eastern Europe was liberalized to the maximum and reached new heights. In 1975, the export quota rose to a record 17 per cent, the share of *Osthandel* in Austria's overall foreign trade balance stood at 14.1 per cent. Despite increasing energy imports (that already caused a deficit in bilateral trade with the Soviet Union since 1971), the overall trade balance with Eastern Europe was highly favourable. In absolute numbers, trade with the East continued to grow even after the boom in the mid-1970s, but the share of Austria's total foreign trade, around two-thirds of which was with the European Economic Community (EEC), fell continuously.[11] Nevertheless, the 1970s and 1980s are one of the most exciting periods in the history of trade with Eastern Europe. While the trade balance went into deficit again, due to increasing energy imports from the Soviet Union, there were still profitable business models with other CMEA countries.

Austria's nationalized industries were the main driver of this development. As a result of the post-war developments in Austria, nationalized industries emerged on a large scale and even survived the end of the occupation period in 1955. This sector (to a large extent consisting of iron and steel industry) was constantly facing structural problems and underwent several reforms, restructuring and mergers; however, no major privatizations took place until the second half of the 1980s.[12] Beginning in the 1950s the nationalized industries increasingly lacked sales markets in the West. Hence, Austrian politicians made arduous efforts in order to find new markets in the East that can be regarded as 'liberal/progressive' economic nationalism.[13] During the 1960s, their efforts remained without striking success. The economic (and oil price) crisis of the 1970s and declining commodity prices further reduced the foreign markets for Austria's nationalized industries. Especially the steel market got tougher; hence, the VÖEST had to focus on other branches. The most promising field was plant engineering and construction. Against this backdrop, gradually the concept 'large-scale orders in return for loans' evolved as the role model for the heyday of Austria's economic relations with the socialist states in the 1970s and 1980s. However, it was not primarily about intensifying economic relations with the socialist states but also about maintaining the number of employees in Austria's nationalized industries, which was an explicit goal of Chancellor Kreisky.[14] Pursuing this business model was one of Austria's reactions to the difficult economic situation and converged with the investment interests of several socialist countries that aimed at modernization through increased imports from the West.[15] To make this trade work Austria expanded its soon well-developed export promotion system which pre-financed exports via state-secured loans (organized by the *Kontrollbank* and decisively shaped by its general director Helmut Haschek, in office since 1972) and thus provided the framework for the *Osthandel* expansion. Due to this development economics started to dominate Austria's *Ostpolitik*.[16] Additionally, it deserves being mentioned that, after 1975, Kreisky even regarded fostering East-West cooperation in the fields of economic and energy politics as major focus of the Conference on Security and Cooperation in Europe (CSCE).[17] Whenever he addressed an international audience on the topic of détente in Europe Kreisky stressed the necessity of cooperation as a means to make détente more concrete. Usually, he provided examples of already developing and potential future East-West cooperation in the energy sector like the import of natural resources from the Soviet Union or the possibility of constructing coal-fired power plants in Poland which would be repaid by the export of electric energy desperately needed by the Austrian economy.[18] Due to the economic giant EEC in Western Europe with its Common Commercial Policy (CCP) and the absence of a trade agreement between EEC and CMEA requested by the Warsaw Pact member states, the economic dimension (the second basket) never prospered throughout the CSCE process.[19] While hopes for a multilateral basis of increasing economic cooperation across the Iron Curtain gradually came to naught, on the bilateral level the 1970s were a dynamic decade – especially for small in-between states like neutral Austria. In relation to Poland and the GDR (and most other smaller CMEA member states), Austria increasingly acted as a regional economic power. Initially the common economic space of the former Habsburg Empire was at the heart of this policy but due to Cold War realities it soon was applied to the entire CMEA area. For the socialist states, neutral Austria became a partner preferred over countries that were fully anchored in the North Atlantic Treaty Organization (NATO) and the EEC and thus had less leeway in developing economic cooperation across the Iron Curtain.

Poland: From détente and cooperation to economic fiasco

This development is best illustrated on the example of Poland. Austrian–Polish relations had led the way in Austria's *Ostpolitik* in the early 1960s, but due to unresolved bilateral questions they entered a period of stagnation by the mid-1960s. In the summer of 1970 finally, the Austrian–Polish treaty on proprietary questions was initialled. Ambassador Johannes Proksch valued this step as the beginning of a 'new era in Austrian–Polish relations'.[20] In early 1971, only six weeks after the Gdańsk massacre of December 1970 (causing the death of forty-five people) Austrian Foreign Minister Rudolf Kirchschläger visited Poland (a disputable step, for which archival sources have not yet delivered a comprehensible explanation). Upon his arrival, in a statement for Polish television, he said: 'Austria has always regarded Poland as a neighboring country in a broader sense. We have many historical and cultural ties with the Polish people.' Next to a further intensification of cultural relations, he mentioned the prospect of increasing economic cooperation.[21] Chancellor Kreisky paid a visit to Warsaw in 1973. In his conversation with Prime Minister Piotr Jaroszewicz he emphasized that Austria truly aimed at 'developing relations to Poland to the maximum'. This meant not only the political, but first and foremost the economic dimension. Both sides cherished high hopes in their future development, although it was obvious that it would need Austrian loans to reach this goal.[22] In 1975, the trade volume rose to 8 billion Austrian schillings (ATS), the Polish deficit amounted to 3 billion ATS. Next to the Soviet Union, Poland had become Austria's most important Eastern trading partner. Since Austria primarily imported fuels, raw materials and foodstuffs, a reduction of the passive Polish trade balance was highly unlikely. Austria provided bridge-over loans amounting to several billion ATS.[23]

Kreisky held the view that increasing trade with Poland would serve as a beacon for other socialist states to expand their trade with Austria. Some ministers of his cabinet already worried if Poland would ever be able to pay back the loans taken out in Austria.[24] In 1976, the *Kontrollbank* warned that the Polish liabilities in Austria were extremely high in international comparison and openly stated: 'Today, Poland is seen as "second hand" on the credit market.'[25] In 1976 the trade volume had even risen to 9.4 billion ATS and the Polish deficit to almost 4 billion ATS. The liabilities at the *Kontrollbank* already amounted to 19.2 billion ATS. Additionally, Poland had taken 5.9 billion ATS in financial loans from private banks. Record trade deficits and record debt resulted in a bleak economic outlook in the Austrian assessments of Poland.[26]

However, Kreisky feared a looming collapse of Western iron and steel industries and in consequence a more far-reaching crisis. His thinking was clearly influenced by the interwar experience of the Great Depression. Given these prospects, he warned of protectionism and criticized rising tariffs discriminating against *Osthandel*. Kreisky opined that without the already existing degree of economic integration in Europe,

> we would have fallen into a quagmire of protectionism in the face of economic development in the world and the difficulties we face in international trade would have become much severe. We know this because of the experience gained in the early 1930s. It is not more protection that can help us now, but as much overcoming of protectionism as possible.[27]

This can be understood as Kreisky's repudiation of 'conservative/defensive' economic nationalism as opposed to his own 'liberal/progressive' approach that included export promotion via loans. However, Kreisky completely misjudged the risks of Austria's expansive loan policy. He believed that in case of a loan default the Soviet Union would step in. When Poland asked for further loans in 1977, Minister of Trade Josef Staribacher recorded what Kreisky said in the economic committee of ministers: 'Kreisky stated firmly that there was no risk in providing further loans – he literally said the risk is zero – because the USSR will never allow Poland to default on an installment. The USSR will step in if Poland has difficulties.'[28] Kreisky disagreed with the West German views of Otto Wolff von Amerongen and Chancellor Helmut Schmidt that the socialist states had already been provided with too many loans. He still saw enormous business potential in the Middle East and Eastern Europe.[29] In a speech given during a visit to Germany he had even stated:

> To me the degree of indebtedness does not seem to be at all alarming, especially if one considers the vast wealth, especially of the Soviet Union, in oil, gas, coal,

> gold, and other important raw materials, and knows that a large part of these credits is used for the more rapid development of these resources, which in turn have led to the increase of trade with the West.[30]

Kreisky's views were not altered by frank statements of Eastern European representatives about the actual economic situation of the CMEA countries. For example, in late 1977, the Czechoslovakian Prime Minister Lubomír Štrougal openly told the Austrian chancellor that 'some COMECON states – not Czechoslovakia – do not have water up to their mouths, but already over their heads'. And his minister of foreign trade, Andrej Barčák, openly confessed: 'The idea that if things get worse in the capitalist West, if the capitalist crisis always announced by Marx comes, then the socialist states can triumph, and their system will prove itself in the best possible way is unfortunately also not true. If the West has difficulties, the East has many more difficulties.'[31]

Consequently, the Minister of Trade Staribacher did not see how Poland could get out of its 'loan mess'. Even in the event of large-scale energy imports (Austria was striving for), he remained pessimistic. Still, he valued the advantages of Austria's loan policy: The capacity utilization of Austria's nationalized industries was significantly more favourable than elsewhere in Europe. According to the general director of the VÖEST, Heribert Apfalter, the 'capacity utilization of Austria's iron and steel sector was still almost 20% higher than in the rest of Western Europe'. This can be regarded as a success of 'liberal/progressive' economic nationalism in its 'Austro-Keynesian' variety. There was no guarantee but a lot of hope that things would remain that way.[32] Until the early 1980s, members of the Austrian government firmly held the view that national corrections to the European economic course were possible. Naturally, global booms and recessions did not leave Austria untouched, but the conviction that the government could passably go against such developments and their repercussions was still in place and fuelled their 'liberal/progressive' economic nationalism. Expanding economic relations with Eastern Europe and securing energy supplies from there was part of this policy. Unsurprisingly this caused the opposition to criticize the resulting growing dependency on the socialist states.[33]

There had been no shortage of warnings about the excessive loan policy towards Poland, but Kreisky, like many others in the West, believed in the so-called 'umbrella theory' according to which the Soviet Union would never let one of its allies go bankrupt. Therefore, his government continued to provide loans for Poland. The sharp rise in interest rates on the international capital markets from 1978/79 onwards became an increasing problem for the socialist states, since more expensive loans had to be taken out in the West to service existing liabilities. Austria was well aware of the function of new loans handed out to Poland. In late 1978, Kreisky had doubts about additional loans for Poland supposedly needed to sustain bilateral cooperation. Minister of Finance Hannes Androsch qualified them as 'financial aid' needed by Warsaw 'for some purchases in Western countries'. In the end, Kreisky remained convinced that Poland would live up to its promised energy deliveries in return for loans.[34] A year later, Kreisky openly said internally that Poland needed a 2 billion ATS financial loan to 'postpone its insolvency'.[35]

However, Kreisky regarded cooperation in the energy sector as a means to maintain détente in times of increasing East-West tensions. During his visit to Poland in 1979, the focus was on negotiations about a large coal supply contract. For this purpose, Poland demanded a financial loan of $300 million, which Austria provided despite Poland's already difficult financial situation that started to cause a decrease in bilateral trade. Here the business model was loans against the long-term 'securing of energy supplies'.[36] Kreisky believed that his concept of cooperation between Austria and Poland in the field of energy could contribute to the development of East-West relations in which the two countries could even create 'a role model'. In his view the 'energy question' was a 'European question' and the Soviet Union would also recognize it as such.[37]

Kreisky defended his economic policy against media criticism. Since Austria, as a creditor state, was interested in strengthening Poland as an 'economic partner', he wanted to help the country 'at a difficult time'. In 1979 he officially still held the view that the 'agreements with Eastern Bloc countries' were 'sufficiently secure'.[38] By the end of the 1970s, Austria had become the third largest Western creditor after France and Great Britain, but ahead of West Germany and was bearing the largest single risk. Kreisky recognized the fatal economic development of Poland but against the background of increasing international tensions, and for the sake of détente, he was not willing to change his policy. It was in this spirit that the new Polish prime minister, Edward Babiuch, was received on an official visit to Austria in June 1980, during which the loan and coal supply agreements were signed.[39]

Austrian diplomats did not hold back phrasing their views about the Polish economy in stereotypical ways. In September 1980, the Austrian ambassador reported about the reasons for the surfacing crisis:

> The background to this is that Poland – as is well known – is in great economic difficulties. The successes of economic policy at the beginning of the 1970s could not be maintained. The crisis that had been brewing since 1975 as a result of the oil crisis, poor harvests, mismanagement and a lack of work ethic was ignored. The restrictions introduced as a result of foreign debt brought optical successes, but further disgruntlement among the population, who had never really been made aware of the seriousness of the situation.[40]

Pejorative reports about the 'Polish economy' as a sequence of mismanagements and incompetence were repeatedly sent to Vienna as the Polish crisis aggravated.[41]

The Austrian government cautiously, but unequivocally condemned the Soviet invasion of Afghanistan, and Austria did not boycott the Moscow Summer Olympics of 1980.[42] In return, Kreisky expected the Soviet Union to balance Austrian-Soviet trade that had turned highly unfavourable due to increasingly costly energy supplies. His pleas in this regard had some effect, and once more Austria benefited from its role as a diplomatic 'ice breaker' for the Soviet Union. In April 1981, Austria became the first Western country to receive Soviet Prime Minister Nikolai A. Tikhonov after the invasion of Afghanistan. In the course of his visit, a large-scale order was placed at the VÖEST, whose dependency on the Eastern markets further increased.[43] However, the Soviet Union made entirely clear that it would not balance the trade deficits of other CMEA member states. Thus, Kreisky's hopes came to naught that the USSR would be willing to use its huge surplus in bilateral trade with Austria to balance the deficits other countries had accumulated in trade with Austria. A total of approximately 60 billion ATS outstanding loans of Eastern European countries caused worries of a moratorium of the major debtor Poland and repercussions for Austria's own creditworthiness.[44] The United States was already highly critical of loan-financed Austrian *Osthandel* as well as assumed violations of the CoCom embargo.[45] Later Kreisky claimed that the United States was 'torpedoing' his *Ostpolitik* in the way of banks which were increasingly pressurized and interviewed when taking up loans themselves.[46]

In 1980, Polish liabilities had risen to some 30 billion ATS. Measured by the number of inhabitants, Austria had become Poland's biggest creditor in the West. Relations were still valued as 'being of privileged character',[47] but the appearance of Solidarność and the accompanying further economic decline of Poland complicated this East-West 'love affair'. However, not least because of the massive Austrian financial involvement, aid for Poland was a major concern for Kreisky throughout the years of crisis.[48] Crisis-related reductions of Polish coal deliveries further complicated the chancellor's position in the winter of 1980/81.

At the end of March 1981, the Polish government announced that it was 'unable to meet its payment obligations'. Austria deferred the liabilities due in 1981 and, despite the lack of coal deliveries, made the 'second half of the Poland loan in the amount of 150 million US dollars' available.[49] Poland was very grateful for this and also hoped for commercial loans. Ambassador Franciszek Adamkiewicz openly admitted in Vienna: 'Until serious work is resumed, a decisive improvement in the supply and economic situation [in Poland] cannot be expected.'[50] Kreisky did not see this very differently. In his memoirs, he blamed the failure of the communist planned economy for the problems.[51]

Despite internal resistance by the Ministry of Finance,[52] in the course of a visit by Polish Foreign Minister Joszef Czyrek in November 1981, the Austrian government continued to show 'willingness to help at least a little, if possible'. In return, however, it expected the coal delivery obligations indispensable for the Austrian energy concept to be fulfilled.[53] Internally, Kreisky stated: 'Austria has given so much money to the Poles that a reminder [regarding coal deliveries] is absolutely within reason.'[54]

Still, after the imposition of martial law on 13 December 1981, Kreisky opposed economic sanctions against Poland. Until his resignation in 1983, he engaged in favour of rescheduling Polish debts and even proposed a 'Marshall plan' for Poland, but the West met his idea without enthusiasm.[55] Given this situation, the unpaid Polish debts affected the Austrian attitude towards Poland. The lack of a debt restructuring agreement (within the framework of the Paris Club) resulted in an 'unsustainable situation' for Austria, which amounted to a 'free moratorium for Poland' and meant considerable financial burdens.[56] In addition, Austrian diplomacy was outraged by Polish statements that Warsaw was 'in no hurry' to service the debt 'in view of the Western boycott measures' and that it would not treat Vienna any better than the other creditors, despite its loan policy and its stance against the boycott.[57] Ambassador Richard Wotava qualified the linking of interest payments with the demand for new loans as an 'impertinence' and got the impression that 'Austria was apparently intended to play the role of an inexhaustible cash cow'.[58] The long term consequences of this situation have not been researched to this day, but they must have meant a considerable burden on private banks' business up until the 1990s, especially in the case of non-state-secured loans provided by private banks. Austrian Chancellor Franz Vranitzky visited Poland in July 1990, where he met president Wojciech Jaruzelski. When asked by Vranitzky about the debt and the Austrian loans, 'President Jaruzelski replied that in his opinion it was not naive of Austria to give loans to the previous government. At that time, too, the country was in a difficult situation. It was perhaps naive on the part of Poland to have asked for further loans of this amount.'[59]

East Germany: Same strategy, fatal outcomes

Another major debtor that caused severe worries in the early 1980s was the GDR.[60] Not least because of diplomatic non-recognition until 1972 and in the absence of common ties in the Habsburg Empire, East Germany was a latecomer in Austria's *Ostpolitik* and *Osthandel*. Until 1970, the entire trade volume never exceeded 2 billion ATS. Following diplomatic recognition and up to the visit of Chancellor Kreisky in East Berlin in 1978, bilateral trade increased only from 2 to 3 billion ATS. Since the end of the 1960s, the GDR was increasingly seeking Western loans. If the GDR wanted to receive loans from Austria, East Berlin in return had to place a large-scale order at an Austrian enterprise. In 1970, a first big deal was concluded. The GDR received an Austrian loan and ordered a complete ethylene plant from the VÖEST in return. It was the first deal of a business model that characterized Austrian-East German economic relations in the late 1970s and early 1980s. The main reason for the expanding economic ties in the run-up to the Kreisky visit of 1978 was Austrian loans given to the GDR, for which Austria's nationalized industries received large-scale orders from the GDR in return.[61]

In the run-up to the visit to East Berlin, the GDR had guaranteed to place orders in the amount of 6 billion ATS at Austrian enterprises, in return the Austrian government approved a loan of the same amount (and a low interest rate) to the GDR.[62] The Austrian system of export promotion was predestined for this proceeding. Another important aspect was the fact that those large-scale orders were organized as compensation deals. This principle of socialist (and especially East German) Western foreign trade implied that the volume of a plant constructed by a Western company was to be compensated over the years with the production of this plant or with other products of the respective country. In the course of the Kreisky visit the GDR placed an order for a rolling mill at the VÖEST.[63] Subsequently the trade volume increased significantly. In view of the prospect of large East German orders for the nationalized industries, Vienna did not let the Polish fiasco deter it from doing business with East Berlin through loans. At the turn of the 1970s, East German orders started to replace the deals, which had collapsed elsewhere (not least in relations with Poland). The domestic political motivation to keep the nationalized industries going without rationalization and job losses was stronger than the increasing warnings about growing East German debts. Already in 1975 Staribacher had appealed to the East Germans that increased economic cooperation would benefit both countries, the GDR 'to achieve and even exceeded the target of the five-year economic plan', and to Austria 'that, even in times of economic recession, foreign orders and thus jobs will continue to be secured'.[64] This approach had not changed since then and the GDR was considered an economically stable partner. Expertise by the Vienna Institute for International Economic Studies of late 1980 did not expect 'serious financial difficulties' of the GDR because of the special relationship with West Germany and the belief that the Soviet would step in if needed.[65]

The VÖEST competed for the order to construct a converter steel work in Eisenhüttenstadt with a total volume of 12 billion ATS. At the beginning of 1980 Austria committed to the extension of the credit line for the GDR, which increasingly faced problems in receiving loans in the West.[66] Now the floor for the Eisenhüttenstadt deal seemed clear. Indeed, Honecker had garnished his Western premiere in Vienna in 1980 by placing the order at the VÖEST.[67] In Kreisky's view it was Soviet interest that the GDR increased its businesses with Austria. But he was not entirely happy with the way the 'gigantic deals' were perceived: One should 'not praise them too much, so that the GDR does not patronizingly declare that it has secured full employment in Austria'.[68]

Despite its 'Polish experiences', the Kreisky government pursued an expansive loan policy in its relations with the GDR. In the first half of the 1980s, the GDR advanced to Austria's second most important economic partner of the CMEA countries. Moreover, Austria had become the second most important Western trading partner of the GDR, after West Germany. East German debt was on the rise and thus the economic policy unsustainable in the long term. Because of costly 'consumer socialism', continuous trade deficits with the West and rising interest rates, the East German balance of payments crisis aggravated towards the end of the 1970s. Despite all internal warnings and massive Soviet complaints about dependence on the West, the concept of the 'Unity of Economic and Social Policy' remained unchanged and all measures taken to reach a favourable trade balance proved insufficient. In view of developments in Poland any change in social policy seemed too risky. Declining Soviet support (raw materials, especially crude oil) and the financial turbulences of Poland and Romania made the situation even worse. Facing a Western credit boycott (after the imposition of martial law in

Poland), in spring 1982 bankruptcy seemed unavoidable. By opting for a going-out-of-business sale during which everything possible was sold for hard currency and by exercising several emergency measures, ironically indirectly still credited with Western money, solvency was secured in the short term.[69]

Interestingly, when it came to securing its solvency, the GDR did rely not only on the Soviet Union and West Germany – as previously assumed – but also on small Austria, which had no relevant financial market of its own. This was only possible due to a convergence of interests (loans against large-scale orders). Since 20 per cent of the GDR's national debt consisted of Austrian loans one can easily measure how important they were for keeping the GDR solvent. This Austrian help resulted in annually concluded skeleton agreements on economic relations that fostered Austrian exports to the GDR. All large-scale orders were not only financed by loans but also organized as compensation deals. To be able to carry out the compensation deals with East Germany the VÖEST founded a trading company named *Intertrading* to distribute GDR products in 1978. Soon it became an almost ungovernable actor in Austrian-East German economic relations that, however, had to rely on loans guaranteed by the Austrian state. In 1982, even oil barters with the GDR that constituted merchant trading were financed by the *Kontrollbank* loans aimed at facilitating Austrian exports. They played no small role in securing East German solvency in the winter of 1982/83.[70] At that time, minister Staribacher wondered in his diary why 'the then Minister of Finance [Hannes] Androsch had given such relatively generous untied financial loans to state-trading countries'. But he was also 'firmly convinced that Kreisky had demanded this of him in order to further improve political relations between the Eastern states and Austria'.[71] Also in case of the GDR Kreisky was convinced that the East German regime would 'receive the necessary help' from the Soviet Union. Furthermore, he considered it 'the biggest mistake to believe that one could now bring the East to its knees financially'.[72] Hence, economic relations with the GDR continued to expand. Along with the business activities of the *Intertrading* and the companies of the Department for Commercial Coordination of the East German state party the bilateral trade volume increased to 9.3 billion ATS in 1984, showing a deficit of 4.8 billion ATS on the East German side, however. Only after the expiration of large-scale orders, the billion Deutschmark loans for the GDR brokered by the Bavarian Prime Minister Franz Josef Strauß in 1983/84 and the severe crisis of Austria's nationalized industries surfacing in 1985 bilateral trade decreased in the mid-1980s. Still further loans were provided and finally, after the collapse of the GDR, unified Germany had to pay them back.[73]

Within a few years, the *Intertrading* rapidly grew; but after entering the oil sector (futures, spot market), it suffered heavy losses and was mainly responsible for the crisis of Austria's nationalized industries in the mid-1980s.[74] In the end, the business constructions and models needed to keep an unreformed nationalized industrial sector alive, sounding the death knell for the nationalized industries. Thereafter restructuring and privatizations were regarded as inevitable.

The fiasco of Austria's nationalized industries in the mid-1980s, the economic importance of the EEC and the attractiveness of European integration are the most important factors that led to a sea change in Austria's integration policy in 1987. The need to modernize the state economy and pressure by the Austrian industrialists were important when the government reconsidered the question of membership in the European Community (EC), but the main driver was the fear of being excluded from the ongoing integration process. The Single European Act (SEA) with its Internal Market Project was most decisive. Austria conducted about two-thirds of its foreign trade with the Common Market. The re-established grand coalition of the Socialist Party and the People's Party accelerated a new policy towards the EC and within less than two years decided to apply for full membership in 1989, albeit under restriction of staying neutral.[75]

Conclusion

The collapse of the Habsburg Empire led to a disintegration of its economic space. Austrian trade with East Central Europe continued to decline in the early stages of the Cold War, but the age of détente led to a revival. Being small, neutral and outside the two major economic blocs helped a lot in this process. Due to its geographic and geopolitical positions, neutral Austria even over-engaged in international comparison. The structural problems of the nationalized industries, the global economic crises of the 1970s and their repercussions on Austria (which were counteracted with a Keynesian approach) were an additional driver for the intensification of *Osthandel*. Even though the development of *Osthandel* in the foreign trade strategy of 'Austro-Keynesianism' could be told without reference to economic nationalism, in the more general reading of the term pursued in this volume it can be considered a variety of 'liberal/progressive' economic nationalism. Because of the experiences with protectionism during the Great Depression in the interwar period, Kreisky rejected any kind of protectionism in the sense of 'conservative/defensive' economic nationalism, particularly of the Cold War economic blocs; however, at the same time he advocated the protection of Austria's national economy. The protection of a national project like the nationalized industries which had become a symbol of Austria's post-war reconstruction and the following economic miracle which had developed into the biggest employer of the country and was thus crucial for the maintenance of full employment is the most striking case of Kreisky's aims. This led to the somewhat paradoxical situation that protection of the nationalized industries and full employment required further opening up in economic and financial relations with Eastern Europe which he pursued and framed as a contribution to the development of détente.

Despite conducting two-thirds of trade with the EEC, neutral Austria was a Cold War in-between and thus already geopolitically an ideal Western partner for the socialist states. Furthermore, the Austrian aims converged with the modernization and financing interests of socialist states. In some cases (Hungary, Romania) their weak economic performance set limits to the expansion of economic relations but others (Poland, GDR) turned into economic partners of the Austrian strategy. Despite its own smallness, with the exception of the Soviet Union, Austria never acted as a junior partner in these relations. Well aware of its economic performance in the post-war and its special political status, Austria tended to behave like a superior economy and thus as a constructive regional power in the sphere of the former Habsburg Empire (and beyond in socialist Eastern Europe) – although at times with a post-imperial touch. However, Austria did not conceal the dependency of its small economy on cooperation with Eastern Europe – not least in the field of energy supply.

How shall we qualify the Austrian approach towards Poland? Was it reckless lending that ignored all warnings and primarily served domestic Austrian interests? Or was it rather a policy that aimed at fostering détente and pan-European cooperation? I would argue that it was both and by the early 1980s there was no way out of the Austrian over-engagement. Throughout the 1970s the Austrian approach had serviced the country's economic needs; however, at the end of the decade it had become unsustainable. Nevertheless, despite internal resistance, Austria aimed at supporting Poland during the years of crisis. Still, the dire economic situation of Poland led to a decline of bilateral economic relations and endless debt rescheduling negotiations. Despite warnings, in those very years, deals with the GDR replaced some of the business with Poland and the loan-financed export promotion strategy remained in place. In consequence, Austria even played a disproportionate role in the GDR's struggle to prevent insolvency. Against this backdrop, in a moment of unbowed support for Kreisky's policy pinched with a dose of resignation, Minister of Trade Staribacher confessed to his diary: 'Austria, I believe, has no alternative from the point of view of employment policy, trade policy, and ultimately overall policy.'[76] Only by the mid-1980s it became obvious that this policy – the 'Austro-Keynesian' variety of 'progressive/liberal' economic nationalism – was unsustainable for Austria as well. The VÖEST crisis led to the unavoidable restructuring of Austria's nationalized industries and in further consequence given the new opportunities of the closing Cold War Austria developed a new approach in its integration policy and opted to apply for membership in the EU.

Notes

1 For the most recent study of this development, see Bartel, *The Triumph of Broken Promises*.

2 Kruizinga, 'Introduction', 4.

3 On the Austrian State Treaty, see Stourzh and Mueller, *A Cold War over Austria*; Suppan, Stourzh and Mueller (eds), *The Austrian State Treaty*.

4 Mueller, *A Good Example of Peaceful Coexistence*, 16–20.

5 On Austrian *Ostpolitik*, see Suppan and Mueller (eds), *Peaceful Coexistence or Iron Curtain?*; Graf, 'Indefinite Coexistence?', 233–59.

6 Bischof and Ruggenthaler, *Österreich und der Kalte Krieg*; Graf and Meisinger (eds), *Österreich im Kalten Krieg*.

7 Rathkolb, 'The Kreisky Era, 1970–1983', 263–93; Kriechbaumer, *Die Ära Kreisky*. On Kreisky's biography, see Petritsch, *Bruno Kreisky*. On Kreisky's foreign policy, see Röhrlich, *Kreiskys Außenpolitik*.

8 On 'Austro-Keynesianism', see Seidel, *Wirtschaft und Wirtschaftspolitik in der Kreisky-Ära*.

9 On Austria's economic relations with the socialist countries, see Resch, 'Der österreichische Osthandel im Spannungsfeld der Blöcke', 497–556; Enderle-Burcel, Franaszek, Stiefel and Teichova (eds), *Gaps in the Iron Curtain*; Enderle-Burcel, Stiefel and Teichova (eds), *'Zarte Bande'*.

10 Karner and Ruggenthaler, 'Austria and the End of the Prague Spring', 419–39.

11 Resch, 'Der österreichische Osthandel', 529–35; Butschek, *Vom Staatsvertrag zur EU*.

12 Stiefel, *Verstaatlichung und Privatisierung in Österreich*.

13 See the chapter by Adrian Brisku.

14 On Austria's nationalized industries, see Kastil, 'Von der Verstaatlichung zur Privatisierung'; for a short overview, see Stöger, 'Die verstaatlichte Industrie', 237–58.

15 Romano and Romero (eds), *European Socialist Regimes' Fateful Engagement with the West.*
16 Graf, 'Kreisky und Polen', 700–3.
17 Gilde, *Österreich im KSZE-Prozess 1969–1983*, 318–30.
18 For example, 'Betrachtungen zur Zukunft der Entspannungspolitik in Europa', Hamburg, 23 November 1976, in, *Kreisky Reden, vol. II*. Vienna: Verlag der Österreichischen Staatsdruckerei, 1981, 642–9.
19 The EEC (although with some delays) had successfully implemented its CCP at the beginning of 1973. From that very moment on, its member states were not allowed to conclude any new bilateral trade agreements and the duration of those existing was limited to the end of 1974. In November 1974 the EEC formally informed the CMEA states that from 1975 onwards no more bilateral trade agreements would be signed or renewed. Instead trade negotiations with the Commission were offered. Since the CMEA states did not reply to the Commission's letter, the EEC council acted unilaterally. It established quotas and other checks for imports which were subject to quantitative restrictions revised every year. Against the backdrop of the economic crisis hitting Western European economies, this arrangement promised no better deals for the East. When core interests were affected the dogma of demanding official CMEA-EEC relations and not negotiating with the Community was not even sustainable for the Soviet Union nor the GDR. Romano, 'Untying Cold War Knots: The European Community and Eastern Europe in the Long 1970s,' 153–73. Mueller, 'Recognition in Return for Détente', 79–100; Kansikas, *Socialist Countries Face the European Community.*
20 Proksch to Kirchschläger, Warsaw, 20 July 1970, Zl. 21.-Pol/70, ÖStA, AdR, BMAA, II-Pol 1970, Polen 2, Gr.Zl. 89.474-6/70, GZ. 90.074.
21 See the statement by Kirchschläger in ÖStA, AdR, BMAA, II-Pol 1971, Polen.
22 Graf and Ruggenthaler, 'Entspannung trotz Krisen?', 173–200. On economic relations, see Franaszek, 'Die Handelsbeziehungen', 185–96.
23 Information über Polen, 21. April 1976, Staatsbesuch des Vorsitzenden des Staatsrates der Volksrepublik Polen, Prof. Dr Henryk Jabłoński in Österreich vom 26. bis 30. April 1976, Kreisky Archive, Box Poland 4.
24 Staribacher Tagebücher, 30 March 1976. For the online edition, see Tagebücher Josef Staribacher. Digitale Ausgabe. Hg. von Kreisky-Archiv und ACDH (https://staribacher.acdh.oeaw.ac.at/).
25 Tel. Auskunft Dir. Castellez; betr. Exportkredit für Polen, [31 March 1976], Kreisky Archive, Box Poland 4.
26 Österreichisch-Polnische Handelsbeziehungen, [early 1977], Kreisky Archive, Box Poland 4.
27 'Betrachtunen zur Zukunft der Entspannungspolitik,' Helsinki, 4 May 1978, in *Kreisky Reden*, vol. II, 723–6, for the quote 724.

28 Staribacher Tagebücher, 8 November 1977.
29 Staribacher Tagebücher, 9 November 1977.
30 'Betrachtungen zur Zukunft der Entspannungspolitik in Europa,' Hamburg, 23 November 1976, in *Kreisky Reden*, vol. II, 642–9, 646.
31 Staribacher Tagebücher, 22 November 1977.
32 Staribacher Tagebücher, 15 December 1977.
33 Staribacher Tagebücher, 23 January 1980.
34 Staribacher Tagebücher, 4 December 1978.
35 Staribacher Tagebücher, 19 November 1979.
36 Polen; wirtschaftliche Aspekte des Besuches des Herrn Bundeskanzlers im November 1979, Vienna, 14 December 1979, ÖStA, AdR, BMAA, II-Pol 1979, GZ. 2.166.18.04/5.III.1/79; Aktenvermerk, Warsaw, 7 December 1979, Zl. 195-Res/79, ÖStA, AdR, BMAA, II-Pol 1979, GZ. 518.01.03/23-II.3/79.
37 Staribacher Tagebücher, 23–26 November 1979.
38 Arbeitsbesuch des Herrn Bundeskanzlers in Polen (24.–26. November 1979); Dokumentation, ÖStA, AdR, BMAA, II-Pol 1979, GZ. 518.01.03/23-II.3/79.
39 Offizieller Besuch des polnischen Ministerpräsidenten Edward Babiuch in Österreich (25. und 26. Juni 1980); Arbeitsgespräch im Bundeskanzleramt am 25. Juni 1980: Résuméprotokoll, Vienna, 30 June 1980; ÖStA, AdR, BMAA, II-Pol 1980, GZ. 166.18.04/26-II.3/80.
40 Zanetti to Pahr, Warsaw, 10 September 1980, Zl. 7-Pol/80, ÖStA, AdR, BMAA, II-Pol, GZ. 166.03.00/81-II.3/80.
41 Zanetti to Pahr, Warsaw, 11 August 1981, Zl. 5-Pol/81, ÖStA, AdR, BMAA, II-Pol, GZ. 166.03.00/252-II.3/81.
42 Meisinger, 'Die österreichische Haltung'.
43 Staribacher Tagebücher, 7 April 1981.
44 Staribacher Tagebücher, 24 June 1980; Staribacher Tagebücher, 10 October 1981.
45 Rathkolb, *Internationalisierung Österreichs seit 1945*, 73–4.
46 Staribacher-Tagebücher, 19 February 1982.
47 Official visit by the Polish prime minister to Austria [25–26 June 1980], Kreisky Archive, Box Poland 2.
48 Kreisky: Sozialdemokraten sollten den Polen helfen, in *Arbeiter-Zeitung*, 8 September 1980, 2.
49 Amtsvermerk. Verschuldung Polens im Westen; Hilfsmassnahmen, Vienna, 1 July 1981, ÖStA, AdR, BMAA, II-Pol 1981, GZ. 166.20.00/11-II.3/81.
50 Gespräch mit den polnischen Botschafter Adamkiewicz, Vienna, 11 September 1981, ÖStA, AdR, BMAA, II-Pol 1981, GZ. 166.03.00/270-II.3/81.
51 Kreisky, *Im Strom der Politik. Erfahrungen eines Europäers*. Berlin: Goldmann, 1988, 219–20.

52 Offizieller Besuch des polnischen Außenministers, Joszef Czyrek, in Österreich vom 9. bis 11. November 1981; Medienecho, Programm und Informationsmappe, ÖStA, AdR, BMAA, II-Pol, GZ. 166.18.02/9-III.1/81. The Ministry of Finance wanted to make new loans 'exclusively dependent on Poland's creditworthiness as a debtor', by which it meant the repayment of non-deferred liabilities. Information für den Herrn Bundesminister. Polen; Besuch des polnischen Außenministers Czyrek; 9. bis 11. November 1981; Ergänzung zur Informationsmappe, Zl. 2.166.18.02/7-III.1/81, ÖStA, AdR, BMAA, II-Pol, GZ. 166.18.02/9-III.1/81.

53 Aufzeichnung. Arbeitsgespräch Pahr-Czyrek 10. November 1981, ÖStA, AdR, BMAA, II-Pol, GZ. 166.18.14/23-II.3/81; Arbeitsgespräch mit BM Dr. Staribacher vom 11. November 1981, ÖStA, AdR, BMAA, II-Pol, GZ. 166.18.02/9-III.1/81; Offizieller Besuch des Außenministers der Volksrepublik Polen, Jozef Czyrek in Österreich vom 9. bis 11 November 1981; Information. Runderlass an alle Berufsvertretungsbehörden, 13 November 1981, ÖStA, AdR, BMAA, II-Pol, GZ. 166.18.14/24-II.3/81.

54 Staribacher Tagebücher, 29 September 1981.

55 On Austria and the Polish crisis, see Graf, 'Österreich und die "polnische Krise"', 201–21.

56 Runderlass an die Botschaften in den EG-Staaten. Polen; Umschuldung, Vienna, 12 April 1983, Vertraulich!, ÖStA, AdR, BMAA, II-Pol, GZ. 166.20.01/23-II.1/83 (therein Polen; Umschuldung 1983, Zl. 166.510/32-III.1/83). On Polish debt rescheduling and IMF accession, see Zaccaria, 'Debito e condizionalità? L'amministrazione Reagan e l'ammissione della Polonia al FMI (1981–1986)', 295–316.

57 Wotava to BMAA, Warsaw, 10 March 1983, Zl. 48-Res/83, ÖStA, AdR, BMAA, II-Pol, GZ. 166.20.01/10-II.1/83; Wotava to BMAA, Warsaw, 3 May 1983, Zl. 103-Res/83, ÖStA, AdR, BMAA, II-Pol, GZ. 166.20.01/22-II.1/83.

58 Wotava to BMAA, Warsaw, 19 May 1983, Zl. 114-Res/83, ÖStA, AdR, BMAA, II-Pol, GZ. 166.20.01/24-II.1/83.

59 Memcon Vranitzky – Mazowiecki/Jaruzelski, Warsaw, 5 July 1990, Botschafter Gerhard Wagner to BMAA, Warsaw, 13 July 1990, Zl. 217-RES/90, ÖStA, AdR, BMAA, II-Pol, GZ 518.01.01/21-II.3/90.

60 On the economic history of the GDR, see Malycha, *Die SED in der Ära Honecker*, 177–322; Steiner, *The Plans That Failed*; Berghoff and Andrea Balbier (eds), *The East German Economy, 1945–2010*; Hoffmann (ed.), *Die zentrale Wirtschaftsverwaltung*; Zatlin, *The Currency of Socialism*.

61 Graf, *Österreich und die DDR*, 381–404.

62 Polze an Krolikowski, Berlin, 1 February 1978, BArch, Abteilung DDR, DC/20/4750, Bl. 90–3.

63 Arbeitsprotokoll der Sitzung des Politbüros des Zentralkomitees am 11 April 1978, SAPMO-BArch, DY 30/J IV 2/2A/2145, Bl. 78–9; Bericht über die Aktivitäten auf

ökonomischem Gebiet während des Besuches des Bundeskanzlers der Republik Österreich, Bruno Kreisky, in der DDR, Berlin, 3 April 1978, SAPMO-BArch, DY 30/3248, Bl. 151–7; also see Kreisky Archive, Box DDR 1, Mappe BK-DDR-Besuch 30 March–1 April 1978. On compensation deals, see Judt, 'Kompensationsgeschäfte der DDR', 117–38.

64 Staribacher to Fleck, Vienna, 18 November 1975, SAPMO-BArch, DY 30/17800.

65 Levcik to Lacina, Vienna, 10 November 1980, Kreisky Archive, Box GDR 2, folder 'Diverses 1976–1981'.

66 Information über den Aufenthalt in Österreich zur Führung von Gesprächen mit der österreichischen Regierung und der Wirtschaft am 18. Februar, Berlin, 19 February 1980, BArch, Abteilung DDR, DC/20/4750, Bl. 33–7. Judt, *Der Bereich Kommerzielle Koordinierung*, 142–74.

67 Niederschrift über das Gespräch unter vier Augen, das der Vorsitzenden des Staatsrates der DDR, Erich Honecker, und der Bundeskanzler der Republik Österreich, Bruno Kreisky, am 10. November 1980 in Wien führten, SAPMO-BArch, DY 30/J IV 2/2/1866, Bl. 36–47.

68 Staribacher Tagebücher, 18 November 1980.

69 Graf, 'Before Strauß', 737–54.

70 Graf, *Österreich und die DDR*, 425–33, 459–70, 497–528.

71 Staribacher-Tagebücher, 2 October 1982.

72 Staribacher-Tagebücher, 7 October 1982.

73 Graf, *Österreich und die DDR*, 535–48.

74 Summer, *Das VOEST-Debakel*, 327–46.

75 Gehler, *Österreichs Weg in die Europäische Union*, 102–6; Graf, 'The Accession of the Neutrals', 91–111.

76 Staribacher Tagebücher, 7 October 1982.

7

National in content and … pragmatic in practice: People's Poland's economic relations with the Western Polish diaspora in the 1970s and 1980s

Martin Gumiela

Introduction

Like other countries during détente, People's Poland explored various ways to strengthen its economic relations across the Iron Curtain. At that time, and especially when People's Poland's economy deteriorated dramatically in the second half of the 1970s, the Polish diaspora in the West (commonly known as 'Polonia') became an important economic link for Warsaw's attempts to find wider access to Western markets. The Polish government thus endeavoured to intensively exploit the economic potential of the Polish diaspora in the West – an economic strategy that other state socialist countries with large diasporas, above all the People's Republic of China, also pursued but at a later time.[1]

Western companies owned by diaspora Poles became favoured by Warsaw in its trade relations with the West, and since 1976, People's Poland allowed limited foreign direct investment (FDI) in the domestic market, encouraging especially Polonia entrepreneurs in the West to set up small and medium-sized private enterprises (so-called 'Polonia firms') in People's Poland. These firms usually received state concessions for the domestic service sector and/or for the production of various consumer goods that state-owned companies were unable to supply (in sufficient quantities). By enabling private enterprises with seed capital from the West (i.e. Polonia firms), the political leadership in Warsaw hoped for an inflow of hard Western currency and Western know-how to Poland as well as to alleviate the disastrous shortage of consumer goods in the country. Scholars often frame the *c.* 800 Polonia firms that were founded in People's Poland until 1989 as a kind of 'concessionary capitalism' or as 'enclaves of capitalism' and thus as a remarkable market liberalization of People's Poland's state socialist planned economy.[2]

However, one could also define the privileging of Western Polonia entrepreneurs in People's Poland's economic relations with the West as a classic nationalist and defensive protectionist measure. The simultaneity of both – liberalizing the economy and nationalist protectionism at the same time – does not have to be a contradiction in terms. Rather, it stresses what various scholars have pointed out in recent years, namely that perceiving economic nationalism in a traditional way as states' protectionist economic measures only is insufficient.[3] According to Eric Helleiner, economic nationalism represents a broad range of varieties, including neo-mercantilism as well as free trade.[4] Vera Šćepanović argues on the example of post-Soviet Estonia that even massive economic liberalization and a total market opening for FDI can represent a facet of economic nationalism since Estonia aimed to protect itself from economic dependence on Russia.[5] Thomas Fetzer considers research works on economic nationalism of scholars such as Šćepanović 'revisionist' since they do not define economic nationalism in a traditional way as individual political measures opposed to economic liberalism and globalization but rather locate it in ideational dimensions.[6] Fetzer claims that in many studies on nationalism, little attention is paid to economic aspects and 'nationalism and economy are treated as analytically separate realms'.[7] Political economy studies, on the other hand, often interpret economic nationalism in its already mentioned traditional way.[8] Further, protectionist economic policies are often labelled *per definitionem* as 'nationalist'; however, economic protectionism and/or autarkic economic policies do not always have to be based on nationalistic motives.[9] That is why Fetzer argues for a stronger relaunch of 'revisionist' approaches in this research field since 'it makes no sense to conceptualize economic nationalism in juxtaposition to economic globalization'[10] and even suggests avoiding the centring on the term 'economic nationalism' itself.[11]

This chapter examines how People's Poland justified limited market liberalization of its state socialist planned economy for Western capital investment with the help of nationalist narratives. In what way did People's Poland perceive economic cooperation with the Western Polish diaspora as a useful path to expand its economic autonomy within the Eastern Bloc in times of a dynamically changing global economy? Further, how did the political decision-makers in Warsaw frame economic cooperation with Western Polonia ideologically over time and how was the nationalist justification of economic opening-up implemented in practice?

People's Poland as a 'small state', torn between East and West

Although a unifying definition of a 'small state' is still lacking, there is consensus that quantitative data only (such as population, GDP or geographic criteria) is insufficient since 'a state's size cannot be adequately boiled down to quantifiable criteria'.[12] Going beyond quantitative criteria, it makes sense to scrutinize qualitative characteristics that focus primarily on the power relations of a given state with other states.[13] A unifying feature could be, for example, that other – larger – states and even immediate neighbour states do not take a particular state's sovereignty for granted. Aware of their own 'weak power', small states seek to secure their independence by forcing alliances with other (larger) states.[14] Finally, small states are also economically dependent on larger states and international/global influences.[15] They usually can only react to economic changes on international markets, which, in the end, shapes their own agency.[16] Referring to mainly qualitative aspects, such as power relations with the neighbouring states, Neal G. Jesse and John R. Dreyer propose the following definition of a small state: 'always weak at global and regional levels, but strong at sub-regional level'.[17] Jesse and Dreyer take Bangladesh as an example to show how crucial the region is in which the respective state classified as 'small' is located. With 157 million inhabitants, Bangladesh has the eighth highest population in the world, but its GDP as well as its military forces, for example, are weak. 'If Bangladesh was located in Central America it might dominate the region, but its location in South Asia ensures that it will be a small state for a long time to come'.[18] The example of Bangladesh highlights that purely quantitative data – such as GDP – may be useful for contextualization. Matthias Maass emphasizes that it is precisely the combination of qualitative and quantitative criteria that can be particularly 'fruitful' in determining whether a state could be considered 'small'.[19]

Considering pure quantitative parameters, People's Poland's GDP per capita in 1973 was lower than that of some socialist 'brother states' with a significantly smaller population such as Czechoslovakia or the GDR.[20] Compared to Western small states such as Luxembourg, which considers itself even a microstate,[21] Poland's GDP per capita was more than double the low in 1973.[22]

With the proclamation of the 'Polish United Workers' Party' (PZPR) in 1948, which brought a political unification of the country under a Stalinist regime,

Poland felt under Moscow's political and increasingly growing economic dependence. At that time, Poland was still mostly an agrarian society and major parts of the population lived in the countryside.[23] Compared to the highly industrialized northwest of Europe, Poland, like parts of East-Central Europe and the European Southeast, was considered peripheral. In order to overcome the stigma of economic periphery, the communist regimes declared catching-up economically with the industrialized West as one of their core economic goals.[24]

After huge efforts of industrialization during the Stalinist period, Poland's now industrialized economy – based on coal and steel – primarily had to satisfy Soviet demands. Since the Soviet Union had blocked Poland's (and Czechoslovakia's) participation in the Marshall Plan, their subsequent joining to the Council for Mutual Economic Assistance (Comecon) led to further significant isolation from Western markets.[25] The party under the leadership of Władysław Gomułka, however, ideologically located Poland as an integral part of the Western civilization, and the political elites in Warsaw were aware that the transfer of Western expertise through economic relations with the West was crucial for Poland's modernization. Therefore, the regime observed the increasing economic integration of Western Europe and the accompanying restrictions against the Warsaw Pact states, such as the Coordinating Committee for Multilateral Export Controls (CoCom), with greatest concern. Since the Soviet Union started to sanction Poland's efforts for a more autonomous foreign policy, for example, by imposing restrictions on Russian oil exports to Poland, the party leadership in Warsaw realized even more that the development of long-term economic relations with the West would 'strengthen Poland's position within the bloc and, in particular, vis-à-vis the Soviet Union'.[26] Thus, in the late 1960s People's Poland found itself in an economic trap. The growing economic unification of the West caused Poland's greater isolation from Western markets; on the other hand, any of Poland's (too) far-reaching attempts towards stronger economic relations with the West inevitably led to severe economic restrictions by the Soviet Union. Aware of its own weakness, Poland tried *to react* by strengthening its economic ties with neutral states, such as Austria or Sweden, and forcing limited bilateral agreements with other Western states in order not to lose its rudimental access to Western markets.[27]

Poles in the West unite … and cooperate with People's Poland!

Poland's foreign economic policy in the 1960s, manoeuvring between East and West, was accompanied by an increasing state-directed nationalism. After 1956, the highest unifying element in People's Poland was no longer class affiliation but national affiliation to the Polish nation.[28] That is why the authorities under Gomułka's leadership started to intensify relations with the Polish diaspora in the West and declared to foster the 'natural emotional bond' between Polonia and their 'motherland Poland'. The Polish state in particular sought to cooperate with those large parts of Western Polonia that were considered 'apolitical economic migration'. At the same time, Warsaw feared the growing influence of politically oppositional Western Polonia networks that were loyal to the Polish government-in-exile in London. Therefore, the state 'Polonia-Association' [Towarzystwo Łączności z Polonią Zagraniczną 'Polonia'] – founded already in 1955 – became People's Poland's central hub for cultural exchange with countless Polonia organizations in the West.[29] The association's founding board was broad and included economists like Oskar Lange or catholic priests to signalize a broad societal movement.[30] From the very beginning, however, the security apparatus played a leading role in the association's agency.[31] In the 1960s, Western Polonia representatives took part in many state celebrations of historical anniversaries such as the 'Polish Millenium' (the 1000 years of Polish 'state' existence) and Polonia organizations undertook fundraising campaigns among the Polish diaspora in order to co-finance such events in Poland.[32]

After Edward Gierek came to power, Warsaw sought for even closer cooperation with the Polish diaspora in the West. In 1971, it launched a considerable mobilization to create a 'national front' for rebuilding the Warsaw castle that German troops blew up during the Warsaw Uprising in 1944. The Polish diaspora in the West played an important role in co-funding the rebuild as the Austrian ambassador in Warsaw stated:

> Western emigration has a special role to play. Committees were formed in many countries, donations were collected in hard currency, and connections with Warsaw were established, with the participation of prominent anti-communists, who were not rejected here. National enthusiasm unites the most contrary positions, and one should be careful not to see in it only a momentary phenomenon.[33]

Gierek's efforts to give (economic) relations with Western Polonia a programmatic framework finally led to official party resolutions, such as the 'cooperation with the Polonia in capitalist countries' in 1971 or the establishing of an interdepartmental commission in 1972, that should work for this purpose.[34]

The intensifying economic relations with Western Polonia were an obvious result of the détente between the Soviet Union and the United States, which raised global hopes for better political and economic relations between East and West and thus became a true 'turning point in the world economy'.[35] However, suppressing the Prague Spring in 1968 was Soviet Union's clear message to all socialist 'brother states' to refrain from fundamental systemic reforms. From East Berlin to Bucharest, the regimes undertook risky manoeuvres (in varying degrees) to foster their relations with the West and, at the same time, to avoid fundamental reforms. In this regard, Hungary and Romania made remarkable liberalization steps giving Western companies limited access to their domestic markets by enabling them to set up joint ventures with state-owned companies. They followed non-aligned Yugoslavia, where such enterprises were legal since the late 1960s.[36]

Gierek's administration closely monitored the ongoing liberalization trends while it intensified imports from the West and enabled the usage of licences of Western companies in Poland.[37] Importing Western technological expertise (that was considered crucial for own economic growth) should be financed by increasing exports of Polish manufactured goods to the West over time. The major goal of that strategy – which scholars define as 'import-led growth' – was to establish and to secure stable and long-term access to advanced Western industries and technology.[38] So-called Eurodollar loans – generously lent by Western banks – became Poland's crucial source for financing that strategy.[39] The economic cooperation with Western Polonia had to play an important role in People's Poland's new foreign trade policy.[40] Gierek himself stated during a meeting with Polonia engineers and technicians in Poznań in 1971:

> We know that we are united by the desire for our country to develop faster … We thank you for that, but we also expect your help. We want the input of your experience, your good will … I am convinced that Polonia can serve its fatherland better than it has done so far.[41]

Successful companies in the West owned by diaspora Poles should act as business connectors to Western markets. An internal paper published under the authority of Polish Prime Minister Piotr Jaroszewicz stated

> the serious possibilities of winning responsible partners for our foreign trade in the Polonia communities – especially in the USA, Canada, FRG, England and France – are still not used. The relevance and need to establish broader cooperation does not only result from the general political assumptions of cooperating with the Polonia but can also bring real benefits … for our economy.[42]

The Gierek administration further defined the twelve to fourteen million members of the Polonia in 'capitalist countries' as a 'natural sales market for many Polish products and our activities should go in the direction of its maximum exploitation'.[43] Thus, a main goal of the state-owned foreign trade association 'Polimar', founded in 1972, was to establish trade relations with companies owned by diaspora Poles in the West and, on the other hand, act as an official business representative of such companies on the domestic market.[44] Polimar cooperated closely with other state institutions such as the Ministry for Foreign Trade or the 'Polonia' Association, both of which were crucial for intensifying People's Poland's economic cooperation with the Polish diaspora.[45] Whether the Polish authorities qualified a potential trading partner in the West as a Polonia entrepreneur mainly depended on her/his 'conscious national belonging', 'knowledge and use of the Polish language' as well as 'national descent'.[46] The political background of Polonia entrepreneurs, however, was not that relevant since Jaroszewicz proposed to

> Revise /in agreement with the MSZ and the MSW [Ministry of foreign affairs and Interior Ministry]/ so-called 'negative lists' for contracts with companies that are owned … by citizens of the Polish People's Republic, who left the country under different circumstances. A flexible assessment should be applied to evaluate possible benefits if such a liberalization could achieve trade or industrial contracts.[47]

Polimar was particularly interested in future business relations with companies in the West owned by diaspora Poles that had 'economic potential', a 'solid reputation', an international standing and experience in international trade.[48] At the same time, Polimar advised Polish state companies to prioritize them in case of equality with potential Western trade partners with non-Polish descent.[49] According to internal government documents, Gierek's institutionalization and intensification of trade relations with Western Polonia brought visible results. For example, the share of companies in the West owned by diaspora Poles as trade partners in the total exports of all Polish foreign trade companies to the United States increased from 16.3 per cent in 1973 to 32.5 per cent in 1974. In 1975, the Polish Airlines 'Lot' generated 55 per cent of its total Western foreign exchange earnings from cooperating with Polonia travel agencies in the West and the state-owned Polish travel agency 'Orbis', even 82 per cent. At that time, Polish state companies planned to export via companies owned by diaspora Poles in the United States and Canada larger amounts of goods produced in Poland such as bicycles, kitchenware or telephones.[50]

Investing in People's Poland as Polonia's 'duty to the nation'

In 1977, the total turnover value of Poland's trade with companies in the West owned by diaspora Poles reached 700 million in so-called 'convertible złoty' [Złoty dewizowy, złd][51] – an accounting currency unit of the Polish Złoty that was used in People's Poland's official foreign trade transactions and statistics with the West.[52] At the same time, it became apparent that the import-led growth strategy did not bring the desired effects. On the one hand, in the second half of the 1970s, Poland's trade balances with Western countries were still import-heavy.[53] On the other hand, the worsening economic situation on global markets brought rising inflation of the US dollar, which made it more difficult to repay the loans. Thus, Poland's national debt was rising rapidly and reached almost $15 billion in 1977.[54] In the mid-1970s, Gierek's administration stated that – despite visible positive effects – the economic cooperation with Western Polonia still would not contribute relevantly to the entire economic relations with the West. At the same time (to highlight a positive feature) trade balances with companies in the West owned by diaspora Poles were, contrary to the general trend, not import-heavy.[55] Nevertheless, there was consensus to expand the cooperation. Literally, the 'cooperation should not be limited to trade, but should be extended to co-production, which has not been realised satisfactorily so far'.[56] In practice, this could mean founding holding companies in the West between Western companies owned by diaspora Poles and Polish state enterprises as it happened in one particular case in West Germany in 1975.[57]

To promote further cooperation, the regime invited Polonia entrepreneurs from the West to a conference (entitled 'Kooperacja '75') that took place at the Poznań international industrial fair in 1975. A total of 106 Polonia entrepreneurs from fifteen countries followed the official invitation and took part in the event – some of them giving presentations in official discussion panels.[58] 'Kooperacja '75' was the largest official meeting between Polonia entrepreneurs and state authorities so far, but it was not the first one since already under Gomułka's leadership Polonia entrepreneurs were regular guests of the Poznań international fair. Such visits were organized by the 'Polonia' Association, and in addition to attending the fair in Poznań, the 'Polonia' Association also invited its visitors on round trips through Poland.[59] The 'Kooperacja '75' event was, however, remarkable because of the state's organizational efforts. It also marked the beginning of institutionalized future annual meetings between Polonia entrepreneurs from the West and high state officials in Poland, labelled as

Polonijne Forum Gospodarcze [Polonia Economic Forum]. During 'Kooperacja '75' significant ideas of future economic cooperation were discussed and as one core outcome the Polish government introduced new legal possibilities for FDI-based private entrepreneurship on the territory of People's Poland, in 1976.[60]

More precisely, in May 1976, particular directives of the Council of Ministers for the first time in People's Poland enabled foreign investors to found small and medium-sized private enterprises with seed capital in Western foreign exchange that could operate in selected sub-sectors of the Polish economy, such as craft and services.[61] Western Polonia investors as the founders of such firms were legally required to appoint proxies, who acted as managers of the particular firms on-site and thus needed to have their permanent residence in Poland.[62] Such firms became known as *Przedsiębiorstwa Polonijno-Zagraniczne, PPZ* [Polonia foreign companies], or simply 'Polonia firms'. Polonia firms were not the first private enterprises in People's Poland because besides the non-collectivized agriculture sector, limited forms of micro-entrepreneurship (mainly in the craft sector as well as in services) were legal nearly throughout the whole existence of People's Poland. However, these private micro-enterprises were mostly subject to severe state regulations, such as high taxation and strict limits on numbers of employees.[63] The Polonia firms in Poland enjoyed more economic freedom from the very beginning of their existence. For example, the firm founders did not need to have a relevant training for the economic sector in which the particular firm should operate. They were required to present an investment plan and cover the whole investment in 'convertible Western currency'. In case of a positive evaluation, the respective voivodeship office issued licences for ten years for the particular firm on the territory of the voivodeship.[64] Although the number of employees was limited, Polonia firm owners could formally request for its extension and some Polonia firms had over one hundred employees already in the early 1980s.[65] The main goals of such FDI-based private enterprises in People's Poland were clear. The Gierek administration hoped for better access to Western know-how, for a production increase of consumer goods on Polish ground instead of importing them from the West and for a further influx of Western currency since People's Poland needed at least $2–3 billion yearly to keep the state solvent at that time.[66] Additionally, the Polonia firms' management concept with the Polonia owner abroad and a representative in Poland was probably another state's attempt to formalize already existing informal economic ties between Western Polonia and citizens of People's Poland. In 1975, 'Polimar' complained about several difficulties in establishing trade relations with companies in the West owned by diaspora Poles and assessed that 'some companies which are operating on the territory of Poland take help from family members or random people in Poland. Such a situation complicates negotiations for cooperation and makes it impossible to establish representations of such companies [by Polimar]'.[67]

In public meetings with Polonia entrepreneurs, high state representatives usually underlined the 'patriotic' aspects of the growing economic entanglements. Wiesław Adamski, the director of the 'Polonia' Association, highlighted in his opening speech during the 'Kooperacja '75' event that all participants are connected by 'the deep love for the fatherland and the proud of its current economic success'.[68] Indeed, the economic crisis in People's Poland was constantly growing towards a new peak: In 1980, Poland's debt was already more than $25 billion but Warsaw was able to repay only a fraction of it. Further, Poland also became indebted to the Soviet Union and it turned out that the Soviet Union itself was unable to help Poland out financially.[69] Thus, the West lost an important guarantee for further loan payments to Poland, because until then Western lenders had assumed that the Soviet Union would help Poland out in case of a serious financial emergency.[70] In the spring of 1981, People's Poland finally had to admit insolvency to its Western lenders and the looming national bankruptcy could be barely prevented by temporary debt restructuring measures.[71]

The precarious economic situation led to massive cuts in the domestic economy that in turn caused social unrest and large-scale protests. The mass strikes of July and August 1980 gave birth to the first independent trade union 'Solidarność' and, further, led to an end of Edward Gierek's decade of party leadership. Already in October 1981, Wojciech Jaruzelski replaced Gierek's political successor, Stanisław Kania. Jaruzelski then cut the growing conflict between the party and the Solidarność by crushing the independent trade union and declaring martial law in December 1981.[72] While imprisonment affected tens of thousands of Poles and severe restrictions subjected millions of Poles at the beginning of martial law, the state socialist regime strove to maintain good relations with Western Polonia entrepreneurs. In the first weeks of martial law high representatives of the state, such as Vice-Prime Minister Jerzy Ozdowski, praised the Polonia firms and promised good long-term conditions for them since they would satisfy the regimes' economic 'need for new solutions'. He rounded up his speech with patriotic phrases by framing Polonia firms as a 'duty to the nation' as well as 'service to the fatherland'.[73] However, it were not only empty promises and praise: During martial law, Polonia firms' entrepreneurs belonged to a tiny group of people that could enjoy the freedom of travel. Already in January 1982, proxies and other senior executives of Polonia firms could receive passports for business trips to the West when state borders were generally closed and business trips to other Comecon countries required special permissions from the authorities.[74] The owners of Polonia firms, who were often foreign citizens, usually obtained a travel visa to Poland without any problems and could then 'move freely throughout the country'.[75]

However, why did the regime care about the Polonia firms, since these enterprises remained a marginal phenomenon, even in the non-agriculture private sector of the Polish economy?[76] It is worth mentioning that in mid-1981, there were only 127 of such firms with a total turnover of about one billion Polish Złoty.[77] Following Dariusz Grala, the Polonia firms became People's Poland's important 'window to the West' during martial law since the economic sanctions imposed by the West hit the already ruined Polish economy even harder.[78] Aware of that, Jaruzelski declared already in January 1982 that 'there will be no war between Poland and the Polonia'.[79] Since state officials framed People's Poland's economic relations with Western Polonia during martial law as 'business as usual',[80] the Polonia Economic Forum also took place in June 1982. Among various state representatives, there were 186 Polonia entrepreneurs, some of whom even co-financed the entire event.[81] Vice-Prime Minister Edward Kowalczyk held the keynote and declared that the 'door is widely open' for further economic cooperation with Western Polonia. Apart from discussing concrete upcoming legislative changes for Polonia firms, Kowalczyk's speech was also full of patriotic pathos. There were phrases of 'same blood' and 'mother Poland' that should be 'defended and supported'.[82] Already in July 1982, the government introduced a new law on 'economic activity of natural and legal foreign persons in the field of small business'. In addition to important amendments and clarifications, the new law prolonged the liberal tax policy towards Polonia firms and exempted them from income tax in the first three years of their economic activities.[83] The remarkable economic liberalizations as well as the demonstrative intensive canvassing of Western Polonia by the regime in times of deepest economic crisis caused a rapid increase of Polonia firms. By 1983, almost five hundred enterprises were operating on Polish territory (until 1989 there were eight hundred Polonia firms on the Polish market).[84]

Pragmatic in practice

In times of high shortage of consumer goods in Poland, the Polonia firms gained nationwide popularity since they were able to offer a broad variety of goods and services. The export activity of Polonia firms, however, was unprofitable for the entrepreneurs due to unfavourable tax regulations and, thus, remained marginal. Until 1989, production was therefore almost exclusively oriented on the domestic market.[85] The Polonia firm 'Konsuprod' (founded with seed capital from West Germany), for example, started with a car wash station in Warsaw in 1977, and then produced, among others, sportswear or paving stones. In 1982, 'Konsuprod' became the first authorized dealer for Western electronic products of Grundig and Bauknecht in Poland.[86] The Polonia firm 'Top Mart' with seed capital from Canada became a well-known producer of jeans with production facilities in Częstochowa and Łódź, and long queues formed in front of the firm's salesroom in Cracow even at night.[87] However, the popularity of Polonia firms was not only because they produced desirable consumer goods for the ravenous domestic market. As private enterprises Polonia firms used Western marketing strategies, aesthetic product packaging and Western-sounded product names. Thus, they produced 'Western-like' commodities in People's Poland, which were much more affordable for ordinary people than the very limited Western consumer goods that were only available for US dollar in so-called 'Pewex' shops or for horrendous prices on the black market.[88]

Besides pathetic speeches on official events where both sides – state representatives and Polonia entrepreneurs – highlighted patriotic motives for their economic cooperation, arguments of purely economic benefits also became visible in the discourse. Regarding the tiny group of Polonia entrepreneurs who decided to undertake business relations with People's Poland, the majority stated already in an internal survey in 1976 that their main motivation for doing business with People's Poland was purely economic benefits and additionally sentimental aspects. Only 22 per cent of them defined 'sentimentality' as their main drive.[89] In the 'Informator Inter-Polcom' (a journal published monthly by the official chamber of Polonia firms in Poland, 'Inter-Polcom') the Polish economist Andrzej Lubbe highlighted, 'Investing in Poland should be neither a charitable act nor the patriotic duty of Polonia. Rather it is a normal activity that should be oriented on bringing profit.' Lubbe further stated that although foreign capital would have 'bad reputation' in socialist countries, the Polonia firms as small private enterprises established with FDI could be a valuable blueprint for any further foreign 'capital import' to People's Poland since FDIs are 'simply necessary for any developed country'.[90] Lubbe's opinion was not isolated since he only highlighted the pragmatic dimension of People's Poland's business relations with Western Polonia. The patriotic narratives declared by the regime and its propaganda of Polonia's 'duty' could suggest that People's

Poland only allowed Western Polonia entrepreneurs to undertake FDI into the Polish market. However, in law acts concerning Polonia firms since 1976, there was no legal regulation allowing only Polonia entrepreneurs to establish Polonia firms in Poland. Although Western Polonia was the main addressee, such a limitation 'could not be taken into account in the legislation – nor was it desired' by the state, as it was already noted in 1984.[91] According to Bernadetta Nitschke, at least in the late 1970s, local authorities were encouraged to approve applications for new Polonia firms only from members of Western Polonia, that is, foreigners with Polish descent and Poles with a permanent right to stay abroad. Applications from those who emigrated from People's Poland and then renounced Polish citizenship had to be refused.[92] However, the local authorities did not implement such guidelines strictly, since the owner of one of the first Polonia firms (founded in 1977) exchanged his Polish citizenship for Austrian citizenship in 1976.[93] There was also flexibility in the interpretation of the 'Polish origin' of some firms' founders. The owner of 'Plastomed', a Polonia firm with seed capital from Austria, which manufactured highly needed specialized medical equipment for the domestic market in Poland, 'as a Viennese did not have to worry about his Polish descent since all residents of the capital on the Danube are a bit Czech, a bit Polish, a bit Austrian'.[94]

That is why already in 1982, some Polonia firms' entrepreneurs began to question the common term 'Polonia firm'. The proxy of the Polonia firm 'Dekor' stated that 'the term "Polonia firm" is not precise for many firms united in Inter Polcom, since among the firms' owners there are, for example, a Turk, a Tunisian and a Hindu with a turban [sic!] ... the unifying factor for all these firms is foreign capital'.[95] Yet, the majority of Polonia firms' owners from the West were of Polish descent. Due to their knowledge of Polish language, their family and, in some cases, already established business ties to People's Poland they had the necessary soft skills and social capital for founding a Polonia firm.[96] For foreign private investors and entrepreneurs without any relations to Poland most state socialist countries were unstable political systems with deep ideological aversion to private entrepreneurship and thus too risky markets.[97] However, if a Western entrepreneur without Polish roots wanted to set up a small private firm ('Polonia firm') in People's Poland based on the mentioned law acts of 1976/1982, the authorities did not prevent him from doing so only because of his non-Polish origin. An economic paper on Polonia firms around 1984 noted in this regard that the first Polonia firms were founded by members of Western Polonia and 'they were followed by foreign investors with no ties to Polonia who wanted to invest their capital in our country'.[98] Giving an example: In Southern Poland,

Polonia entrepreneurs ran forty-nine out of sixty-three registered private firms with foreign capital ('Polonia firms') by 1985.[99] According to an internal document, in 1986, 60 per cent of all these private firms in Poland were owned by entrepreneurs 'of Polish descent or Polish citizens with consular passports'.[100] The Polish journalist Aleksander Paszyński summed up People's Poland's cautious opening to Western FDI in the form of 'Polonia' firms, which the regime publicly legitimized with mostly nationalist narratives, very well in 1982:

> I use the term 'Polonia firms' only because that is what our ritualised language calls the back door for the inflow of foreign capital into Poland. No one speaks it aloud, but anyone who can think knows that capital has no nationality in these days. We like the white and red national colours and the word 'patriotism' is even overused. If some cooks find the meal tastes better in such a sauce, so be it.[101]

However, already in 1983, Jaruzelski's regime began to 'pull the emergency break' because the dynamic development of these private firms in 1981–3 caused growing ideological concerns within the party and, on the other hand, People's Poland's economic situation began to slightly improve. The authorities withdrew the liberal tax concessions between 1983 and 1985, and an amendment to the law of July 1982, introduced in 1985, requested a significantly higher seed capital for new firms.[102] Polonia firms and their entrepreneurs faced strict observation by different departments of the security service and since 1982, many of these firms additionally became targets of intensive controls by various state institutions, such as the Supreme Audit Office.[103] The state press conducted a negative press campaign against Polonia firms reporting on their numerous law violations discovered during countless state inspections. Complaints about some entrepreneurs' reckless financial enrichment and accusations of selling overprized poor quality goods or of buying raw materials from state companies instead of importing them from the West became common[104] – although there was no legal requirement for Polonia firms of importing raw materials from abroad.[105] The narratives of romantic-patriotic investment motivations of Polonia entrepreneurs began to decrease and besides the commonly known term 'Polonia firm', these firms were increasingly referred to simply as 'foreign small manufacturing enterprises' [zagraniczne przedsiębiorstwa drobnej wytwórczości – ZPDW].[106] State representatives still highlighted 'open doors' but criticized 'numerous irregularities' within Polonia firms, emphasizing that the state's opening-up for Western (Polonia) FDI was not about 'sentiments' but, in the end, about purely economic benefits for 'both sides'.[107] Growing dismissive attitudes of political decision-makers in Warsaw and the negative public debate on Polonia firms in the state media finally led to even greater uncertainty within Western Polonia itself.[108] This overall negative change towards Polonia firms became visible in 1985, as significantly fewer new firms were founded after 1983 than between 1981 and 1983 and various internal reports made the restrictive laws of 1983–5 responsible for this.[109]

However, more restrictive laws on Polonia firms and the regime's negative propaganda campaign were not a fundamental turning point in People's Poland's opening-up for Western FDI since the government under Zbigniew Messner advocated a radical acceleration of economic reforms launching the 'second stage of reforms'. Due to the continuously high debt to the West ($31.3 billion), the state still urgently needed a large inflow of Western foreign currency.[110] In April 1986, the first law on joint ventures was introduced in People's Poland and until 1990, several successful joint ventures between Western companies and Polish state companies were established on the domestic market.[111] In addition, from 1985 onwards, the state noticeably scaled back the notorious controls in the private sector and members of the party elites began their own entrepreneurial activities in the growing private sector. It was a time when faith in socialism began to wane visibly even among high party members.[112] The timing of such further liberalization of the state economy for Western FDI was not coincidental since Jaruzelski could count on Moscow's goodwill in this regard. In the Soviet Union, Mikhail Gorbachev sought to open up the Soviet economy for Western investments in order to restore broken economic relations with the West and Moscow officially ratified its joint venture law in January 1987.[113] According to Grala, the reforms of the 'second stage' in the last years of People's Poland had already brought fundamental changes towards a market economy. Thus, 'the Balcerowicz Plan after 1989 no longer reformed a planned economy, but a system that was already subject to the dynamic changes of a market economy'.[114]

During that time, various state actors evaluated the past and ongoing economic cooperation with Polonia as mixed. Seeking for already large Western investment capital at that time, the government was critical of the low (re) investment activity of Polonia firms.[115] A programmatic paper that intended to present economic cooperation with Polonia until 1990 described Polonia's overall financial potential in the West as weak. Therefore, it proposed continuing cooperation with Polonia in the sector of small private enterprises.[116] A working group on 'ethnic capital', founded in 1987, proposed to use the experiences with small private foreign enterprises (Polonia firms) for further market openings, arguing at the same time that it is precisely 'small business' that is essential for the growth of any 'developed' economy.[117] Indeed, state representatives continued to make promises towards Polonia entrepreneurs: At the Polonia Forum 1988, Prime Minister Mieczysław Rakowski declared to stop 'thinking in the categories of a small merchant' and promised 'maximum liberalisation'.[118] Although some existing Polonia firms recorded continuous remarkable growth and in 1988, Polonia firms had already seventy thousand employees, the foundings of new firms, however, continued to stagnate in the second half of the 1980s.[119] Thus, contemporary analyses especially urged to liberalize the restrictive tax regulations established in 1983–5.[120] By offering better tax conditions to joint ventures than to Polonia firms,[121] the state proved, in the end, that it was already more interested in preparing ground for major FDI in the state sector itself. An internal party paper stated euphorically that the first joint ventures in People's Poland promised to have 'dimensions … of a significant scale, comparable to the potential of many foreign trade companies'.[122] With a total turnover of 224 billion Polish Złoty and a share of just 0.8 per cent in the total exports of the Polish economy in 1987,[123] Polonia firms, on the other hand, became economically less significant for Warsaw's growing appetite for Western FDI in the very last years of People's Poland's existence.[124]

Conclusion

In the 1970s, People's Poland perceived companies in the West owned by diaspora Poles as important pioneers for establishing future Western sales markets for Polish exports. They thus became the spearhead of People's Poland's 'import-led growth' strategy. The 'national consciousness' of the Polonia entrepreneurs was a core aspect, because with the help of the propagated 'national unity' Warsaw sought to build up long-term trade relations with Western Polonia (and thus in the West) that could last even when the détente between East and West came to an end. As the economic crisis in People's Poland worsened the regime intensified its nationalist mobilization for economic cooperation within Polonia and extended it beyond simple trade relations, enabling to found small and medium-sized private enterprises with seed money from the West in selected sub-sectors of craft and services since 1976. While these FDI-based private enterprises became commonly known as 'Polonia firms' in the Polish public, People's Poland legally created a backdoor for Western investors without restricting it exclusively to Western Polonia. The Jaruzelski regime kept this back door open, especially during the severe crisis of martial law. While the propaganda framed Polonia entrepreneur's investment in Poland as a 'patriotic fulfilment of duty', Western Polonia again had to serve as an 'icebreaker'. Here, Polonia entrepreneurs should pave the way for further private investments from the West where the ethnic origin of the investors no longer played an important role. With 1983, Warsaw not only introduced more restrictive laws for this form of private entrepreneurship in Poland but also began to speak more openly about the pragmatic economic aspects of such an opening-up while patriotic narratives became rarer. Finally, Soviet Union's perestroika reforms significantly expanded People's Poland's economic scope. When Warsaw opened up its state economy for large Western FDI in the second half of the 1980s, economic cooperation with Polonia, as well as Polonia firms with its marginal share in the overall Polish economy, lost priority even more.

Summing up, extended economic cooperation with Western Polonia should help People's Poland to maintain its economic ties with the West.[125] Despite the changing forms of cooperation in the 1970s and 1980s, Polonia acted as an important 'icebreaker' to provide People's Poland broader access to Western markets and thus also to fulfil Warsaw's long-standing efforts to strengthen People's Poland's economic autonomy within the Comecon bloc. The nationalist narratives for the economic mobilization of Western Polonia – which ultimately did not meet Warsaw's expectations – corresponded to the state socialist regime's nationalist premise of the nation as the most important unifying collective identity. At the same time, the nationalist legitimization increasingly served as a 'cover up' for ideologically unorthodox market liberalization for FDI that went beyond economic cooperation with Western Polonia only.

Notes

This chapter has been written as part of the research project 'A Breach in the System. The "Polonia Firms" 1976–1994', funded by the Austrian Science Fund (FWF), project number: I 4877.

1 See, for example, Nyíri, 'From Class Enemies to Patriots'.

2 See Grala, 'Przedsiębiorstwa z kapitałem'; Sikora, 'Koncesjonowany kapitalizm'; Nitschke-Szram, 'Ekonomiczny wymiar'.

3 Fetzer, 'Beyond "Economic Nationalism"', 236.

4 Helleiner, *The Neomercantilists*, 8.

5 Šćepanović, 'National Interests', 210, 220–1.

6 Fetzer, 'Nationalism and Economy', 964.

7 Ibid., 963.

8 Fetzer, 'Beyond "Economic Nationalism"', w.p.; Fetzer, 'Nationalism and Economy', 963.
9 Shulman, 'Nationalist Sources', 367.
10 Fetzer, 'Nationalism and Economy', 964.
11 Fetzer, 'Beyond "Economic Nationalism"', w.p.
12 Maass, 'The Elusive Definition', 66–7.
13 Ibid., 72.
14 Jesse and Dreyer, *Small States in the International System*, 8–9; Maass, 'The Elusive Definition', 73.
15 Pillarisetti, Lawrey, Siddiqui and Lai Teck Choo, 'Small Economies', 2.
16 See Introduction in this book.
17 Jesse and Dreyer, *Small States in the International System*, 10.
18 Ibid., 13.
19 Maass, 'The Elusive Definition', 80.
20 See Maddison, *The World Economy*, 185, 349.
21 See Thomas Kolnberger's contribution in this book.
22 Maddison, *The World Economy*, 179, 185.
23 Wasilewski, 'Społeczeństwo Polskie', 356–7.
24 Romero, 'Socialism between Détente and Globalisation', 12.
25 Jarząbek, 'Polish Economic Policy', 293.
26 Ibid., 294–5.
27 Ibid., 297.
28 Porter-Szűcs, 'From Homo Sovieticus', 556.
29 See Cenckiewicz, 'Geneza Towarzystwa', 161–8; Nitschke, 'Walka o "dusze" Polonii', 65–79; Nitschke, 'Działalność Towarzystwa', 159–85.
30 Nitschke, 'Działalność Towarzystwa', 161.
31 Cenckiewicz, 'Geneza Towarzystwa', 162–3.
32 Nitschke, 'Działalność Towarzystwa', 177–82.
33 Österreichisches Staatsarchiv, AdR AAng II-Pol 2.Republik 5, 1801 Polen 1971, An den Herrn Bundesminister für Auswärtige Angelegenheiten, Wien, Warschau, am 27. März 1971.
34 Nitschke-Szram, 'Ekonomiczny wymiar', 209–10, 212.
35 Grala, 'Przedsiębiorstwa z kapitałem', 79; Pula, *Globalization under and after Socialism*, 74.
36 Pula, *Globalization under and after Socialism*, 69–71, 83. For joint ventures in Hungary and in Yugoslavia, see Erwin Eichmann, 'Joint Ventures in Hungary', 257–94; Artisien and Buckley, 'Joint Ventures in Yugoslavia', 111–35.
37 Komornicka, 'From "Economic Miracle"', 85–6.
38 Pula, *Globalization under and after Socialism*, 79–80.
39 Ibid., 76–7.

40 Archiwum Akt Nowych, further AAN, 2/1140/13/7, Towarzystwo Łączności z Polonią Zagraniczną 'Polonia' w Warszawie. Ośrodek ekonomiczno-prawny. Współpraca ekonomiczna z Polonią 1970–4, Tezy do wystąpienia Towarzysza Ministra W. Adamskiego na spotkaniu z pełnomocnikami dyrektorów naczelnych przedsiębiorstw h.z. d/s aktywizacji współpracy gospodarczej z Polonią w krajach kapitalistycznych, w.p.

41 AAN, 2/1140/13/14/2, Polonijne Spotkania Gospodarcze 'Kooperacja-75'. Poznań 9–11 września 1975 rok.

42 AAN, 2/1140/13/9, Opracowania, Informacje, Notatki, Opinie nt współpracy gospodarczej z Polonią 1972–87, Plan pracy z Polonią w krajach kapitalistycznych, Warszawa, dn. lutego 1972, 4.

43 AAN, 2/1140/13/7, Tezy do wystąpienia St. Długosza na spotkanie z tow. W. Kraśko, 15 February 1975, w.p.

44 AAN, 2/1140/13/8, Współpraca z Polonią Zagraniczną w dziedzinie gospodarczej. Towarzystwo Handlu Zagranicznego Polimar S.A. Realizacja programu współpracy z Polonią Zagraniczną, 1–16.

45 AAN 2/1140/13/12/2, Firmy Polonijne. Współpraca z Polską 1970–4, Dot.: współpracy gospodarczej z Polonią zagraniczną, 30 March 1973, 1–3; Dotyczy działalności polonijnej Polimaru, Warszawa, w grudniua 1972 r., 4; Nitschke-Szram, 'Ekonomiczny wymiar', 211.

46 AAN 2/1140/13/12/2, Firmy Polonijne. Współpraca z Polską 1970–4, Dot.: współpracy gospodarczej z Polonią zagraniczną, Notatka informacyjna, without pagination.

47 AAN, 2/1140/13/9, Plan pracy z Polonią w krajach kapitalistycznych, Warszawa, dn. lutego 1972, 5.

48 AAN 2/1140/13/12/2, Wstępne założenia programu działalności THZ 'Polinar' SA w zakresie rozwoju współpracy gospodarczej z Polonią w krajach kapitalistyvznych, Warszawa, w grudniu 1972 r., 4.

49 Ibid., Polecenie służbowe, w sprawie zasad współpracy z Polonią, Warszawa, 24 June 1974, 1.

50 AAN, 2/1140/13/7, Tezy do wystąpienia St.Długosza na spotkanie z tow. W. Kraśko, 15 February 1975, w.p.

51 AAN, 2/1140/13/9, Czesław Leśniak, Polonia w handlu zagranicznym z Polską, 1.

52 Budziński, 'Kontakty gospodarcze PRL', 95. Until 1971, there was a stable exchange rate (1 USD = 4 złd) and until 1982, when it was finally abolished, the rate was slightly fluctuating from 1 USD = 3.6 złd to 3.3 złd, see Budzowski, 'Ewolucja polskiej polityki', 84–5.

53 See, for example, Budziński, 'Kontakty gospodarcze PRL', 95.

54 Pula, *Globalization under and after Socialism*, 76–7.

55 AAN, 2/1140/13/9, Czesław Leśniak, Polonia w handlu zagranicznym z Polską, 1–2.

56 AAN, 2/1140/13/14/1, Kooperacje 75. Założenia programowo organizacyjne Polonijnego spotkania gospodarczego 'Kooperacja 75', Poznań w dniach 9–11. IX 1975, 1.

57 AAN 2/1140/13/12/2, Umowa o powołaniu 'Polintra' spółki importowo-eksportowej z ograniczoną odpowiedzialnościa, w.p.

58 AAN 2/1140/13/14/2, Polonijne Spotkania Gospodarcze 'Kooperacja-75'. Poznań 9–11 września 1975 rok, 6–10.

59 AAN, 2/1140/13/7, Notatka, Warszawa, 19 listopad 1970, without pagination.

60 Florian Dłużak. 'Firma Top Mart była pierwsza'. Almanach Polonii 1984, Wydawnictwo Interpress: Warszawa, 1983, 227–8; Nitschke-Szram, 'Ekonomiczny wymiar', 212.

61 Sikora, 'Koncesjonowany kapitalizm', 127; Rozporządzenie Rady Ministrów z dnia 14 maja 1976 r., Dziennik Ustaw Nr. 19, Poz. 123.

62 Rozporządzenie Rady Ministrów z dnia 14 maja 1976 r., Dziennik Ustaw Nr. 19, Poz. 123., § 6.

63 See Kochanowski, *Rewolucja Międzypaździernikowa*, 329–64; Grala, 'Przedsiębiorstwa z kapitałem', 79–80.

64 Rozporządzenie Rady Ministrów z dnia 14 maja 1976 r., Dziennik Ustaw Nr. 19, Poz. 123, §7, § 10.

65 Archiwum Państwowe w Katowicach, further APwK, 12/551/0/9/1/2542, Akta Kontroli. Przedsiębiorstwo Polonijno-Zagraniczne 'Bumet' w Gliwicach, Protokół Kontroli 11–13.

66 See Grala, 'Przedsiębiorstwa z kapitałem', 80–2.

67 AAN, 2/1140/13/8, Współpraca z Polonią Zagraniczną w dziedzinie gospodarczej. Towarzystwo Handlu Zagranicznego Polimar S.A. Realizacja programu współpracy z Polonią Zagraniczną, 9.

68 AAN 2/1140/13/14/3, Ośrodek ekonomiczyno-prawny. Polonijne Spotkania Gospodarcze "Kooperacja-75, Przemówienie Sekretarza Generalnego Towarzystwa 'Polonia' min. Wiesława Adamskiego otwierające obrady, 1.

69 Jarząbek, 'Polish Economic Policy', 303–4.

70 Budziński, 'kontakty gospodarcze PRL', 100.

71 Peters, '»Rette sich, wer kann!«', 108–9.

72 See Eisler, *'Polskie miesiące'*, 98–102.

73 Business as usual. Wicepremier Jerzy Ozdowski wśród członków 'Inter-Polcomu', in: *Informator Inter-Polcom 1* (1982): 2–4.

74 Stola, *Kraj bez wyjścia?*, 165.

75 Archiwum Instytutu Pamięci Narodowej, further AIPN Wr 020/573, Sprawa operacyjnego sprawdzenia kryptonim 'Sitwa', Plan przedsięwzięć operacyjnych w sprawie oprac. sprawdzenia krypt. 'Sitwa', Jelenia Góra, 10 February 83, 12.

76 Grala, 'Przedsiębiorstwa z kapitałem', 84, 86.

77 Przedsiębiorstwa Polonijne a kryzys gospodarczy, in *Informator Inter-Polcom* 2 (1982), 19.
78 Grala, 'Przedsiębiorstwa z kapitałem', 84.
79 AAN 2/1140/13/48, Polonijne Forum Gospodarcze 82. Programy, Informacje, Wystąpienia, Pisma i Korespodencje dot. organizacji forum. Wycinki prasowe 1982, Sekretarz Generalny Towarzystwa 'Polonia'. Ambassador Wojciech Jaskot, 2.
80 See Business as usual. Wicepremier Jerzy Ozdowski wśród członków 'Inter-Polcomu', in: *Informator Inter-Polcom 1* (1982): 2–4.
81 AAN 2/1140/13/48, Sprawozdanie, 1–14.
82 Ibid., Drzwi do współpracy szeroko otwarte. Przemówienie wicepremiera Edwarda Kowalczyka na VIII Forum Polonijnym w Poznaniu, in Kurier Polski, 22.czerwca 1982.
83 Dziennik Ustaw Nr.19. Poz. 146. Ustawa z dnia 6 lipca 1982 r., 343; Grala, Przedsiębiorstwa z kapitałem, 82–5; Sikora, 'Koncesjonowany kapitalizm', 127.
84 Grala, 'Przedsiębiorstwa z kapitałem', 84, 86.
85 Ibid., 83, 90.
86 'Prezentujemy firmy: Konsuprod'. In *Inter-Polcom Informator* 5–6 (1982): 28–9.
87 Florian Dłuzak, 'Firma Top Mart była pierwsza'. Almanach Polonii 1984, Wydawnictwo Interpress: Warszawa, 1983, 226–9.
88 Grala, 'Przedsiębiorstwa z kapitałem', 80, 92.
89 AAN 2/1140/13/25, Korespondencja dot. m.in. organizacji Forum Gospodarczego – 76, Informacja Instytutu Ekonomiki Handlu Zagranicznego Uniwersytetu Gdańskiego o wynikach badań w zakresie oceny rezultatów pierwszych polonijnych spotkań gospodarczych 'Kooperacja 75', 4, Tablica 6.
90 Andrzej Lubbe, Import kapitału – odstępstwo od zasady czy powrót do stanu normalnego? *Inter-Polcom Informator* 4 (1982), 31–4.
91 Florian Dłużak. 'Firma Top Mart była pierwsza'. Almanach Polonii 1984. Wydawnictwo Interpress: Warszawa, 1983, 227.
92 Nitschke-Szram, 'Ekonomiczny wymiar', 216.
93 See AIPN BU 1368/13544, Akta Osobowe Cudzoziemca, Decyzja, Wiedeń, 8 November 1976 r., 72.
94 Prezentujemy firmy. Plastomed, in: *Inter-Polcom Informator* 3 (1982), 28.
95 Prezentujemy firmy. Dekor, in: *Inter Polcom Informator* 5–6 (1982), 24.
96 Aleksander Paszyśnki, Co z tego mamy?, in *Inter Polcom Informator* 5–6 (1982): 10.
97 Andrzej Lubbe, Import kapitału – odstępstwo od zasady czy powrót do stanu normalnego? *Inter-Polcom Informator* 4 (1982): 33–4.
98 AAN 2/1140/13/38, Konferencja naukowa, maj 1984. Seminarium nt. Współpracy gospodarczej z Polonią zagraniczną. Referaty, wystąpienia, Inwestycje bezpośrednie kapitału polonijnego w kraju założenia, wyniki, perspektywy, 8.

99 AAN 2/1140/13/55, Jubileusze, Notatki, 1983–85, Zagraniczne Przedsiębiorstwa Drobnej Wytworczości na terenie działalności oddziału Krakowskiego Towarzystwa Łączności z Polonią Zagraniczną 'POLONIA' w roku 1985, 1.

100 AAN 2/1140/13/57, Polsko-Polonijna Izba Przemysłowa-Inter-Polcom, Informacje o działalności, sprawozdania, oceny, wnioski 1984–8, Ocena dotychczasowej współpracy ze środowiskami polonijnymi, 4.

101 Aleksander Paszyśnki, 'Co z tego mamy?', *Inter-Polcom Informator* 5–6 (1982): 10.

102 Grala, 'Przedsiębiorstwa z kapitałem', 80, 83; Nowelizacja ustawy z dnia 6 licpa 1982 roku, *Inter Polcom Informator* 4 (1985): 2–7.

103 See Sikora, 'Koncesjonowany kapitalizm'; Lesiakowski, 'Kierunki działalności kontrolnej', 51–72.

104 AAN 2/2514/0/-/24/1104, Maria Guzowska, Gotówka na stół. Doświadczenia spółdzielni 'Świt', in: *Express Wieczorny*, 5 December 1985; AAN 2/2514/0/-/24/1104, Firmy Polonijne. Materiały ogólne. Krytycznie – o pierwszych doświadczeniach. Firmy Polonijne w świetle kontroli, in: *Trybuna Ludu* Nr. 57, 9 March 1983.

105 See Stanowisko, 'PPIH Inter-Polcom w sprawie wyników kontroli PIH i Ministerstwa Finansów', *Inter-Polcom Informator* 1 (1983): 7.

106 See for example: Alfabetyczny wykaz ZPDW stan z 15 stycznia 1987 r. in: *Inter Polcom Informator* 3–4 (1987): 15.

107 See AAN 2/1140/13/53, Polonijne Forum Gospodarcze 1983. Informacje, Notatki, Programy, Przemówienia, Korespondencje dot. Organizacji Forum; AAN 2/1140/13/58, X Polonijne Forum Gospodarcze, Porgram, wystąpienia, streszczenia. X Polonijne Forum Gospodarcze, Poznań 1984, Wystąpienia. Tadeusz Przyborowski, Pełnomocnik Rządu ds.Zagranicznych Przedsiębiorstw Drobnej Wytwórczości, 18.

108 AAN 2/1140/13/9, Program Współpracy z Polonią do 1990 r., 7.

109 AAN 2/1140/13/71, Sprawozdania Ministerstwa Handlu Wewnętrznego z działalności PPZ (Przedsiębiorstw Polonijno-Zagranicznych) 1987, Departament Obrotu Towarowego, Uwagi na temat funkcjonowania zagranicznych przedsiębiorstw drobnej wytwórczości, październik 1987, 4.

110 Grala, *Reformy gospodarcze w PRL*, 292–5.

111 AAN 2/940/0/47/1349, Instytut Koniunktur i Cen Handlu Zagranicznego w Warszawie, Opracowanie naukowo-badawcze: Inwestycje zagraniczne w Polsce stan faktyczny i perspektywy, Ewa Sadowska – Cieślak, 16.

112 Grala, *Reformy gospodarcze w PRL*, 271.

113 Ironside, 'Because of Him', 247–8.

114 Grala, *Reformy gospodarcze w PRL*, 325.

115 AAN 2/1140/13/66, Forum Gospodarcze 1986, Informacje, dok. organizacyjne, teksty wystąpien, oferty. Andrzej Głowacki, Pełnomocnik d/s Zagranicznych

Przedsiębiorstw drobnej wytwórczości, Panie Przewodniczący, Panie i Panowie! 25–6; see also Nitschke-Szram, 'Ekonomiczny wymiar', 217–18.

116 AAN 2/1140/13/9, Program Współpracy z Polonią do 1990 r., 6.

117 AAN 2/1140/13/72 Kapitał Etniczny, Uwarunkowania wykorzystania kapitału etnicznego w polskiej gospodarce. Tezy, 2–3.

118 AAN 2/1140/13/35, Polonijne Forum Gospodarcze 1988, 1989, Tezy do przemówienia premiera Mieczysława F. Rakowskiego na XIV Polonijnym Forum Gospodarczym '88, 4–5.

119 Between 1985 and 1989 only 119 new Polonia firms were founded, see Grala, 'Przedsiębiorstwa z kapitałem', 86.

120 AAN 2/1140/13/57, Polsko-Polonijna Izba Przemysłowa-Inter-Polcom, Informacje o działalności, sprawozdania, oceny, wnioski 1984–8, Ocena dotychczasowej współpracy ze środowiskami polonijnymi, 6.

121 A total of 75 per cent income tax compared to 50 per cent income tax for joint ventures + tax exemption in the first two years of activity. See AAN 2/1140/13/32, Dokumenty dot. działalności Towarzystwa 'Polonia' na rzecz rozwoju współpracy gospodarczej Polski z Polonią zagraniczną. Programy, informacje, sprawozdania, 1977–87, Informacja o stosunkach gospodarczych z Polonią i związanymi z tym problemami finansowymi, 12 July 1988, 2; Grala, 'Przedsiębiorstwa z kapitałem', 83.

122 AAN 2/1354/0/2.2.10/XX-121, Polska Zjednoczona Partia Robotnicza. Komitet Centralny w Warszawie. Wydział Polityki Kadrowej, Towarzysz Marian Woźniak, Członek Biura Politycznego. Sekretarz Komitetu Centralnego PZPR, Warszawa, 9 March 1987.

123 AAN 2/1140/13/32, Informacja o stosunkach gospodarczych z Polonią i związanymi z tym problemami finansowymi, 12 July 1988, 1–2.

124 See, for example, Sikora, 'Koncesjonowany kapitalizm', 128.

125 Grala, 'Przedsiębiorstwa z kapitałem', 79.

Part IV

State-Building through Globalization

8

Economic nationalism in socialist Yugoslavia: The Slovenian and Croatian responses to globalizing market forces in the 1970s

Benedetto Zaccaria

Introduction

This chapter shows how globalizing market forces in the late 1960s and 1970s affected Yugoslavia's federal balance by focusing on the foreign economic relations of the Socialist Republics (SRs) of Slovenia and Croatia. Per se, Yugoslavia's SRs were part of a broader multinational federal framework. However, they were able to develop autonomous foreign economic policy initiatives which were sanctioned and sanctified by Yugoslavia's 'confederal' constitution of 1974, which endowed federal units a form of 'proto-statehood'.[1]

Accordingly, the SRs of Slovenia and Croatia are optimal examples of small 'sub-state' or 'non-state' entities susceptible to external market pressures, stemming in particular from the neighbouring European Economic Community (EEC). What Ljubljana and Zagreb did develop was a 'liberal' variety of economic nationalism which started to develop in the late 1960s, targeting integration into the Western European market. In this chapter, I refer to economic nationalism as an economic agenda which encompassed a well-defined republican entity and which was pursued by republican authorities for the exclusive interest of their respective republican constituencies. As a strategy carried out within a federal framework, economic nationalism during the 1970s was not intended as a way to make the republics economically and politically independent, according to the 'classic' notion of economic nationalism in Central and Eastern Europe (based on protectionism and nation-building) in the twentieth century.[2] In the case of the SRs of Croatia and Slovenia, the meaning of economic nationalism was radically different: it was based on the goal of republican autonomy within a federal setting and on the opening of republican markets to international partners. By doing so, this chapter follows Adrian Brisku's argument about the multiple historical varieties of economic nationalism – well beyond the simple reading of it as a defensive/protectionist practice – and the link between economic nationalism and national-economic building.

This chapter considers in particular the joint attitude of Ljubljana and Zagreb towards the federal centre rather than the internal deliberation within each republican leadership. It is based on primary sources from the *Arhiv Jugoslavije* in Belgrade, in particular the correspondence between the republican institutions of the SR of Slovenia and the SR of Croatia (economic secretariats and local chambers of commerce) and the Federal Secretariat for External Trade (*Savezni Sekretarijat za Spoljnu Trgovinu*, SSST) in Belgrade. These papers reveal the efforts by the SRs of Slovenia and Croatia to face economic globalization through trade liberalization by, at the same time, reinforcing their republican autonomy. In terms of context, this study does not argue that the republican leaderships of Slovenia and Croatia had overlapping economic agendas: business, trade and investment plans abroad did not stem from joint planning.[3] Nor does it suggest that the two republics were unique examples of trade and investment initiatives with foreign partners stemming from republican frameworks.[4] However, this chapter emphasizes that coordination was developed between the two republics to address the question of autonomy from the federal centre and, at the same time, integration with the Western European market.

All in all, far from offering a 'teleological' narrative of Yugoslavia's history, this chapter suggests that Yugoslavia's increasing integration in the global economy of the 1970s offered new room for its northern republics to turn internationalization, economic liberalization and globalization into a tool to shape republican economic agendas. In concluding this, it does not offer any 'revisionist' account on Yugoslavia's internal dynamics, yet offers archive-based evidence on the nexus between economic and national questions and leaves the ground open for future research concerning trans-regional networks in the Adriatic-Danube region.[5]

The national question in Yugoslavia and the economy

The notion of economic nationalism is strictly linked to the broader 'national question' in Yugoslavia. The rise of this question has been largely treated by historians, who have highlighted the controversial relationship between the socialist project of a multinational Yugoslavia and the self-determination rights of its constituent nationalities. In particular, historians have emphasized that the establishment of socialist Yugoslavia in 1945, as a federal state made up of six republics (Slovenia, Croatia, Serbia, Bosnia-Herzegovina, Montenegro, Macedonia) and two autonomous provinces (Vojvodina and Kosovo), did not solve the management of nationality affairs. What would be the place of the single nation/people (*narodi*) in the new federal system? What would be the relationship/coincidence between the *narodi* and the *republike* envisaged by Yugoslavia's first constitution of 1946? Would a new 'Yugoslav' national identity emerge, overcoming the existing nationalities? What attitude would the socialist leadership take vis-à-vis the national question, in both ideological and pragmatic terms? Scholarly agreement exists about the centrality of these 'national' conundrums in the evolution of socialist Yugoslavia. While this is not the place to consider them individually, it is possible to identify a periodization about the 'national question' on the basis of the existing literature.[6]

After a first phase characterized by Soviet-style party centralism which lasted until the Tito-Stalin split (June 1948), the 1950s were marked by the attempt of Yugoslavia's ruling party – the League of Communists of Yugoslavia (LCY) – to launch a soft Yugoslav nation-building process through 'cultural, linguistic, economic, legislative and political reforms'.[7] In this process, which was paralleled by the introduction of the self-management system, two alternative views emerged within the LCY: one privileging republican autonomy (mainly espoused by Yugoslavia's leading ideologue, the Slovenian Edvard Kardelj) and one favouring centralism (mainly sponsored by Serbian Aleksandar Ranković).[8] In the mid-1960s, Kardelj's line would prevail, favoured by a parallel process of market-oriented (so-called 'liberal') reforms which rejected socialist 'Yugoslavism' as a project that 'denied individual republics the right to play a significant role'.[9] As noted by Tomaž Ivešić, the abandonment of 'Yugoslavism' was 'a starting point for the national rebirth of Croats, Montenegrins, Muslims, and Slovenes'.[10] The 'liberal' period lasted between the mid-1960s and the early 1970s. It coincided with a major process of constitutional amendments and reforms which, between 1967 and 1971, gradually turned Yugoslavia into a confederal state, based on increasing devolution of economic powers to the republics. This trend would reach its apex in the early 1970s during the 'Croatian spring', a mass movement that publicly rediscovered the question of Croatian national identity. The 'Croatian spring' would be harshly suppressed by the LCY leadership, although the purges against the so-called liberals across Yugoslavia between 1971 and 1972 would not mean a revival of 'Yugoslavism' as a state ideology. On the contrary, the decentralization process continued and would be sanctified by Yugoslavia's 1974 constitution, which made the federation an 'empty shell' and made decision-making at the federal level dependent on intra-republican consensus.[11] According to Hilde Katerine Haug, the aim of this decentralization process was that of granting widespread autonomy to each constituent party of the federation, in order to dispel fears of 'centralization' and harmonize intra-republican and provincial relations on the basis of the socialist model of self-management.[12] The 1974 constitution would even enhance the 'national question', spurring the recriminations of the Serb republican leadership against the quasi-republican status of its 'autonomous provinces' and, consequently, the counter attitude of the northern republics (particularly Slovenia). What the historiography on the national question in Yugoslavia has emphasized is therefore the gradual identification of republics (in territorial terms) and Yugoslavia's constituent nations. The constitutional reforms of the 1970s crystallized Yugoslavia as a state without a 'Yugoslav' nation, or alternatively, a multinational state with competing national agendas.

The economic side of the 'national question' has also been addressed by political scientists and historians, who have mainly focused on the internal disparities within the federation – between the 'developed' North and the 'underdeveloped' South – and on recriminations by republican leaderships about the allocation of financial resources for development programmes and infrastructural planning.[13] Instead, the international 'implications' of the national question in Yugoslavia have been less considered by historians. Indeed, international historians have mainly emphasized the role played by Yugoslavia in the Cold War global framework, as a pillar of Western containment policies against the Soviet Union after the split between Josip Broz 'Tito' and the Soviet leader Josip Stalin,[14] and as a leading actor of the Non-Aligned Movement (which was officially established in Belgrade in 1961).[15] These studies tend to offer a portrait of Yugoslavia as a unitary actor, thereby diminishing the 'national' question and its consequences in terms of republican autonomy in international affairs. Only recently have historians addressed the question of the para-diplomatic activities of the Yugoslav republics in order to understand how the national question affected Yugoslavia's foreign policy: crucial in this regard are the studies by Borut Klabjan[16] and Jure Ramšak[17] on the external economic activities of the SR of Slovenia. They have pointed out that the 1974 constitution had deep consequences on the development of a foreign – or rather 'regional' – para-diplomatic activity by Ljubljana towards the bordering countries. One of the most important results of this activity was the establishment of the 'Alps-Adriatic Working Community' in 1978 between the SR of Slovenia and Croatia, the Italian regions of Veneto and Friuli-Venezia Giulia, and the Austrian federal states of Carinthia, Styria and Upper Austria. Both Klabjan and Ramšak mainly focused on the genesis of Slovenia's embryonic 'diplomatic' organization during the 1970s and on the relationship between Ljubljana and the federal centre, showing that until the late 1980s there was not a patent competition between the two levels, and that republican interest and federal ones often coincided. The following sections aim to contribute to this strand of historiography in order to emphasize the nexus between the national question and the emergence of republican foreign policy interests. In doing this, this study also deals with recent literature on 'small nations' in the international system, in that it addresses the reaction of Yugoslav republics towards global economic trends, and their search for 'equal partners' among regional actors in both Italy and Austria.[18]

Yugoslavia's 'liberal' turn of 1965: International and domestic dimensions

The mid-1960s marked the development of autonomous republican economic agendas by the SRs of Slovenia and Croatia. This was the consequence of an ambitious liberalization programme in the economic sphere adopted by the LCY leadership in December 1964. The goal was that of accelerating the country's integration in the international market. This process was linked to the dynamics of regional integration taking place in both European blocs and, at the same time, to a decade-old internal debate within the LCY between the advocates of centralization and decentralization.[19] As for the process of regional integration in Western Europe, the Yugoslav leadership was keen to maintain and foster commercial and economic ties with the booming economies of the six founding members of the EEC, namely the Federal Republic of Germany, France, Italy and the Benelux countries.[20] Domestic motivations added to international ones. They were linked to the rapid transformation of Yugoslavia's economy since the early 1950s. This transformation was connected, since its outset, to the country's gradual integration in the international economy, which the 1964–5 'turn' intended to accelerate. What was needed was access to Western technology and hard currency to modernize Yugoslavia's industrial sector, which had been developing since the mid-1950s to the expenses of the agricultural one. This industrial 'modernization' also served political goals.[21] As in the countries of the neighbouring socialist camp, modernization was a synonym of stability in a period when consumerism and the attraction of Western models was growing steadily.[22] Yugoslavia was particularly exposed to such 'Western' attraction, which was fostered by its Western counterparts, including the United States and its Western European neighbours.[23]

However, the 'stabilization' dimension of the post-1965 reforms had, since the beginning, a collateral effect. Indeed, post-1965 economic and monetary reforms were followed by the adoption of several constitutional amendments between 1967 and 1971 which encouraged the decentralization of the economic system. In this process, republican authorities – that is, the economic secretariats and chambers of commerce of the individual republics – were increasingly seen by the management of local enterprises as their main reference points.[24] This trend concerned in particular the SR of Slovenia and Croatia. There is archival evidence that the late 1960s were marked by increasing requests by republican authorities to enhance their autonomy in the field of foreign trade, to favour the economic enterprises located in their territories. Indeed, the enterprises of the two SRs of Slovenia and Croatia were those to be most exposed to international competition. In particular, their economic activities were closely linked to the Italian and Austrian markets. The latter were, at the same time, import and export markets. They were sources of technology, goods, know-how, credits which needed, in turn, the development of exports to gain hard currency. This was a unique case of privileged relationship with Western partners which the other Yugoslav republics lacked due to geographical reasons. It must be noted that Ljubljana and Zagreb were able to exploit a favourable trend of diplomatic relations between Belgrade, Rome and Vienna which, starting from the mid-1950s, had created an innovative convergence between a socialist yet non-aligned country (Yugoslavia), a member of the Atlantic Alliance and the EEC (Italy) and a neutral country and member of the European Free Trade Association (Austria).[25]

It was this very geographical proximity which offered the authorities of the two republics the occasion for confronting the federal authorities – in particular, the SSST – and also raising the question of republican interests at the federal level. In particular, a specific republican agenda emerged vis-à-vis the question of border trade between Yugoslavia and Italy.[26] This border region had been a matter of international contention after the end of the Second World War, with Belgrade and Rome claiming the city of Trieste and its border region. The original plan envisaged by the 1947 Peace Treaty with Italy to create a 'Free

Territory of Trieste' under UN administration was never implemented due to Cold War reasons, and a de facto solution was only reached in 1954, when the London Memorandum of Understanding divided the 'Free Territory of Trieste' in two zones, A and B, under the respective administration (but not sovereignty) of Italy and Yugoslavia. The two countries aimed to put political questions aside in order to develop economic cooperation, which was needed by Belgrade to face economic isolation from the Soviet bloc, and by Italy to expand economic relations towards the Balkan region and, at the same time, secure the stability of its eastern border. In this context, cross-border provisions were concluded in the mid-1950s, which provided for duty-free transit of selected goods between enterprises located in the border zones in order to favour the economic integration between zones A and B.[27]

Gradually, for both the SR of Slovenia and Croatia, the border with Italy emerged as the main gateway to the EEC.[28] Enterprises and chambers of commerce were particularly interested in the development of industrial cooperation with Italy in the border area near the city of Trieste, which would allow enterprises operating in this area to have free duties access into Italy and, consequently, into the Common Market. To do so, they also aimed at expanding the provisions of the 1962 Alpe Adria agreement which provided for the circulation of goods for the organization of joint industrial fairs in the border regions with Italy and Austria.[29]

The 'shock of the global' and its aftermath in Yugoslavia

The integration of Slovenian and Croatian enterprises in the Western European market was even exacerbated by the end of the *Trente Glorieuses* and the 'shock of the global' of the early 1970s.[30] This period was marked by stagflation of Western European economies, which was spurred by the collapse of the post-war monetary system in 1971 and the ensuing 'oil shock' of 1973. These dynamics had huge consequences in Yugoslavia, which suffered from the rise of oil prices and, at the same time, the crisis of economic growth of its Western European partners.[31]

Indeed, in the aftermath of the monetary, financial and energy shocks of the early 1970s, Yugoslavia's dependence on the global economy even strengthened. Foreign credits, goods and technology to foster internal investments were needed to face the consequences of economic recession in Western Europe. In this context, republican economic agendas starkly developed to face these external shocks. Republican autonomy was encouraged by a set of constitutional amendments adopted in 1971, which gradually shifted decision-making in international economic matters from the federal government (Federal Executive Council) to the republics, whose 'statehood' was also affirmed. Indeed, amendment XX, 3 stated that

> the republics are *states* based on the *sovereignty* of *the people* and on the power of and self-management by the working class and all working people, and are socialist, self-managing democratic communities of the working people and citizens, and of nations and nationalities having equal rights.[32]

On the basis of this provision, which reflected Kardelj's attempt at solving the national question by institutionalizing a mechanism to prevent disagreement in federal decision-making,[33] the representatives of the SRs of Slovenia and Croatia expanded their regional networks with 'equal' sub-national partners beyond the borders with Italy and Austria. Indeed, throughout 1972 Ljubljana and Zagreb reinforced direct links with regional authorities in Italy to develop alternative channels of economic diplomacy which bypassed federal authorities. For instance, this was the case of initiatives taken by Milan Zjalić (vice-president of the Executive Council of the SR of Croatia) to establish direct relations with the president of the Lombardy region, Piero Bassetti, in order to plan a system of water channels linking Italy and Croatia, thereby favouring economic integration between Southern France (Marseille), Northern Italy (Genoa and Trieste), Slovenia and Croatia (Rijeka and Koper) to face the competition of Northern European harbours.[34] Direct relations were also established between representatives of the Executive Councils of Slovenia and Croatia and the representatives of the Friuli-Venezia Giulia region, for instance within the framework of the Trieste international fair held in January 1972.[35] At the same time, a detailed plan to develop water transports in the Danube river was drafted by a joint consortium named *Gruppo di studio italo-sloveno* (Italian-Slovenian Study Group) which involved Slovenian republican authorities (including the chamber of commerce of Slovenia and the Republican Secretariat for urban planning) and the Italian *Consorzio per l'Idrovia Litoranea Veneta* (Consortium for the Venetian coastal waterway) based in the city of Treviso.[36] A report drafted by the Executive Council of the SR of Slovenia in July 1972 noted that the project of a waterway linking the Danube river to the Adriatic Sea through Vukovar, Šamac, Zagreb, Ljubljana, Vipava and the Soča/Isonzo river was considered a long-term development goal of Slovenia, in order to link Slovenia to European and Yugoslav waterways.[37]

What is interesting about these joint initiatives involving Italy's northeast (Lombardy and Veneto) is that they coincided with the establishment of Italian regions with proper regional governments in 1970. While Friuli-Venezia Giulia, a 'special statute' region, had already been established in 1963 – soon developing 'regional' contacts with the neighbouring Yugoslav republics – the institutionalization of Italian regions led to an unprecedented phenomenon of regional diplomacy in Italy, a subject which still has to be systematically researched by historians. Regional actors in this border zone also included Austria's *Länder*, originating an unprecedented transnational regional network among sub-national entities belonging to different states, organizations, international alignments, and yet being able to develop autonomous economic initiatives.[38]

Also, it must be noted that the trend of trans-regional cooperation resisted the reaction of the orthodox leadership of the LCY against 'bureaucratic' and 'managerial' forces which were accused of corrupting the socialist nature of Yugoslavia, challenging the party leadership and also unleashing republican nationalisms. As noted above, between late 1971 and 1972 the tension between the party echelons and the republican leaderships had led to a purge of 'liberals', mostly involving the very elites which had promoted the process of economic reform in Slovenia, Croatia, Serbia and Montenegro.[39]

However, this did not mean the end of republican economic agendas. The purges were intended to strengthen the political role of the LCY, but – again under the impulse of Kardelj – they did not question the republican status set by the 1971 constitutional amendments. Between 1973 and 1974, the SRs of Slovenia and Croatia continued to develop republican initiatives in the field of international economic relations, which were promoted by joint efforts by the chambers of commerce of the two republics to foster cross-border commerce with Italy.[40] Representatives of both republics urged the SSST to speed up the process of negotiations with Austria and Italy in order to enlarge the scope of the Alpe Adria and the existing border trade arrangements.[41] In doing so, they reflected the bottom-up requests coming from enterprises and small businesses which since the 1960s had developed transnational connections in the fields of textile production, automation, the chemical and pharmaceutical industry, etc.[42] These enterprise included Centromerkur, Elektrotehna, Kemija-Impex, Contal, Jugotekstil, Slovenija-Avto, Metalka, Slovenija-Sadje, Prehrana (based in Ljubljana); Adriacommerce (Koper); Jadran (Sežana); Primorje-Export (Nova Gorica); Toko (Domžale); Intercommerce (Umag); Kemikalija, Textil, Vajda Koopexport, Voće (Zagreb). The aim was to overcome what Milan Šamec (a member of the Executive Council of the SR of Croatia) defined, during a meeting with Federal and Croatian authorities which took place in Zagreb in March 1973, as an 'artificial border' dividing the economic zone around the Trieste area.[43]

Similar calls to overcome the 'unnatural' border were made by the Executive Council of Slovenia the year before.[44] Crucial in their strategy was the aim to contain the impact of Western European integration in their economic sectors, to avoid isolation and favour integration and joint production initiatives. In other words, this was a 'survival' strategy in an unstable international economic framework. In this context, the SRs of Slovenia and Croatia were blamed to pursue anti-federal agendas which isolated Yugoslavia's central and southern republics – in primis Serbia, Montenegro and North Macedonia – as mere sources of raw materials and labour for the richer 'North'. This was in particular the position of the Federal Secretariat for the economy, which in February 1973 sent a report to the SSST about the unfair regime favouring over sixty Slovenian and Croatian enterprises which were granted facilitated access to the Common Market via Italy through existing border arrangements.[45] The report noted that special trade provisions established in the 1950s were now 'anachronistic'. As noted above, they were established in very different economic and political circumstances, in order to preserve the economic unity between zones A and B. Now they were creating, instead of solving, regional imbalances. This was an explicit criticism towards the 'para-diplomatic' activities of the SRs of Slovenia and Croatia which seemed to privilege the Western European market and to disrupt the Yugoslav one.

Economic decentralization and the federal demise

This dynamic was confirmed after 1974, when the adoption of a new constitution even increased the autonomy of republican economic interests vis-à-vis the federal centre.[46] The new constitution confirmed the republics as state entities; no sovereignty was instead designated with the Yugoslav state itself.[47] The 'regional' interests of the SRs of Slovenia and Croatia continued to consolidate in this context and they reinforced each other. Two examples of republican initiatives involving the field of international economic relations can be mentioned. First, the signing of the Osimo Treaty with Italy in November 1975, which definitively solved the border question by confirming de jure the provisions of the above-mentioned 1954 Memorandum of Understanding. The Osimo Treaty was primarily negotiated by Slovenian Boris Šnuderl, a former member of

Yugoslavia's government (Federal Executive Council) with deep links with the Slovenian business and banking communities.[48] Second, the signing in 1978 of the above-mentioned 'Working Community of States and Regions of the Eastern Alpine Regions' showed the expansion of the regional dimension of cooperation in the Danube area which overcame the Italian-Yugoslav framework and left autonomy to republican centres: it covered areas such as trans-Alpine traffic links, port traffic, generation of energy, agriculture, forestry, water management, tourism, etc.[49] Both initiatives responded to precise foreign economic agendas which had to face the integration of the industrial sectors of the two republics in the Western European market and beyond. In particular, the Treaty of Osimo envisaged the creation of a free industrial zone across the two countries – the first ever connecting the EEC with a non-member state – allowing for the free circulation of the products of this zone within the Common Market.[50]

The question of autonomy also concerned the difficult implementation of a Yugoslav common policy of economic development due to intra-republican economic competition[51] and, linked to that, the lack of federal coordination in the attraction of Western financial credits towards the federal republics.[52] This had huge consequences for the unity of the Yugoslav market, as the president of the Federal Executive Council, the Montenegrin Veselin Djuranović, openly denounced during a Federal Executive Council meeting on 8 March 1979.[53]

However, it must be noted that, despite criticism coming from the Secretariat for the economy, the 'liberalization' agenda of the Northern republics was not hampered by the SSST or the Foreign Affairs Federal Secretariat (*Saveznom sekretarijatu za inostrane poslove*, SSIP). In official relations with third parties, including the EEC and its member states, SSST and SSIP representatives confirmed their willingness to enhance its integration in the Western European economic system.[54] This was, to a great extent, the consequence of the agency of its republican constituencies which impacted on, and shaped, federal stances: in other words, there was not a competition between the federal centre and the northern republics. Rather, the question was about the lack of a federal centre: by the end of the decade, intra-federal coordination in the field of foreign economic relations proved extremely hard, endangering the foreign trade balance and the growing spiral of foreign indebtedness in the late 1970s.[55] This also questioned the unity of the federation as a single creditor vis-à-vis Western commercial banks.[56]

The republican search for autonomy did not mean, however, a call for political independence or secession. The 'Yugoslav framework' was used by republican authorities themselves to achieve their economic interests, as shown, for instance, by the prominent role played by republican authorities of Slovenia and Croatia during the negotiations for the 1980 Cooperation agreement between the EEC and Yugoslavia in April 1980. This agreement also served the political interests of Yugoslavia 'as a whole', due to its significance in terms of continuous economic and financial support by their Western European partners which aimed to preserve Yugoslavia as a stable, united and independent federation.[57] As shown by Ramšak, similar instances of republican initiatives drawing on Yugoslavia's prominent role in the Non-Aligned Movement concerned economic/financial initiatives by enterprises and republican banks, in particular *Ljubljanska Banka*, in countries such as Iran, Egypt, Algeria, India, Kenia, Central African Republic, Venezuela and Colombia.[58]

Things would only change in the late 1980s and early 1990s, when economic nationalism turned into political nationalism in a radically altered internal and international environment. It must be noted, however, that republican economic agendas had fostered the 'European' self-perception of Ljubljana and Zagreb and created a solid network of regional relations which would prove crucial to include Slovenia and Croatia in the architecture of the 'new Europe' after the fall of the Berlin Wall. Indeed, Slovenia's and Croatia's partners in the Alpe Adria framework would stand as open supporters in the process of independence between 1990 and 1991.[59]

Conclusion

By the end of the 1970s, the integration of Yugoslavia in the international economy meant the early crisis of the federal government and the emergence of republican economic interests. This economic process started to develop in the mid-1960s. The 1965 'liberal turn' was a response to the liberalization of trade which took place in Western Europe. The development of economic relations between Yugoslav, Italian and Austrian enterprises indeed favoured enterprises in Yugoslavia's northern republics. This generated republican interests which, in the long term, led to the emergence of republican economic strategies. This encroached with the rise of the national question in Yugoslavia and the confederal reform of the constitution in the early 1970s. In the long term, this led to a sort of economic nationalism on the part of the republican leaderships which would haemorrhage federal finances. The members of the Federal Executive Council recognized this threat, but Yugoslavia's decentralized economic system created a solid link between enterprises and republican authorities. De facto, the SRs of Slovenia and Croatia were non-state actors which developed embryonic national agendas in the economic realm: these agendas were exclusive and corresponded to the republican borders. For them, liberalization of international trade and integration in the broader process of Western European integration were meant to reinforce autonomy towards the federal centre – which was gradually disbanded – and craft a 'Western European' economic identity. Recurring references to the 'artificial' border with Italy and the economic homogeneity with the North Italian and Austrian regions bear witness to this process.

In conclusion, the Yugoslav response to the challenge of economic integration with Western Europe was built on an unsustainable commercial balance which was fostered by republican economic agendas. This exposed Yugoslavia to the debt crisis of the 1980s: a trend which had been forecast within the Federal Executive Council in the late 1970s but which the lack of federal power was unable to prevent. This greatly reduced the possibility of an effective policy response to the second oil shock of 1979 and the harsh economic environment that followed it. It also led to the gradual disintegration of Yugoslavia's internal market.[60]

An additional conclusion of this chapter concerns the evolution of Yugoslav northern republics according to the paradigm of 'smallness'. Although no explicit reference to 'smallness' emerges from the documentation under scrutiny, from the analysis above it is possible to infer that republican authorities in both the SRs of Slovenia and Croatia were fully aware of their sub-national status within the federal framework, and until the late 1980s questions about international sovereignty were not considered. However, the focus on the economic domain was clearly leaving political questions to the proper sphere of 'Yugoslav' foreign policy, which republican authorities used in order to achieve their preferences. By acting as regional actors, Ljubljana and Zagreb were also able to take advantage from the parallel process of regionalization in Northern Italy during the 1970s and Austria's federal arrangement. The self-perception of republican leaderships as representatives of regional/'small' states made the search for broader regional frameworks consequential. In this regard, the move from Yugoslavia towards the European Union and the North Atlantic Treaty Organization can be interpreted as a post-Yugoslav 'compensation of weakness'[61] through the inclusion in larger political-economic and military structures.

Following the interpretation suggested by Brisku,[62] the variety of economic nationalism described in this chapter is one of 'liberal' and 'progressive' opening to the Western European market – as it was based on enhanced competition and cooperation. Yet, at the same time, this opening was meant as a 'protection' against globalizing market forces.

Notes

The research leading to this article started within the framework of the research project 'PanEur1970s – Looking West: the European Socialist Regimes Facing Pan-European Cooperation and the European Community' which has received funding from the European Research Council (ERC) under the European Union's Horizon 2020 research and innovation programme (grant agreement no. 669194) and later developed within the project 'Open Borders' Cold War Europe Beyond Borders. A Transnational History of Cross Border Practices in the Alps-Adriatic Area from World War II to the Present', which has received funding from the ERC under ERC 2021 Advanced Grant funding scheme (ERC grant agreement n. 101054963).

1 Dragović-Soso, 'Yugoslavia's Political Endgame', 482.
2 Berend, 'Economic Nationalism in Historical Perspective'. For a historiographical review on the concept(s) of 'economic nationalism', see Adrian Brisku's chapter in this volume.
3 As recent research has shown, since the mid-1960s decision-making in the business sector rather depended on a combination of market policies and self-management prescriptions. See Vejagić, 'Persistent Centralisation'.
4 Papović, 'Cold War Diplomacy'.
5 In this regard see, for instance, Ruzicic-Kessler 'The Path to Interregional Cooperation in Cold War Europe'.
6 On the evolution of the national question in Socialist Yugoslavia, see Haug, *Creating a Socialist Yugoslavia*; Budding, 'Nation/People/Republic: Self-Determination in Socialist Yugoslavia'; Ivešić, 'The Yugoslav National Idea'; Brunnbauer and Grandits, *The Ambiguous Nation*; Abram, 'Integrating Rijeka'.
7 In this regard, see Ivešić, 'The Yugoslav National Idea'.
8 On the divergent positions of Yugoslav intellectuals around the national question, see Cosovschi, 'Between the Nation and Socialism in Yugoslavia'.
9 Haug, *Creating a Socialist Yugoslavia*, 163.
10 Ivešić, 'The Yugoslav National Idea', 156.
11 Jović, *Yugoslavia: A State That Withered Away*, 95–140; Pavlowitch, 'Yugoslavia: Internal Problems and International Role', 84.
12 Haug, *Creating a Socialist Yugoslavia*, 374.
13 On economic history and political science studies using the notion of 'economic nationalism' in the context of Socialist Yugoslavia, see, for example, Dallago and Uvalić, 'The Distributive Consequences of Nationalism'; Todorovic, 'Regional

Economic Nationalism in the Former Yugoslavia'; Lazarević, 'Disparities and Economic Nationhood in Yugoslavia'. Historians of socialist Yugoslavia have also used the term 'economic nationalism' when addressing Slovenian and Croatian economic policies in the 1980s. See for instance Jović, *Yugoslavia: A State That Withered Away*, 17. On the connection between economic reforms and the national question in Yugoslavia, see Jakir, 'The Economic Trigger'.

14 Lees, *Keeping Tito Afloat*; Heuser, *Western 'Containment' Policies in the Cold War.*

15 Jakovina, *Treća Strana Hladnog Rata.*

16 Klabjan, ' "Transnacionalne politike, nacionalna diplomacija"?'.

17 Ramšak, ' "Socialistična" gospodarska diplomacija'.

18 For a recent account on the question of 'size' in international relations, see Kruizinga, *The Politics of Smallness in Modern Europe.*

19 See Unkovski-Korica, *The Economic Struggle for Power in Tito's Yugoslavia.*

20 Obadić, 'A Troubled Relationship'.

21 Zaccaria, 'From Liberalism to Under-Development'.

22 Romero, 'Socialism between Détente and Globalization'.

23 Zaccaria, 'From Liberalism to Under-Development'.

24 Arhiv Jugoslavije, Belgrade (Archives of Yugoslavia, AJ), Fond 751, Pov. 2757, F 154, Socialistična republika Slovenija, Republiški sekretarijat za gospodarstvo, 12 February 1968, Analiza regionalnih in sejemskih sporazumov v pogojih novega deviznega režima, 12 February 1968.

25 Ruzicic-Kessler, 'The Path to Interregional Cooperation'.

26 AJ, 751, Pov. 2953, F 277, Državni Sekretarijat za Inostrane Poslove, Poziv na sastanak, Pitanje izmena u sastavu i delokrugu rada mešovite jugoslovensko-austrijske i stalne jugoslovensko-italijanske mešovite komisije za pogranični promet lica, Belgrade, 13 January 1968.

27 Ruzicic-Kessler, 'Italy and Yugoslavia'.

28 AJ, 751, Pov. 2953, F 277, Gospodarska Zbornica SR Slovenije Savezni sekretarijat za spoljnu trgovinu, 22 December 1969.

29 AJ, Fond 751, File 416, SSST, br. 02–322, Belgrade, 12 February 1970.

30 Ferguson et al. (eds), *The Shock of the Global.*

31 Calic, 'The Beginning of the End'.

32 Quoted in Haug, *Creating a Socialist Yugoslavia*, 205. Haug also shows the difference with articles 1 and 2 of the 1963 constitution, which read:

> 1. The socialist Federal Republic of Yugoslavia is a federal state of voluntarily united and equal peoples and a socialist democratic community based on the powers of the working people and on self-government. 2. The Socialist Federal Republic of Yugoslavia comprises the Socialist Republics of Bosnia and Herzegovina, Croatia, Macedonia, Montenegro, Serbia and Slovenia. The

territory of the Socialist Federal Republic of Yugoslavia is unified, consisting of the territories of the socialist republics.

33 Haug, *Creating a Socialist Yugoslavia*, 208–9.
34 AJ, 751, F 826, Savezni sekretarijat za spoljnu trgovinu, Beleška o razgovoru M. Hadžića, saveznog sekretara za spoljnu trgovinu sa G. Maccotta, ambasadorom Italije I g. Battistini, novim ekonomskim savetnikom Abasade Italije, 17 April 1973.
35 AJ, 751, F 687, 1972, Generalni Konzulat u Trstu, Socijalističke Federativne Republike Jugoslavije, Informacija o otvaranju 24 Medjunarodnog sajma u Trstu i Jugoslovenskom danu na istom, undated but February 1972.
36 AJ, 751, F 687, Skupščina Socialistične Republike Slovenije, Izvršni Svet Zvezni Izvršni Svet, Beograd, undated but September 1972.
37 AJ, 751, F 687, 1972, Skupščina Socialistične Republike Slovenije, Izvršni Svet, Številka: 90-pov. 264/67, Ljubljana, 31 July 1972.
38 Among the studies on this subject, see Ruzicic-Kessler, 'The Path to Interregional Cooperation'; Klabjan, '"Transnacionalne politike, nacionalna diplomacija?"'.
39 Lampe, *Yugoslavia as History*, 299–302; Ramet, *The Three Yugoslavias*, 227–63.
40 AJ, 751, 1973, F 826, Privredna Komora SR Hrvatske, Odbor za sajemske sporazume, Savezni Sekretarijat za spoljnu trgovinu. Predmet: Dostava Bilješki sa sastanka dne 20 March 1973 u Zagrebu – malogranični promet s Italijom – Sajamski sporazumi za 1973. Godinu, Zagreb, 30 March 1973.
41 AJ, 751, 1973, F 826, Privredna Komora Socijalističke Republike Hrvatske, Zagreb, Savezni Sekretarijat za Spoljnu Trgovinu, Predmet: Prijedlog za sastanak Mješovite radne grupe, Zagreb, 30.5.1973; Ibid., Savezni Sekretarijat za Spoljnu Trgovinu, pov. br. 02-2241/1, Beleška o rezultatima sastanaka u vezi sa problematikom pogranične razmene sa Italijom održanim u Privrednoj komori SR Slovenije 13. I 14 November 1973. godine.
42 See AJ, 751, F 154, 1968, Gospodarska Zbornica SR Slovenije, Služba za tržišće, Pov. 17/1-68-03 B/D, 29 March 1968.
43 AJ, 751, 1973, F 826, Privredna Komora SR Hrvatske, Odbor za sajemske sporazume, Savezni Sekretarijat za spoljnu trgovinu. Predmet: Dostava Bilješki sa sastanka dne 20 March 1973 u Zagrebu – malogranični promet s Italijom – Sajamski sporazumi za 1973. Godinu, Zagreb, 30 March 1973.
44 AJ, 751, F 687, Skupšćina SR Slovenije, Izvršni Svet, Urad za zunanje zadeve, Stevilka: 90-pov. 1/64, Ljubljana, 21 January 1972, Zadeva: SFRJ-Italija, Novo besedilo videmskega sporazuma o obmejnem prometu OSEB.
45 AJ, 751, F 776, 1973, Savezni Sekretarijat za Privredu, Stavovi o institutu malograničnog i susedskog prekomorskog prometa, Strogo Poverljivo, undated but January 1973.
46 See Adamović, 'The Foreign Trade System of Yugoslavia'.

47 Haug, *Creating a Socialist Yugoslavia*, 292. As reported by Haug, Art. 3 of the 1974 constitution stated that: 'The socialist republics are states based on the sovereignty of the people and the power of and self-management by the working class and all working people. They are socialist, self-managing democratic communities of working people and citizens and of nations and nationalities having equal rights.'

48 Zaccaria,'Yugoslavia, Italy, and European integration'; Škorianec, *Osimska pogajanja*.

49 Ruzicic-Kessler, 'The Path to Interregional Cooperation', 201.

50 Zaccaria, *La strada per Osimo*, 123–7.

51 See, for instance, AJ, KPR-II-5-C-2/317, Kabinet Predsednika Republike, Informacija o radu na unapredjenju medjurepubličke saradnje u sprovodjenju Rezolucije o ekonomskoj politici u 1975- godini, Beograd, 13 February 1975.

52 AJ, Fond 130, File 4211, Stenographic notes of the 63rd meeting of the SIV, 19 March 1979.

53 AJ, Fond 130, File 4211, Stenographic notes of the 61st meeting of the SIV, 8 March 1979.

54 Zaccaria, *The EEC's Yugoslav Policy in Cold War Europe, 1968–1980*, 129–69.

55 Dyker, *Yugoslavia: Socialism, Development and Debt.*

56 I refer to Emanuele Parrillo's doctoral research which is currently ongoing at the University of Nottingham: 'Whitehall, the Clearers and British financial diplomacy towards Yugoslavia. 1979–1983'.

57 Zaccaria, 'From Liberalism to Underdevelopment'.

58 Ramšak, '"Socialistična" gospodarska diplomacija'. On Slovenia's 'commercial diplomacy' after 1974 see also Udovič and Jačimović, 'Osamosvojitev držav in 'pozaba' zgodovinskih dosežkov'.

59 Klabjan, '"Transnacionalne politike, nacionalna diplomacija?"'.

60 Estrin, 'Yugoslavia: The Case of Self-Managing Market Socialism'.

61 I borrowed this expression from the chapter by Kruizinga and Gram-Skjoldager, 'Conclusion', 207. It refers to the chapter by Adrian Brisku in the same volume (Brisku, 'Dealing with Smallness in Habsburg Bohemia, Ottoman Albania and Tsarist Georgia in the late-19th and early-20th century'), which deals with the development and consolidation of national identities and sub-state entities within imperial settings.

62 See Adrian Brisku's chapter in this volume.

9

Elastic Estonia: Late 1980s economic debate in a small nation, from self-management to independence

Kevin Axe

Introduction

Late on 24 September 1987, Edgar Savisaar, head of a small department in Soviet Estonian State Planning Committee, arrived in the city of Tartu bearing the result of quiet discussions about economic autonomy and reforms with trusted colleagues. Having decided only the day before to publish the resulting proposal, he only had time to secure the signatures of three fellow planners, plus a sociologist he met while walking to the offices of Tartu's main newspaper. The proposal's four signatories became celebrities within Estonia, while the proposal used liberal economic ideas from socialists abroad as a key step towards independence.

The publication of the resulting proposal for a 'self-managing Estonia', soon known by the acronym IME (Estonian for 'miracle'), brought economic reform discussions among local economists into the open. This sparked the creation of working groups staffed by a new generation of planners aiming to create an economically autonomous Estonia within the Soviet framework, guided by imported ideas about self-management and marketization. While calling for Estonia to become economically autonomous within the Soviet Union, it ultimately played a major role in its independence, as the public discussion it triggered soon turned to political self-management, and eventually to full independence. By starting marketization early, IME began Estonia's complete economic transformation earlier than elsewhere in the Soviet Union.

I argue that Estonia's small size and long history of intense trade with neighbours along the Baltic Sea Region made it receptive towards what became the 'liberal/progressive' form of economic nationalism. Local elites used this sense of economic nationalism as a tool against their Soviet superiors, ostensibly to improve the all-union economy, but effectively to build a separate one and gain power for themselves, spreading proto-neoliberal economic ideas in the process. This was by no means a steady, assured process. Wide-ranging policies and plans were argued over, drafted, then abandoned, as goals and political circumstances swiftly shifted. Estonia's elites are greatly interconnected thanks to their small number, aiding relatively agile and elastic decision-making and marketization. Even as two competing reformist factions developed, which eventually formed rival political parties, they cooperated well before independence. The combination of small state nimbleness and interconnectedness, and mid-level planners and scholars harnessed economic nationalism and a history of experimentation to create relatively cohesive plans and promote self-management, then ultimately independence and 'neoliberal' marketization to a swifter and more radical degree than elsewhere in the former Soviet Union.

As an occupied state, and the least populous union republic, Estonia could hardly expect much policy freedom. In 1989, Moscow alone had nearly six times Estonia's population.[1] Yet Estonia was able to turn this weakness into a strength and survival strategy. Its small elite community harnessed its strong interconnectedness to create consensus and act decisively, moving ahead of the rest of the former Soviet Union in marketization and currency reform. In 1988, it even became the first union republic to declare sovereignty from the Soviet Union, although Lithuania was the first to declare full independence. Estonia's small size helped ethnic Estonians present a united front to Soviet authorities and the outside world, while avoiding stagnation and the powerful, sclerotic bureaucracy that sabotaged waves of reform elsewhere.[2]

Economic nationalism played a key role in Estonia's perestroika-era economic and political developments, and the resulting state. Like neoliberalism, economic nationalism can be a vague term, and refers not just to specific policies but also the goals and aims behind them, especially an intention to promote the survival of a nation or state. This loose goal allows for a wide variety of ideas, from free markets to state socialism.[3] Neoliberalism can likewise be a form of economic nationalism, rather than simply its globalist antithesis.[4]

In Estonia, proto-neoliberal policies focused on creating and defending a market economy partially protected from interference by interest groups and the larger public fit key aspects of national self-image, such as a high degree of individualism. It also matched the independence movement's goal of replacing the Soviet Union with a 'return to Europe', defined to include integration with the global economy. Neoliberalism can thus be a form of economic nationalism, rather than simply its globalist antithesis. This desire to restore the imagined spirit of interwar capitalist Estonia, from its trade ties with the West to its individualistic entrepreneurial model, matches 'the essence of Geneva School neoliberalism' as summed up by Quinn Slobodian: 'Integration is not the creation of something new but the restoration of something lost.'[5] Many scholars have rightfully pointed out that neoliberalism's focus on private ownership and individualism spoke to the aversion most Estonians had to big government, which state socialism had combined with oppression, as well as a cultural tradition of individualism, and interwar capitalist experience. For transition elites, liberal economic policies offered a way to simultaneously further national sovereignty and economic development, while furthering the 'return to Europe'. Economic geographer Robert Mikecz argues that 'when economic policies are examined in view of the national self-image and motivation of policymakers, the incongruence between economic nationalism and liberal policies disappears'.[6] This is consistent with what Adrian Brisku classifies elsewhere in this volume as the 'liberal/progressive' form of economic nationalism, which is open, outward-looking and based on cooperation with other states. It also matches both Soviet reforms that experimented with autonomy and marketization, and the neoclassical and neoliberal ideas that would come to be associated with the modern Estonian state.

This chapter combines contemporary editorials and newspaper columns by reformist economists, planners and politicians, as well as their later memoirs and interviews, to show how Estonian actors harnessed Estonia's small size and popular support for economic nationalism to lay the groundwork for the neoliberal model Estonia soon adopted. As Lars Fredrik Stöcker argues elsewhere in this volume, a sense of relative deprivation and lost opportunity was certainly a motivator driving Estonian marketization, but only in engagement with other factors. I will use an intellectual historical approach to explain how outside ideas found fertile soil in Estonia, greatly influencing its economics and politics as it moved towards independence. Sources written by reformers during and immediately following the transition period demonstrate the evolution of Estonia's economic nationalist debate, while later sources by reformers provide further context and motivations, albeit through biased perspectives influenced by transformed interests.

This section chronologically follows IME's aftermath, beginning with the public and governmental debates it sparked. This was intensified by an increasingly popular and uncensored media, and further aided by the interconnectedness of local elite networks, and ties between nationalism and economic policies. This proposal led to the creation of official and unofficial working groups, which shared members and findings, which were made into policy. The public and official discussions that followed moved rapidly, and many radical ideas were soon abandoned for being insufficient, as the body politic moved towards outright independence and radical marketization.

A 'miraculous' economic nationalist proposal and reorientation

In August 1987, in an office one floor below the office of the chairman of Estonia's Planning Committee, Edgar Savisaar quietly held a brainstorming session with about a dozen trusted planners and scholars with backgrounds in economics and management.[7] A planner and trained historian, Savisaar ran the development scenario department, but had greater ambitions. He would soon become one of Estonia's most famous and controversial figures, cofounding Estonia's primary opposition group Rahvarinne ('Popular Front'); proposing the Baltic Way demonstration; serving as acting prime minister, mayor of Tallinn and long-reigning head of the Centre Party; and becoming frequently entangled in scandals and court cases.[8] The meeting's discussants, generally members of a young new generation of economists (soon to become prominent themselves), primarily aimed to wrest economic powers back from Moscow.[9]

Although later accounts of Estonian marketization often ignore the roots of the resulting policy, modern Estonia's market economy was not miraculously created ex nihilo. Rather, it resulted from years of economic debate over, and experimentation with, foreign marketization thought, especially from Hungary.[10] One example is a 1985 experiment based on Hungarian policies that enabled state enterprise employees to earn extra money by working for groups they managed themselves at their workplaces, beyond the end of their typical shifts. This programme was popular with employees and improved both the productivity and quality of goods and services, although some critics worried that it simply amounted to better incentives for working overtime.[11] By 1986, marketization experiments had made Estonia the main laboratory for the most radical Soviet economic trials, complete with a new wage system, support for family farming and more independence for the consumer goods industry. These added up to the most liberal economic reforms in the Soviet Union at the time.[12] Reforms centred around autonomy had been occasionally tried since the 1960s, but until perestroika were routinely cancelled by cautious authorities once they began to bear fruit and upset the status quo.[13] However, during the perestroika era, these and other reforms were returned to and expanded upon.[14] Savisaar's forward-thinking approach was inspired by the future studies techniques of American James Dator and Raoul Üksvärav, an Estonian economist who studied management theory in the United States in 1964. Üksvärav had already inspired Savisaar to promote the creation and discussion of 'future scenarios', although the ideas discussed had been percolating in the minds of participants for a while.[15]

These discussions soon resulted in the unsanctioned IME proposal, which called for regional self-management as a means of creating economic autonomy for Estonia within the Soviet Union, albeit ostensibly to help aid the greater Soviet economy.[16] This was the first independent economic plan for a segment of the Soviet Union to function autonomously from the overall Soviet economy. The proposal envisioned a role for Estonia somewhat akin to the Grand Duchy of Finland's autonomous status within late czarist Russia, complete with separate currency.[17] Self-financing was emphasized to further reduce Moscow's administrative power.[18] Everything economic within Estonia's territory, from all-union enterprises run by Moscow to rail networks, as well as taxes and budgets, were to be controlled by Tallinn. The economy would be run on a market basis, with an emphasis on competition over planning. Trade with the rest of the Soviet Union would be treated as foreign trade, conducted through a free market using a separate national currency and based on direct ties between producers and consumers. The proposal referenced some of its inspirations: Chinese reforms (including special economic zones (SEZs)); Hungarian market economic reforms (including enterprise-level autonomy ideas); Bulgaria; and the Russian economists Abel Aganbegyan, Oleg Bogomolov, Gavril Popov and Tatjana Zaslavskaya.[19] These inspirations had been a topic of discussion among Estonian economists for years, but IME brought these conversations into the public sphere.

On 26 September 1987, the proposal was published in the popular newspaper *Edasi*, entitled 'Ettepanek – kogu Eesti NSV täielikule isemajandamisele' ('Proposal: Entire Estonian Soviet Socialist Republic to Full Self-Management'). Hurrying to publish, Savisaar only attained signatures from two co-planners (Tiit Made and Siim Kallas) before the piece was published (Savisaar repeatedly said the other planners were either travelling or declined to support the document publicly, but two planners argue Savisaar decided to limit the signatures to the most prominent planners).[20] Kallas was an editor trained in economics at Estonia's leading newspaper, *Rahva Hääl* ('People's Voice'), while Made was a TV political commentator who had worked at the Soviet embassy in Stockholm.

The fourth signatory, Mikk Titma, is a sociologist who Savisaar claims to have happened across en route to *Edasi*'s offices.[21]

The proposal's Saturday unveiling created a two-day gap before authorities returned to their offices on Monday and could issue official responses. Meanwhile, the public reaction was swift.[22] Vladislav Zubok calls IME 'nothing short of a camouflaged bomb planted under the Moscow-centred pyramid of power', noting 'an idea similar to republican "self-accounting" was at the root of the demise of Yugoslavia'. Zubok writes that this was possible because Savisaar was a man who 'knew the Soviet system inside out' and 'received the full support of both Gorbachev and [All-Union Council of Ministers Chairman Nikolai] Ryzhkov'.[23] While biased due to his role in planning IME, economist Ivar Raig goes as far as to count IME's publication as one of three pillars of Estonian independence, alongside the state's 1988 declaration of sovereignty, and the Soviet unveiling of the secret portion of the Molotov-Ribbentrop pact (thus proving its occupation of Estonia was illegal).[24] According to economist Erik Terk, the publication of IME was timed to perfection. Had it been finished earlier, censors would have blocked its printing, and there was still too little interest in market economics (as differentiated from market socialism, Terk notes that the proposal never uses the word 'socialism', but instead refers to market economics).[25] Although Estonia's Soviet leadership was surely aware of the meetings – the planners met one floor down from a leader's office, and all of the planners were part of the state apparatus – Estonia's leaders found themselves on the defensive, and hardliners were increasingly replaced with officials who slowly came out in favour of independence.

Policy by editorial: Reformers gain a public following

IME's publication coincided with a growing independence movement, empowered by increasingly independent and vocal republican media. Activists initially coalesced around leaked plans by an all-union ministry to build large phosphorite strip mines in northeastern Estonia. These plans were revealed in February 1987 on television, radio and by the leading Estonian newspaper, triggering protests that came to be known as the 'phosphorite war'.[26] Although outwardly focused on the potentially disastrous environmental impact of the proposed mines (one of the few issues where Soviet authorities generally tolerated public disagreement), many Estonians were quietly animated by nationalist fears that the importation of workers from the rest of the Soviet Union would render Estonians a minority in their own republic. The Estonian press played a major role, arguing openly against Soviet plans, albeit without criticizing major officials.[27] Soviet journalists already had a tradition of taking complaints from readership and interceding on behalf of the people. If a complainant's rights seemed to be violated, journalists could write official complaints to institutions, which then had a month to respond. This granted citizens actual influence over Soviet bureaucracy, while letting authorities gauge the concerns of their populace. While environmental protests were generally tolerated, censorship remained, and coverage of an August 1987 protest of the Molotov-Ribbentrop Pact was suppressed.[28] Although the mining plans were cancelled around the time IME was published, many ethnic Estonians had mobilized and begun learning the arts of demonstrations and collective action, united by mass media consumed to an impressive degree.[29]

Grassroots organizations and informal elite networks such as academic clubs helped promote changes among elites and the greater populace. Many influential planners and economists were members of a close-knit young generation that had studied together at four universities. Many participated in the Club of Young Economists, a discussion group for junior local economists featuring debates, presentations by foreigners and regular trips to Hungary to witness economic experiments.[30] Reformist scholars were adept at using mass media to gain public support, especially from ethnic Estonians. Indeed, Estonia's smallness meant that the nationalist goals of autonomy, then full independence, were tinged with a necessary and pragmatic appreciation of outside economic thought, internationalization, economic liberalization and globalization. Separation from the USSR, scarce natural resources and a tiny domestic market mandated further integration with the rest of the world, a goal welcomed by those nostalgic for the 'good old days' of interwar Estonia. Thus, reformers sought strategic openness, focusing on policies needed to pivot towards historic trade partners across the Baltic, enacting a 'return to Europe'.[31] Accordingly, a liberal, non-mercantilist state was born for nationalistic reasons.

The beginning of perestroika initially changed little, but the phosphorite war proved to be a fateful catalyst, showing the press that it could speak openly, even if it avoided criticizing major officials. Within a few years of the start of perestroika and glasnost, newspapers were hosting economic reform discussions sparked by IME, and publicizing and legitimizing demonstrations, allowing people across Estonian society to express their views and aspirations.[32] In February 1987, Estonian radio began popular weekly open political discussions and debates among local intellectuals. That October, Estonian television likewise began airing a two-hour prime-time programme about democratic change. In 1988, appeals and resolutions by new political movements, and coverage of their meetings, began to appear in newspapers, amid a rapid breakup of publishing taboos. Estonian publications attained record circulation as they delved into formerly forbidden topics such as Soviet repression, interwar Estonia and criticism of senior officials.[33] Peeter Vihalemm states that 'journalists spoke publicly in the spring of 1988 about problems for which they could have been fired for discussing privately in 1980' and that, beginning in 1988, they 'enjoyed virtually unlimited freedom' because 'political control over their content was abandoned', while by 1989, the Estonian word for 'comrade', *seltsimees*, 'had completely lost its original function and was thereafter only used in a derogatory and ironic manner'. During this time, newspapers stopped using Soviet place names and titles, and censorship was quietly fading away. In 1989, the Estonian Communist Party officially stated that there were no longer any 'forbidden items' that could not be publicized, save for 'extremist positions', a half step leading to a greater level of decrees expanding press freedom the following year.[34]

In February 1990, the Estonian parliament seized control of Estonian radio and TV from authorities in Moscow, and declared that broadcasting, which had begun to adopt Western standards, should aim for the promotion of political pluralism. The official complete abolishment of Estonian censorship occurred in fall 1990.[35] To a lesser degree, these changes were echoed elsewhere in the Soviet Union.[36] These changes demonstrate that Estonia had begun 'acting' as if it were a free country, much like in contemporary Poland.[37]

Meanwhile, senior researchers such as Rein Otsason (head of the Estonian Academy of Sciences' Institute of Economics) harnessed newspapers to publish and gain support for proposals such as replacing food subsidies with cash payments, sparking further public discussion. This was aided by Estonia's small size, as journalists and scholars often shared personal ties.[38] Publishing economic proposals in popular newspapers to gain public support and push the government towards further reforms and spread imported economic thought became a common tactic for Estonian economists. This 'policy by editorial' propelled Estonia further towards marketization. This heated debate soon led to clear public interest in not just economic self-management but political self-management as well, all in the name of perestroika.[39]

Attempts by Soviet authorities, including the KGB, to discredit IME and combat dissidents in the media were unsuccessful, while rules mandating the communist party nominate editors were ignored. In the first four months after IME's publication, Estonian newspapers published nearly one hundred editorials in favour of the proposal, and only five against, despite authorities pressuring experts to publicly oppose it.[40] By the end of 1988, 236 substantial pieces on IME had been published, many written by experts and public intellectuals. This discussion also took the form of dozens of research groups, interdisciplinary symposia, plus TV, radio and in-person discussions. The economic growth and self-governance of the *sovnarkhoz* (regional economic council) reforms of the Khrushchev Thaw were invoked as inspiration to expand upon. Many who wrote pro-IME articles displayed anger towards Gorbachev's 21 February 1987 speech in Tallinn, where he described Estonians as ungrateful for the gifts of peace and prosperity they had supposedly received from the rest of the Soviet Union.[41] The importance of restoring personal responsibility, in part by returning self-management of Estonia to locals, was another prominent theme, a sign of Estonia's coming neoliberal realignment.[42]

Critiques of Estonian self-management often backfired by revealing the extent to which Estonian affairs were managed in Moscow, and how plans were often compromises between monopolistic ministries, giving IME's proponents the opportunity to argue that the Estonian economy was overly centralized.[43] Raig recalls this public discussion as the point when the majority of Estonian economists saw how popular marketization was among the public and began openly supporting it.[44] Annus argues that 'the sum of in-depth analyses and the mood, expectations, and aspirations [IME discussions] generated – certainly contributed to Estonia's rapid economic success in the 1990s'.[45] She argues that Estonian protests against Soviet imperialism found common cause with 'a neoliberalist-style aversion to state control', partially because 'Estonian neoliberal ideas … were strongly bound to the cultural values of the nation state. The smallness of the Estonian nation played a role here – for a culture of scarcely more than a million people, national survival was a legitimate concern of state policy'.[46] By harnessing local debates and nationalistic ideas, and reshaping outside ideas accordingly, Estonian reformers were able to adapt, spread and institute the proto-neoliberal ideas that soon formed the basis for a new state.

A heated state and public debate: A policy census solidifies

On 16 November 1987, the Estonian Council of Ministers discussed the IME proposal and declared it unworkable, but this did not affect the surrounding debate.[47] As its director, Rein Otsason was asked to give the official response of the Estonian Academy of Sciences' Institute of Economics. Later, following

Estonia's return to independence, Otsason wrote that 'our opinion was 95% positive', although his working group critiqued one unnamed 'particular aspect' of IME, likely its currency proposal.[48] Some scholars with ties to planning IME, such as sociologist and Rahvarinne cofounder Marju Lauristin, held public discussions in packed auditoriums. Its ideas were also shared on TV and radio.[49] Even after the IME working groups published their reports, these public forums would continue, expanding to include further topics, such as land reform.[50] Public opinion surveys on IME-related topics were also launched, and had their results publicly published.[51] Through these mechanisms, outside ideas, localized in the form of the IME proposal, quickly spread across Estonia and elsewhere in the Soviet Union, becoming especially influential in Latvia and Lithuania.[52]

In April 1988, Karl Vaino, the leader of Estonia's Communist Party, came out in favour of the IME proposal. This was especially surprising, as Vaino was born and raised in Russia, and was generally seen as loyal to Moscow over Tallinn. Indeed, when he lost his positions two months later, he moved to Russia, where he spent the last thirty-four years of his life without once returning to Estonia.[53] Confusingly, Karl Vaino's replacement was Vaino Väljas, whose possible nationalist inclinations had pushed authorities in Moscow to send him abroad as an ambassador, first to Venezuela, then Nicaragua. Väljas was a personal friend of Gorbachev, granting his government more flexibility, while his arrival meant that, for the first time, the top three posts in Soviet Estonia were in the hands of ethnic Estonians born and raised in Estonia (Arnold Rüütel led the Supreme Soviet (Estonia's powerless parliament), and Bruno Saul led the Council of Ministers).[54] These men were arguably more open to nationalist arguments in favour of more local autonomy (Saul even claimed to have presented a proposal akin to IME in 1984). Taking such measures would also increase their own political power. This allowed Estonia's government to break ties with Moscow sooner than elsewhere (such as Latvia, which retained more foreign-born leadership).[55] Meanwhile, the politburo agreed to let Estonia take control of several economic sectors within its borders, albeit with delays caused by Moscow's bureaucracy.[56]

Kristian Gerner and Stefan Hedlund argue that this first phase of the Estonian transition was largely one of consent, as both sides saw this process as a positive-sum game, offering opportunities to both sides. The leadership hoped that Estonia could lead by example, showing the rest of the Soviet Union how perestroika's opportunities for meaningful reform could be harnessed, a view reflected among members of the intelligentsia, and – according to public opinion surveys – the larger public. Such a success would also aid Moscow's reformers in their debates over the fate of the Soviet Union, the same reformers that some in the Baltic states saw as allies in their bids for autonomy.[57] Support from leadership in Tallinn and Moscow opened the way to the next step in what would become Estonia's market transition. However, in April 1988, the politburo decided on a compromise that left all sides unhappy, transferring a mere seven economic sectors to republican control, while removing republican control of the construction material industry. Annus describes this as the point from which those seeking radical reform, which included the Estonian Communist Party's leader and much of the rest of republican leadership, 'together with activated masses numbering in the hundreds of thousands – now found itself in direct and open opposition to the central government in Moscow'.[58]

The growing desire for independence, and its nationalistic tendencies, was demonstrated by the currency reform debate. IME proposed a self-managing economic zone largely free of Moscow's central planning diktats, partially through the creation of an inflation-resistant national currency, the 'convertible rouble', soon dubbed the *koru*. The *koru* was potentially akin to the convertible *chervonets*, which in 1922 circulated in the Soviet Union alongside the inflationary *sovznak*.[59] In the ensuing debate, the Scottish pound was sometimes discussed, as it provided a model for creating a locally issued currency without fully leaving the rouble zone.[60] IME signatory Tiit Made and economist Vambola Raudsepp even suggested adopting the Finnish *markka*.[61] Estonian planners instead chose to establish a new national currency, the *kroon*.[62] On 1 January 1990, Estonia became the first post-Soviet state to establish its own independent central bank, predating independence, and had even released the first tender for printing *kroon* banknotes in December 1989.[63]

The *kroon* was introduced on 20 June, when Estonia largely shuts down to celebrate midsummer. A date of special significance to ethnic Estonians, this decision was a reminder of the nationalistic side of Estonian currency reform. The *kroon* made Estonia the first state to leave the rouble zone, against the advice of IMF advisers, but with last-minute aid from its experts after it became clear that Estonian currency reform was going to proceed regardless. Ardo Hansson, an American with Estonian parents, protégé of Jeffrey Sachs and member of the three-man committee in charge of the *kroon*, describes the reforms as primarily a political project, especially earlier on, and recalls Savisaar having more of a flair for the dramatic than market sense, even if there was a consensus among Estonian planners that creating a new currency was vital.[64] Thus, as with other policy changes, currency reform was not solely undertaken by technocrats for economic purposes, but carried out in engagement with political debates, challenges and goals.

In an example of economic nationalism, marketization gained popular support in part because it was seen as moving as far from the Soviet planned economy as possible. Indeed, politicians in the 1990s stated that they were endeavouring to create a system as different as possible than the Soviets had imposed. In its first platform, Rahvarinne called for a market economy, which it notably termed a 'normal economy'. This built on oft-expressed public desires to become a 'normal country' and 'return to the West', restoring Estonia to its historic place within Europe, as a state that primarily traded with Germany and other states along the Baltic Sea, instead of mostly with Russia. This partially nationalistic urge, which took the form of a greater connection with the outside world, was shared by much of the ethnic Estonian public, a populace that often wished to go against the policies and legacy of the Soviet occupation and to some extent restore the interwar Estonian republic. Successes in making changes to the Soviet system inspired further demands, as the horizon of expectation shifted. The independence movement's messaging also took advantage of traditional beliefs, often implying that Estonians should be like the head of a family farm or household, focused on improving local surroundings, rather than serving as a mere cog in a foreign empire.

In the late 1980s, economists in Eastern Europe ostensibly continued to focus on reforming socialism, rather than transitioning to an alternative system.[65] Although reform economists in Estonia may have become more radical, at an earlier point, than many of their counterparts elsewhere in the socialist world, it is difficult to determine with much accuracy at what point their discussions came to a consensus (market, proto-neoliberal or otherwise). Likewise, it is difficult to determine when this consensus took shape privately or publicly, or even which economists of this era were indeed true believers in socialism in the first place. Claims made in later memoirs or interviews reflect the opinions of today, in which being in favour of reforms and independence create prestige and social capital in Estonian society. Thus, all such claims must be treated cautiously. However, the actions of the working groups created following IME's publication are helpful in tracing the creation of a marketization consensus and plans to realize this common belief.

Duelling working groups, shared support and findings

In early 1988, the Academy of Sciences formed an official working group to study IME's tenets. The group had over fifty members, led by Otsason.[66] While Otsason had been instrumental in bringing Hungarian-style marketization to Estonia (and became known as the 'father' of Estonia's post-Soviet currency, although his true role is disputed), some critics feared the working group was a scheme to co-opt and sabotage the IME proposal. Shortly after Rahvarinne's April 1988 establishment, it created several alternative IME working groups, which were soon combined into the 'IME Problem Council'. Both working groups aimed to create programmes by November. The Problem Council had no set member list, but at least twenty-five people met and contributed regularly, especially economists from the Academy of Sciences and Estonia's major universities. The Problem Council aimed to both create policy and serve as a watchdog for the governmental working group. The groups included many people with legal backgrounds (and future members of parliament), who drafted legislation.[67] The world of Estonian scholars and planners is so small that the groups shared members and worked closely together.[68]

Juhan Saharov conducted interviews of members of Savisaar's working group, who were clear about their motivations, although it is impossible to know to what degree they changed between the 1980s and the 2010s. Economist, sociologist and IME planner Ivi Proos told Saharov that IME was a 'project to use the micro-economic model in a macro-economic environment', while Erik Terk recalled, 'we had no way of knowing how it would end … we did not imagine independence; the realistic aim back then was to negotiate as many economic rights from Moscow as possible', and Raig explained that 'the evolutionary outcome of the previous economic proposals that were rejected in the past … grew more radical through the years'. As for their actual goals, Proos recalled, 'national independence was not what we wanted to achieve with the proposal of economic self-management … it was just an idea for a new economic model – let us try to control the Estonian national economy and budget all by ourselves, like our best kolkhozes did'.[69]

In August, Valeri Paulman, chairman of Estonia's Planning Committee and deputy chairman of the republican Council of Ministers, tried to interfere in this process, but was forced to resign. He was then replaced in both positions by Otsason. As a sign of the close cooperation between reformers and the press, the newspaper *Noorte Hääl*, voice of the Estonian Komsomol, printed draft proposals from the Problem Council. These appeared in a column written by Raig, who had, like Otsason, spent time in Hungary and become a prominent promoter of its market reforms, as well as one of IME's planners. As the president and founder of the Club of Young Economists, Raig had already organized presentations and debates over Hungarian reforms. These discussions especially focused on the works of Hungarian economist János Kornai (who Raig translated and corresponded with). Raig also organized Club of Young Economist excursions to Hungary, in which participants met with local economists, then led discussions of their findings after returning home. These influences quickly became clear, as *Noorte Hääl*'s economics section became a major source of public information on IME-style reforms.[70]

Otsason later described the relations between the working groups as poor, stating 'We did not manage to cooperate amicably. Discussions were rather combative and the conclusions reached were quite dissimilar.'[71] Mäeltsemees believes Otsason was by then in favour of IME, but sought a slower, more careful reform process.[72] Otsason describes the currency problem as the main difference between the two working groups. He decided that establishing a national currency was imperative, but the rival group preferred IME's recommendation that Estonia establish a stopgap currency, the *koru*, which could be introduced and guaranteed by the Soviet central bank, instead of Estonia's own. Indrek Toome, who became the head of Estonia's Council of Ministers (de facto prime minister) in November 1988 and chose Otsason as his deputy, describes the *koru* as 'surrogate money'. Otsason's poor opinion of the IME working group reflects his tense relationship with Savisaar, which became fodder for political cartoons.[73]

Toome describes Savisaar and Otsason almost coming to blows at times during meetings to decide currency reform. The combatants made up two thirds of the Monetary Reform Committee, which was tasked with creating a new currency. Its members dubbed themselves the 'Golden Trio', but Kragh described it as more akin to the Holy Trinity, with Savisaar as the Son and Otsason as the Holy Ghost.[74] Terk connects this personal conflict to tension between members of the Savisaar-affiliated Rahvarinne, and of Vaba Eesti ('Free Estonia'), an independence movement founded by Toome in 1990. Vaba Eesti met across from Tallinn's town hall in an early classicist building recently renovated by one of its critics, Rahvarinne member Ignar Fjuk.[75] It also sometimes operated in opposition to Rahvarinne in the Supreme Council (the Supreme Soviet's new name following its democratic elections in March 1990). Vaba Eesti's members tended to be more senior reformist communists, such as Otsason, Sillaste and Toome, as well as IME signatories Kallas and Titma. Savisaar was briefly a member, but then began to claim it was an extension of the Estonian Communist Party, with a degree of state support.[76] Although in September and October 1989, the Estonian government had decided to follow Savisaar's recommendation to initially introduce purchase cheques prior to introducing a national currency, Otsason convinced it to reverse these decisions in November

1989, debating the matter on TV with Bo Kragh, a Swedish banker and Savisaar ally.[77] These conflicts demonstrate that while pro-independence factions were deeply interconnected, and Estonian planners were in general agreement about their goals regarding independence and the ensuing state, their debates could still be heated.

The motivations of many reformers remain unclear, as the pressures to appear a socialist for the sake of one's career were replaced by pressure to appear in favour of Estonian independence. This was especially true of younger economists, who had less of a reputation or career to lose, and more to gain from radical change. In socialist Europe, economic reforms and proto-neoliberal ideas were often promoted by technocratic administrators and enterprise managers seeking to increase efficiency and rationality – places lacking such 'counter-elites' saw radical economic reforms arrive more slowly.[78] Accounts by Otsason and Savisaar are sometimes contradictory, especially regarding support from Toome or aspects of planning currency reform, with Savisaar giving Kallas credit for Estonia's currency reform, although Otsason has generally become known as the 'father of the kroon'.[79] While we cannot be certain of motivations, we can track the spread of proto-neoliberal ideas gaining popularity and power in Estonia, even if sometimes initially cloaked in Leninist terminology. Otsason occupied the middle ground between the younger generation pushing reforms, and the few older conservatives in Estonia pushing back, such as Paulman. Otsason had originally earned a reputation as a reform-minded market economist. He came to adopt the 'wait and see' attitude typical of much of Estonia's leadership at the time, although he proposed Estonia create its own currency, going beyond even the Problem Council's *koru* proposal. More radical reformers thus used public pressure and publications to push Otsason and like-minded administrators towards further change.

Ultimately, the plans released by both working groups were similar enough to be synthesized into one proposal, although the Problem Council's had a more bottom-up focus, with more specific and wide-ranging findings, covering social, cultural and regional topics in addition to proposed economic regulations. By the time the IME working groups released their proposals in November 1988, economic self-management failed to suffice for many Estonians. The public conversation had largely shifted from economic to political self-management, albeit within Soviet borders, although this would in turn be replaced by open calls and demonstrations for independence.[80]

Once green-lit by authorities, the IME project moved swiftly over the span of a year. A final version of the IME project was created in February 1989, after a three-week meeting at a resort by the seaside village of Lohusalu, near Tallinn. In March, it was revised by the Estonian Council of Ministers whose draft appeared in Estonian newspapers the following month. On 18 May, Estonia's Supreme Soviet passed on a revised IME plan, thus aiming to make Estonia economically self-sufficient. While 241 voted in favour, with one against and one exemption, a further bill calling for economic self-regulation to begin on 1 January 1990 passed unanimously.[81] This was despite grudging pushback from officials in Moscow, one of whom predicted the bill would lead to a confederated USSR, and angrily described it as more political than economic, an absurd, nationalistic effort bound to fail.[82] However, this step was insufficient for many, as it called for further negotiations with Moscow, leading reformers to focus on the Supreme Soviet elections in March 1990 as a means of continuing their quest for further independence.[83]

On 29 May, the Estonian Council of Ministers again met to discuss IME, creating twenty working groups (themselves composed of 102 smaller working groups) to create draft pieces of legislation, with deadlines set from August to October. Savisaar was appointed chairman of the Planning Committee, which was tasked with IME's implementation. When working groups finished draft laws, they were assessed by an expert panel within the Planning Committee, then passed to leading newspapers and the Council of Ministers.[84] Thus, the IME plan was drafted in the span of months and realized less than two and a half years after its initial publication. However, its enactment a mere twenty months before Estonian independence meant that it was overshadowed by other events.

Some Problem Council members soon took senior positions in the Estonian government, using their IME-related proposals to quietly begin Estonia's transition to independence and a market economy by creating drafts for new policies from taxation to banking to pricing.[85] The working groups demonstrate that, despite occasional conflict, Estonian transition elites were in general agreement about the state they wished to create, and that independence-minded factions shared many members. Estonia's small size was an asset as its future was discussed and planned out, as its planners were able to draw upon interpersonal relations that came from years of familiarity, usually tracing back to relationships established in Estonia's few universities.

The extraordinary ease IME-related legislation had in passing demonstrates the degree to which the Overton Window shifted, as previously unsanctioned ideas became the centre of official economic policy. However, this Window continued to move towards local control of Estonia, rendering the legislation too little, too late. Regardless, the resulting discussions and legislation helped kickstart the creation of today's neoliberal Estonian state, giving Estonia an advantage in marketization compared to other Soviet socialist republics. Thus, Estonian neoliberalism can be traced to the IME programme, and to the intra-socialist ties among scholars that produced it, aided by Estonia's small size and the unifying effects of economic nationalist arguments.

A special economic dead end: An autonomy proposal offering too little, too late

In the late 1980s, Estonia's pattern of importing and localizing outside economic ideas was enriched by increased connections beyond the Soviet sphere and influenced by global economic trends. This thought diversification proved useful, even if some ideas ultimately led to dead ends as Estonian planners sought increasingly radical changes and began proposing new economic models, some based on exotic examples, such as Hong Kong's relationship with China, or Mongolia's with the Soviet Union.[86] One failed proposal was the SEZ, an area where trade and business law differ from the surrounding state.[87] Some Estonian economic reformers considered pitching an increasingly sovereign Estonia to foreign investors as a type of SEZ. This would take advantage of Estonia's small size and long coast, enabling the republic to operate as a hub of trade between the Soviet Union and the West, especially Finland and Sweden. Plans varied widely, with proposed locations including five separate cities; a rayon; two islands; and all of Estonia, potentially joined with Latvia and Lithuania.[88] Estonia might have its own tax legislation and currency, ostensibly following Lenin's ideas of federation.[89] This idea had prominent proponents, was based on trips to China and Shannon, Ireland, by delegates such as Otsason and Estonian foreign minister Arnold Green, and was broached with the public via newspaper editorials and televised discussions.[90]

The proposal for an Estonian SEZ was ultimately vetoed by the working groups tasked with creating a new economic system. While they officially set out to create market socialism, as increasingly expansive forms of sovereignty – and ultimately independence – gained popularity, SEZs came to be seen as insufficiently independent. This was partially because they left authorities in Moscow with too much power. China had also failed to impress many Estonian scholars, who saw it as too poor, agrarian, unitary and planned, with insufficiently high labour and production quality standards, to serve as a model, even for a niche policy like SEZs. The public sphere had even less interest in China.[91] The moment for SEZs had passed, and more radical ideas were in vogue among both the public and a younger generation of planners and economists. A *Rahva Hääl* article jointly written by both working groups stated that while SEZs would be relatively easy to set up, they were too narrow a solution, and risked continuing the resource extraction and labour importation that had triggered the 1987 phosphorite protests. An SEZ, even if it encompassed the entirety of Estonia, would require more Soviet bureaucracy and use rules created in Moscow, ceding too much legal power to all-union authorities, while the IME proposal called for Estonia to be given complete economic control over its territory.[92] SEZs would also fail to allow for IME's goal for all economic profits to remain within Estonia.[93] This idea occasionally returned for economic political reasons as late as the early 1990s (especially to combat Russophone successionists in northeast Estonia), and the country now has similar 'free trade zones' in three ports.[94] However, the SEZ concept mainly serves as an example of interest in both capitalist and socialist reforms, and its rapid rise and fall demonstrates the swiftness of Estonia's economic transition.

Conclusion

Enabled by perestroika's relative permissiveness, Estonia was a hotbed of economic experimentation and discussion, both behind locked doors and in public publications and forums. These discussions were led by local scholars and policymakers who adapted market economic regional and workplace self-management ideas – especially from socialist states – experimented with these reforms and created their own forms. This culminated in the 1987 IME proposal for an economically independent Estonia remaining within the Soviet Union. This proposal intensified and publicized reformist economic trends, pushing the state towards privatization, decentralization and ultimately independence, preparing the way for Estonia's market transition. This process of foreign ideas arriving via transnational networks, undergoing a process of filtration and localization through domestic structures, then being spread by local agents, moved so quickly that even liberal ideas such as SEZs were quickly abandoned as insufficiently radical and replaced with more economically nationalist ideas, as the Overton Window shifted towards political sovereignty, then full independence. By this point, Estonia was not simply a recipient of proto-neoliberal ideas, but had become a hub, exporting its take on outside thought across the Soviet Union, a pattern that continued after independence.

I argue that Estonia's small size, resultingly interconnected and effective elites, and a long history of trade along the Baltic Sea Region made local reformers receptive towards a 'liberal/progressive' form of economic nationalism. This was used as a tool to gain autonomy and power, spreading proto-neoliberal economic ideas. The adaptation of proto-neoliberal economic policies by local economists with nationalist sympathies demonstrates that neoliberalism and globalization can be forms of economic nationalism, rather than its antithesis, and casts doubt on Cornel Ban's argument that radical neoliberal policies are correlated with brief, shallow periods of exposure to its ideas. Estonian reformers often focused on redirecting Estonia's economy, tightly interwoven with the rest of the Soviet Union, outwards to join the global economy, especially historic trade partners along the Baltic rim. Thus, Estonian statehood and self-management would be reinforced by globalization, as the resulting economic development and ties with outside states were seen as a means of increasing national sovereignty, even as they were ostensibly intended to improve the overall Soviet economy. IME's creators and other proponents not only spread proto-neoliberal economic thought through public discussions and publications but also harnessed public pressure to gain powerful positions within the governments of Soviet Estonia (often while highly visible members of its opposition) and its independent successor state. This was aided by Estonia's small size, which resulted in a dense network of connections and the ability to swiftly change the direction of the ship of state. By creating a relatively cohesive plan for economic self-management, then using it to gain public support and state power, a generation of young, reform-minded Estonian economists with nationalist sympathies set in motion the especially rapid and radical shock therapy policies that were hallmarks, and exports, of newly independent Estonia, and the basis for its 'Baltic Tiger' reputation.

Notes

Research supported by the Cluster of Excellence 'Contestations of the Liberal Script (SCRIPTS)' and the German Research Foundation (DFG) (project number EXC 2055–390715649).

1 Colton, *Moscow*, 758; Statistics Estonia, 'RV02111: Population by Age and Sex, 1 January (1950–1999)', 2011, https://andmed.stat.ee/en/stat/Lepetatud_tabelid_Rahvastik.Arhiiv_Rahvastikun%C3%A4itajad%20ja%20koosseus.%20Arhiiv/RV02111 (accessed 14 September 2023).

2 Miller, *Struggle to Save*; Feygin, 'Reforming the Cold War State'.
3 Hall, 'Japanese Spirit', 119, 124; Pickel, 'Economic Nationalism', 122; Koch, 'Political Geography', 14.
4 Helleiner, 'Economic Nationalism'.
5 Slobodian, *Globalists*, 272.
6 Mikecz, 'Cornerstone', 587–8; Ther, *Europe Since 1989*, 27.
7 Terk and Tõnisson, 'IME programm'. 135; Kümmel (2002), 'IME avaldusele söandas nime alla kirjutada vaid neli inimest', *Eesti Päevaleht*, 25 September.
8 Zubok, *Collapse*, 85.
9 Saharov, 'Economic Term to a Political Concept'.
10 Piirimäe, 'Gorbachev's New Thinking'.
11 Saharov, 'Economic Innovation as an Icebreaker'.
12 Lassiter, Bisping and Horton, 'Central Banking', 333.
13 Taagepera, *Estonia*.
14 Sjöström, Sten, 'I Estland provas Sovjets reformer', *Dagens Industri*, in ERA (Estonian National Archives, ERA), Tallinn, 5006.1.174.
15 Saharov, 'Future Scenarios to Sovereignty Declarations'; Kümmel, 'IME avaldusele'.
16 Gerner and Hedlund, *Baltic States*; Kallas, Siim, Tiit Made, Edgar Savisaar and Mikk Titma (1987), 'Ettepanek: kogu Eesti NSV täielikule isemajandamisele', *Edasi*, 26 September.
17 Kallas and Sõrg, 'Currency Reform', 53.
18 Kukk, *Eesti majanduse*, 113.
19 Kallas et al., 'Ettepanek'.
20 Annus, *Neoliberalism*, 9.
21 Taagepera, *Estonia*, 128. There are doubts about this being a chance meeting, as the man, sociologist Mikk Titma, had state connections that could aid this project. See Kümmel, 'IME', and Terk and Tõnisson, 'IME programm', 135.
22 Kümmel, 'IME avaldusele'; 'Majandusmõte 2: Intervjuu Edgar Savisaarega' (1988), *Edasi*, 19 April.
23 Zubok, *Collapse*, 56.
24 Interview with Ivar Raig, 1 November 2021.
25 Interview with Erik Terk, 13 October 2021.
26 Lauk, 'Restoring Democratic Discourse'; Vihalemm, *Baltic Media*, 173; Raudsep, Rein (1997), 'Kümme aastat fosforiidisõjast', *Eesti Loodus*, July, http://vana.loodusajakiri.ee/eesti_loodus/EL/vanaweb/9707/soda.html (accessed 22 September 2023).
27 Lauristin and Vihalemm, 'Estonian Mass Media'.
28 Vihalemm, *Baltic Media*, 211, 25.
29 Vihalemm, 'Media Use in Estonia', 17–18; Lauristin and Vihalemm, 'Estonian Mass Media'.
30 Noorte Teadlaste Nõukogu and Noorte Majandusteadlaste Klubi, *Kroonika*.

31 Palm, 'Suurupi Program', 283–98.
32 Saharov, 'From an Economic Term'.
33 Lauristin, and Vihalemm, 'Estonian Mass Media'; Taagepera, *Estonia*, 127, 131; Lauk, 'Restoring Democratic Discourse'; Ruutsoo, 'Emergence of Civil Society', 99.
34 Vihalemm, *Baltic Media*, 174, 212; Lauk, 'Restoring Democratic Discourse', 7; Interview with Alari Purju, 30 June 2022; Ruutsoo, 'Emergence', 99.
35 Ruutsoo, 'Emergence', 99; Vihalemm, *Baltic Media*, 25.
36 A popular Soviet joke had a man phoning a friend to ask, 'Have you read the article on the first page of *Pravda* today?' 'No, what does it say?' 'Sorry, I dare not tell you on the phone.' Quote from Åslund, *Russia's Capitalist Revolution*, 32.
37 Kotkin, *Uncivil Society*, 102.
38 Rein Otsason, Juhan Sillaste, Arvo Sirendi, Madis Habakuk and Arvo Kuddo (1988), 'Ettepanek: Maksta dotatsioon sularahas kätte', *Rahva Hääl*, 11 May; Lauk, 'Restoring Democratic Discourse'; Interview with Alari Purju, 30 June 2022.
39 Saharov, 'From an Economic Term', 135.
40 Taagepera, *Estonia*, 130.
41 Annus, 'Neoliberal Twist', 4; Aunma, *Isemajandav Eesti*, cited in Annus, 'Neoliberal Twist', 2; Annus, Neoliberalism or Postmodernism, 9.
42 Annus, *Neoliberalism or Postmodernism*, 10; Vihalemm, 'Peremehetunne'.
43 Taagepera, *Estonia*, 130; Interview with Sulev Mäeltsemees, 5 November 2021.
44 Interview with Ivar Raig, 20 October 2021.
45 Annus, 'Neoliberal Twist', 20.
46 Annus, 'Neoliberalism or Postmodernism', 4–5.
47 Proos, Ivi, Edgar Savisaar and Erik Terk (1988), 'Aeg Edasi Minna', *Edasi*, 25 February; Sepp, 'Estonia's Transition', 19.
48 Aare, *Otsasoni Kolm Elu*, 28.
49 Saharov, 'From an Economic Term', 131; Terk and Tõnisson, 'IME programm', 134.
50 Raig, 'Saaremaa eksperiment', 161.
51 Terk and Tõnisson, 'IME programm', 137.
52 IME-Probleemnõukogu (1988), 'Üks Eesti–Üks IME', *Noorte Hääl*, 1 November.
53 Vaino's grandson, Anton Vaino, is now Putin's chief of staff. Vaino should not be confused with his successor, Vaino Väljas. As Väljas' surname translates to 'out', after he came to power he was greeted by signs reading 'Hurraa, Vaino Väljas!' These could be seen as a sign of support, or translated as 'Hurrah, Vaino Väljas!' or 'Hurrah, Vaino is out!' Quote from Krikmann, 'Jokes in Soviet Estonia', 54.
54 Notably, Rüütel also served as Estonia's president from 2001 to 2006. As native Estonians were distrusted by Soviet authorities, Estonia's Soviet leadership was primarily composed of Estonian-Russians who spoke Estonian as a second language. Their heavy Russian accents and inability to pronounce the word 'Estonians' ('eestlased') led to them being mocked as 'Yestonians' ('jeestlased').

55 Taagepera, *Estonia*, 118; Feldmann, 'Fast Track', 553.
56 Taagepera, *Estonia*, 130; Gerner and Hedlund, *Baltic States*, 80.
57 Gerner and Hedlund, *Baltic States*, 100.
58 Annus, 'Neoliberal Twist', 4.
59 Kallas and Sõrg, 'Currency Reform', 53.
60 Gerner and Hedlund, *Baltic States*, 100.
61 Savisaar, *Peaminister*, 545; Kallas and Sõrg, 'Currency Reform', 54.
62 Gerner and Hedlund, *Baltic States*, 100.
63 Lassiter, Bisping and Horton, 'Central Banking', 333; Knöbl, Sutt and Zavoico, 'Estonian Currency Board', 5; Kallas and Sõrg, 'Currency Reform', 56.
64 Interview with Ardo Hansson, 30 June 2022.
65 Bockman, *Markets in the Name of Socialism*, 80.
66 Interview with Kalev Kukk, 21 October 2021; Interview with Sulev Mäeltsemees, 5 November 2021.
67 Interview with Alari Purju, 30 June 2022.
68 Interview with Erik Terk, 13 October 2021.
69 Saharov, 'From an Economic Term', 135.
70 Terk and Tõnisson, 'IME programm', 137–8.
71 Aare, *Otsasoni Kolm Elu*, 28.
72 Interview with Sulev Mäeltsemees, 5 November 2021.
73 For examples, see Aare, *Otsasoni Kolm Elu*, 32 and Saldre, Alfred (1990), 'Kui löök on terav, siis tuleb (oma) värav!' 7 December, ERA.5006.1.174.
74 Savisaar, *Peaminister*, 315.
75 Kultuurimälestiste register, '3069 elamu Raekoja plats 17 fassaad, 18.-20. saj.', https://register.muinas.ee/public.php?menuID=monument&action=view&id=3069 (accessed 14 September 2023); Savisaar, *Peaminister*, 54.
76 Savisaar, *Peaminister*, 54, 57.
77 Aare, *Otsasoni Kolm Elu*, 28–32; Savisaar, *Peaminister*, 315; Interview with Erik Terk, 13 October 2021.
78 Mark et al., '1989', 60.
79 Aare, *Otsasoni kolm elu*, 27–35; Savisaar, Peaminister, 545, 744–5.
80 Terk and Tõnisson, 'IME programm', 139; Saharov, 'From an Economic Term', 136.
81 Proos, 'IME hetkeseis: IME-õppe korraldamisest töökollektiivides', *Tootmis-Majandusõpe* 6, October 1989, ERAF (Estonian National Archives, Tartu) 1.48.125; Eesti NSV Ülemnõukogu, 'Eesti NSV seadus "Eesti NSV isemajandamise alused" ' (1989), *Riigi Teataja*, 18 May, https://www.riigiteataja.ee/akt/24003 (accessed 14 September 2023).
82 Lobovnii, 'О проектах документов по вопросам перехода Эстонской ССР на хозяйственный расчет', 1989, ERA.5006.1.153; Sukhanov, 'Замечания к

проекту Закона Эстонской ССР 'Основы хозрасчета Эстонской ССР', 1989. ERA.5006.1.153.

83 Terk and Tõnisson, 'IME programm', 143.

84 Proos, 'IME hetkeseis'.

85 Aare, *Otsasoni Kolm Elu*, 137, 139, 141.

86 Interview with Jüri Sepp, 11 December 2021.

87 Slobodian, *Crack-Up*, 10–11.

88 Tserepanov (1988), 'Majanduse Eritsoonid', *Rahva Hääl*, 31 August; Köörna, 'Erimajanduspiirkond?', *Õhtuleht*, 13 October; Erilaid (1988), 'Erimajanduspiirkonna kehtestamises Eesti NSVs', *Õhtuleht*, 13 October; Mäeltsemees, Sulev, Ivar Raig and Raivo Rajamäe (1987), 'Ettepanek: viia üks rajoon isemajandamisele', *Noorte Hääl*, 16 December; Interview with Sulev Mäeltsemees, 5 November 2021.

89 Conor O'Clery (1988), 'Promises to Baltic States worry Kremlin', *The Irish Times*, 29 October.

90 Interview with Erik Terk, 13 October 2021; Interview with Ivar Raig, 1 November 2021; Joe Carroll (1988), 'Estonians Study Irish Development', *The Irish Times*, 29 October; 'Irish-Soviet Cultural Exchange – 1988', 1988, ERA.5006.1.55, Tallinn; O'Clery, 'Promises to Baltic States'; Interview with Ivar Raig, 20 October 2021; Kask (1988), 'Erimajanduspiirkonnast ja suveräniteedist', *Noorte Hääl*, 29 October. For an example editorial, see Arno Köörna's column 'Hiina ime ja Eesti IME' ('Chinese miracle and Estonian IME/miracle') in the 9 October 1988 issue of *Edasi*.

91 Interview with Erik Terk, 13 October 2021; Interview with Viktor Trasberg, 14 December 2021; Interview with Jüri Sepp, 11 December 2021; Interview with Alari Purju, 6 December 2021.

92 Köörna, 'Erimajanduspiirkond?'; Kask, 'Erimajanduspiirkonnast ja suveräniteedist'; TAMI Ajutine Teaduskollektiv and IME Probleemnõukogu (1988), 'Erimajanduspiirkond. Meie seisukoht', *Rahva Hääl*, 21 October; Interview with Kalev Kukk, 21 October 2021.

93 Siegl (1988), 'Eine Volksfront mit dem Wunsch nach völliger Souveränität', *Frankfurter Rundschau*, 24 June.

94 Interview with Erik Terk, 13 October 2021; Savisaar, *Peaminister*, 505, 581–7; Estonian Investment Agency, 'Free Zones', Invest in Estonia, https://investinestonia.com/business-in-estonia/infrastructure-and-premises/free-trade-zones/ (accessed 14 September 2023).

Conclusion: 'Icebreakers' in the economic entanglements of Cold War Europe

Adrian Brisku, Martin Gumiela and Lars Fredrik Stöcker

The interlinked dynamics of the collapse of the 'Fordist model', the oil shocks and the end of the Bretton Woods system of fixed exchange rates, accompanied by the ideological crises of Marxism-Leninism and Keynesianism, initiated an accelerated chain of economic changes that unfolded from the 1960s through the 1980s, affecting small (nation-)states in East and West alike. This period of accelerated economic change has predominantly been conceptualized through the prism of US-led post-1945 globalization, compounded by the simultaneously unfolding decolonization process that in turn paved the way for an unprecedented economic integration between the 'First' and the 'Third World'. Breaking with the traditional model of colonial dependence, global trade and exchange now relied on the cooperation of equal sovereign states interlinking the 'Global North' with the 'Global South'. Offering an alternative to this Western-centred account, Mark, Kalinovsky and Marung bring up their narrative of the so-called 'alternative globalizations',[1] asserting that not only the West but also the East developed economic and financial entanglements with the Global South amid the economic crises and changes of the late-Cold War era. Entanglements between the socialist East and the Global South, as they state, were also motivated by political and ideological reasons, though such motivations cannot be excluded for the entanglements between the West and the South. More recently, a third account on the globalization dynamics – much aligned with the 'alternative globalizations' narrative – suggested by Besnik Pula points to an era of 'socialist globalization'[2] that began in the 1970s as a corollary of the suppression of systemic economic reform with the socialist bloc after 1968, which in turn led to the experimentation of various forms of opening up of the formerly closed planned economies to the West.

What is clear in hindsight and exhibited in the contributions of our volume is that globalization indeed transcended the Iron Curtain and affected states on both sides equally. The small (nation-)state approach deployed in our volume adds proto-states like the ethno-federal republic of Estonia in the USSR and Croatia and Slovenia in Yugoslavia to the traditional small states perspective, revealing similar patterns of reactions to economic crises, changes and globalizing dynamics as in sovereign small states. As the cases presented in this volume illustrate, Estonia, Croatia and Slovenia, similarly to sovereign Soviet-bloc states like Czechoslovakia and Poland, used openings such as border trade arrangements with non-socialist states as a strategy to protect their declared 'national' interests vis-à-vis the central authorities while simultaneously opening up in the ongoing global socialist entanglement. The multileveled dynamics of political and economic change shattered the strict Cold War geopolitical and geo-economic bipolarity and centrality. States in East and West gradually started to overcome their respective limitations of Moscow's autarkic Comecon policy and export restrictions, opening new avenues for economic interaction. Détente and socialist globalization fostered economic entanglements across the blocs and beyond, allowing particularly smaller (nation-)states unprecedented freedom in their pursuit of potential foreign economic partners. This particularly applied to Europe's small neutral states, as exemplarily illustrated by the case of Austria in our volume, which used its neutral status and subsequent credibility as an asset to increase its room for economic manoeuvre across the two blocs.

What our volume asked and sought to answer was whether small-state responses to the interlinked chain of economic changes and crises that shaped the late-Cold War period in East and West displayed similar coping mechanisms and strategies such as the use of new economic openings and opportunities to escape the hegemonial logic of the bipolar world. Did size in the Cold War economy of divided Europe matter, and, if yes, could it be used as a strategic asset? How were national economic needs and interests discursively framed, discussed and negotiated and how were they translated into viable foreign economic strategies? In what way did the all-encompassing de-ideologization of the Cold War impact trade and capital flows? Did national economic interest always trump ideological and political dogmas? And, most importantly, how were liberal or protectionist policies, or a mixture of both, strategically employed to foster and serve nationally defined interests?

As the contributions have shown, all of the small (nation-)states discussed developed their own strategies of opening up to foreign markets and capital flows in times of ongoing détente and globalization, thus confirming the common assumption that small states by definition are inherently dependent on open trade. Of course, the degree of market opening as well as the underlying motives varied. While some states, such as Estonia or Luxembourg, implemented maximum market liberalization as a strategy of national survival, Poland or Czechoslovakia, for instance, followed a more cautious approach to economic globalization, containing their market openings with the help of protectionist and defensive economic measures. As different as the degrees of opening were the strategies of finding access to global markets. The Estonian SSR and the federal republics of Slovenia and Croatia in state-socialist Yugoslavia chose, as has been mentioned above, a course of regional integration with their Western neighbours, which yielded new macro-regional dynamics such as the emergence of the common Nordic-Baltic market and the Alps-Adriatic-Working Community. People's Poland, on its part, used the large Polish diaspora in the West as an important link to gain access to foreign markets. Czechoslovakia or Greece under the rule of the military junta as well as the GDR expanded their bilateral relations with trade partners in the Global South and/or on the other side of the Iron Curtain in order to expand their economic rooms for manoeuvre. Although not all of those strategies were particularly successful, as the cases of Austria's *Ostpolitik* or Czechoslovakia's ventures in Africa show, they all shared similar degrees of pragmatism that finally helped them to pursue their own national economic interests beyond the political and ideological restraints of the Cold War bloc divide.

Accordingly, major ideological differences did not prevent states on opposite ends of the political spectrum like the GDR and the military junta in Greece from establishing bilateral economic relations. Likewise, Austria, under the government of the social democratic chancellor Bruno Kreisky, followed a pronouncedly pragmatic foreign economic policy course, pursuing potentially profitable economic relations with both Eastern bloc states and the colonels in Greece, thus bridging the ideological abyss in both directions. As 'rule-takers' facing a series of drastic economic changes that they were unable to contain or control, small states had to rely on realpolitik in order to survive economically in a swiftly globalizing world. However, it was precisely the pragmatic economic agency of small states that significantly accelerated the ongoing erosion of the Iron Curtain and turned small-state actors into particularly important bricks on the European geopolitical chessboard.

The economic pragmatism displayed by small states in East and West opened up new avenues across the bloc divide, which in turn contributed to increasing their political agency as well. The Greek junta regime, for example, pushed for closer bilateral economic relations with states on both sides of the Iron Curtain, hoping to gain political recognition in the East and West. Luxembourg became a global player in international financial markets with the help of its internationalized domestic banking sector, generating important political capital that made the micro-state an important actor of European economic and political integration. Pragmatic economic relations could further give rise to concrete political demands, such as Austria's proposal for a 'Marshall Plan for Poland'. In the federal socialist republics of Yugoslavia and the Soviet Union, cross-border economic relations boosted the periphery's political self-confidence vis-à-vis the political centre, as the examples of the Estonian SSR and Socialist Republics of Slovenia and Croatia show. By striving for the greatest possible economic integration with international Western markets, late-Soviet Estonia in particular hoped for providing the ground for maximum economic and political independence from the Soviet Union. Political and economic policies, as the contributions of this volume have consistently illustrated, can thus not be clearly separated.

In a similar vein, the discursive framing of national economic interest, whether debated internally or externally, for example, vis-à-vis a political hegemon, was inextricably linked to discourses about political legitimization. The historical case studies presented in this volume therefore help to overcome the inherent biases of IPE scholarship, which ignores or downplays collective national sentiments and national mobilization as factors having a significant impact on the formation and practical implementation of economic policies. As the contributions demonstrate, collective self-perceptions of being a small state and/or small nation could efficiently be used to legitimize tangible national economic measures, such as maximum liberalization in the case of Estonia or Luxembourg. Playing on the strings of patriotism, the state-socialist regime in People's Poland sought to mobilize the economic potential of the Polish diaspora in the West while, at the same time, legitimizing its course of marketization in the eyes of Polish society and the hegemonic Soviet neighbour alike.

Thus, varieties of economic nationalism, as reconceptualized by Brisku, often appeared simultaneously in concrete national contexts, being and defined and reinforced through nationally framed historical discourses which, in the end, represented and echoed practices and formative experiences of national economy-building. The following examples illustrate that particularly well: in its independence process, Estonia acted ultra-liberal towards Western markets while, at the same time, pursuing a pronouncedly protectionist course towards the former Soviet Union. In doing so, it relied on a nationalizing rhetoric, evoking its historically grown cultural and economic affiliation with the West. In a similar vein, also Luxembourg understood the European and global entrenchment of its domestic market as a cornerstone of its national history and state sovereignty. Thus, for Luxembourg, being a global actor on international finance markets secured the survival of both state and nation. Building upon nationalist discourses and patriotic kinship networks, socialist People's Poland legitimized limited market openings, implicitly declaring the absence of any ideological contradiction as long as (only) Western entrepreneurs with ethnic Polish roots would undertake direct investment into the domestic economy. Here, too, careful attempts of market liberalization went hand in hand with nationally framed legitimizing strategies. In order to protect its own steel industry, Austria cooperated economically with states of the Eastern Bloc and partly legitimized such economic measures with post-imperial discourses on the common economic space in the Habsburg Empire and with the proclaimed necessity of avoiding interwar 'defensive/protectionist' practices. Here, forms of cooperative, 'liberal/progressive' economic nationalism as well as facets of aggressive economic nationalism become visible. Similarly, Slovenia and Croatia justified economic cooperation with Austria's and Italy's border regions by evoking memories of common historical economic spaces that had been forcefully disintegrated by the 'unnatural' redrawing of state borders in the twentieth century. Croatia's as well as Slovenia's cooperative economic nationalisms were at the same time intended to strengthen their respective national autonomy within federal Yugoslavia and to demonstrate their 'historically justified' place in uniting Western Europe. Therefore, this volume does not present isolated examples of varieties of economic nationalism. The bouquet of historical case studies discussed in our volume, by contrast, reflects how various nationalist economic measures reappeared in different constellations in small nation states throughout divided Europe.

Clearly thus, one of the main concerns informing our perspective in this volume was to place the 'national' into the 'global' in times of increased economic liberalization. More poignantly, it inquired into the role of nationally framed discourses regarding the economic sphere and national interest of small states during the opening up of their national economies to global market forces. Our approach, which reconceptualizes economic nationalism in terms of 'varieties' and thus moves beyond the framing of this political-economic phenomenon in terms of the 'false' and exclusive dichotomy of economic nationalism versus economic liberalism present in much of the IPE literature, finds that the 'national', discursively and in practice (policy), does not dissipate even when economies are opening up or become part of larger economic spaces. In fact, as the case of Luxembourg illustrates, 'hyper-liberal' and globalization policies – compounded simultaneously with some 'defensive' policies – allowed for securing national prosperity and stability within the larger European economic space. Similarly, access to the EU and integration with European markets was considered, as the case of Austria in the late 1980s but also of many small states after the end of the Cold War has shown, as a sine qua non for their economic survival. Additionally, as the proto-states in both the Soviet Union and Yugoslavia demonstrated, the liberalization of the centralized decision-making hierarchies triggered nationalist mobilization and agendas, which in turn were driven by national economic strategies and particularistic economic interests. The case of Estonia, in particular, highlights how policies of economic openness with its 'hyper-liberalization' of trade and investment policies could be and were dressed in a nationalist cloak. Like Luxembourg and Estonia, even Greece under the rule of the authoritarian colonel junta pursued liberal economic policies of opening up their domestic market to FDI and sought access to global markets as a 'defensive' survival strategy, which closely connects to their self-awareness of being small (nation-)states.

By insisting on contextualizing the national economic trajectories in all of the cases here, our volume demonstrates how small (nation-)states discursively linked their policy options and legitimized certain modes of actions by referring to historical continuities, discursively framing, for instance, Austria and Poland as a former 'common economic space' or Estonia's economic orientation towards its Nordic neighbours as a historical return to economic 'normality'. And evidently, although the choice between following globalizing trends and keeping a more protectionist path was more difficult for smaller states, they, on both sides of the Iron Curtain, did pursue a variety of choices, which in turn were driven by a perceived threat to sovereignty and the subsequent need to sustain or expand their economic and political flexibility.

Certainly, smallness could be an asset, strategically deployed by smaller states for greater room for manoeuvre in a bipolar world. Navigating between globalized Western markets and the gradually globalizing socialist orbit allowed for a flexibility that helped to overcome structural sea changes. Luxembourg, for instance, efficiently played on its defining smallness in order to handle the challenge of transitioning into a post-industrial era. The Estonian SSR likewise employed the flexibility of being small as an asset, when small elite circles effectively mitigated the risk of oppositional mobilization and the creation of competing camps, which hampered similar economic ambitions by more promising economic powers like the Ukrainian SSR. And yet while an asset also for Austria, the country was not sheltered from economic failure when it stubbornly insisted on providing loans – driven by the goal of shielding the domestic heavy industry sector global market pressure – to severely indebted socialist states. This failure was an outcome of Austria's overestimation of the socialist bloc's internal stability and Moscow's readiness to protect its subordinate socialist sister states by bailing them out. At the same time, smallness being a discursive and thus relative concept can change depending on the circumstance and constellation. For instance, in bilateral and trilateral entanglements between small states, power imbalances may emerge between them with some of them self-styling as regional powers. This could be observed in Sweden's self-perception as a hegemonic economic actor in the nascent regional market in the northern Baltic Sea region in the late 1980s and 1990s. Similarly, a post-imperial attitude could be observed in Austria's entanglement with Poland. Additionally, both Sweden and Czechoslovakia could become 'teachers' vis-à-vis postcolonial states in the Global South, which in some respect elevated them to a higher level than that of an ordinary small state.

Finally, and significantly, the volume showed that most of the small (nation-) states discussed functioned as 'icebreakers' in the bipolar world of the 1960s to 1980s, stretching the limits of bipolarity by testing new forms of East-West relations in trade and finance or becoming autonomous players in the Global South which, as the case of Czechoslovakia illustrates, offered an alternative path to securing hard currency and know-how. Divided Europe's small states forged new patterns of small-state cooperation and alliances – with three or more states pursuing similar trade policies – beyond ideological abysses, as is shown by the examples of Greece, Austria, Poland and the GDR, or the Estonian SSR focusing on expanding its old border trade relations with Finland and Sweden. And they could and did foster long-lasting processes of regionalization, whereby the border trade of the most affluent and economically efficient republics in the Yugoslavian Federation and the Soviet Union expanded into nascent regional markets integrating, respectively, Slovenia with Austria and Italy and the Nordic neutrals Sweden and Finland with the Baltic states.

As prominent historian Bo Stråth elucidated in his recent book *The Brandt Commission and the Multinationals*, two 'planetary perspectives' emerged in the last three decades of the twentieth century to largely overcome the various manifestations of economic nationalism in the Global North and South. The first 'planetary' vision was developed by the Brandt Commission in the 1970s, promoting a kind of 'global Keynesianism' which sought to enhance economic cooperation and development between the North and South. This vision faded into history as, in the mid-1990s, another 'planetary' perspective emerged. Developed by proponents of global corporations, this concept, which came to be known as the neoliberal grand narrative, envisioned 'a planetary enterprise in a single world'. Under the impact of the multiple global crises since 2008, even this vision was eventually (and lastingly) shattered.[3] What we seem to be left with are visions of economic interaction and entanglement from a (nation-)state perspective, which can assume various and, at times, seemingly contradictory forms, as our volume has shown, independently of the relative and perceived size of national economies.

Notes

1 Mark, Kalinovsky and Marung, *Alternative Globalizations.*
2 Pula, *Globalization under and after Socialism.*
3 Stråth, *The Brandt Commission and the Multinationals*, 347.

Bibliography

Aare, Juhan. *Rein Otsasoni kolm elu: Three Lives of Rein Otsason*. Rakvere: VR Kirjastus, 2006.

Abdelal, Rawi. 'Nationalism and International Political Economy in Eurasia'. In *Economic Nationalism in a Globalizing World*, edited by Eric Helleiner and Andreas Pickel, 21–43. Ithaca, NY: Cornell University Press, 2005.

Abdelal, Rawi. *National Purpose in the World Economy: Post-Soviet States in Comparative Perspective*. Ithaca, NY: Cornell University Press, 2001.

Abram, Marco. 'Integrating Rijeka into Socialist Yugoslavia: The Politics of National Identity and the New City's Image (1947–1955)'. *Nationalities Paper* 46, no. 1 (2018): 69–85.

Adamović, Ljubiša S. 'The Foreign Trade System of Yugoslavia'. *Eastern European Economics* 20, nos. 3–4 (1982): 144–65.

Ahde, Pasi, and Teet Rajasalu. 'On the Economics Structure of Estonia and Finland before the 1990s'. Discussion Paper, no. 422. Helsinki: The Research Institute of the Finnish Economy, 1992.

Ahrens, Ralf, and Astrid M. Eckert. 'Industrial Policy in Western Europe since the 1960s: Historical Varieties and Perspectives'. *Jahrbuch für Wirtschaftsgeschichte / Economic History Yearbook* 58, no. 1 (2017): 23–33.

Albrecht, Catherine. 'Economic Nationalism among German Bohemians'. *Nationalities Papers* 24, no. 1 (1996): 17–30.

Alesina, Alberto, and Enrico Spolaore. *The Size of Nations*. Cambridge, MA: MIT Press, 2003.

Allen, Mathew. 'The Varieties of Capitalism Paradigm: Not Enough Variety'. *Socio-Economic Review* 2, no. 1 (2004): 87–108.

Alloul, Houssine, and Michael Auwers. 'What Is (New in) New Diplomatic History'. *Journal of Belgian History* 48, no. 4 (2018): 112–22.

Alogoskoufis, George, Historical Cycles of the Economy of Modern Greece from 1821 to the Present (10 February 2021). Department of Economics Athens University of Economics and Business, Working Paper no. 01-2021, Available at SSRN. https://ssrn.com/abstract=3801664 or http://dx.doi.org/10.2139/ssrn.3801664, accessed 15 April 2024.

Amnesty International. *Report on Torture*. London: Duckworth, 1973.

Amnesty International. *Torture in Greece: The First Torturers' Trial 1975*. London: Amnesty International Publications, 1977.

Annus, Epp. 'Neoliberalism or Postmodernism? Decolonizing Soviet Estonia, 1987–1991'. Unpublished manuscript, 2023.

Annus, Epp. 'Revolutionaries with a Neoliberal Twist: The Idea of Economic Self-Management in the late 1980s Estonian SSR'. Unpublished manuscript, 2023.

Artisien, Patrick F. R., and Peter J. Buckley. 'Joint Ventures in Yugoslavia: Opportunities and Constraints'. *Journal of International Business Studies* 2 (1985): 111–35.

Åslund, Anders. *How Capitalism Was Built: The Transformation of Central and Eastern Europe, Russia, the Caucasus, and Central Asia*. 2nd edn. Cambridge: Cambridge University Press, 2013.

Åslund, Anders. *Russia's Capitalist Revolution: Why Market Reform Succeeded and Democracy Failed*. Washington, DC: Peterson Institute, 2007.

Aunma, Enel (ed.). *Isemajandav Eesti: kirjanduse nimestik 1987/1988*. Tallinn: Eesti NSV Vabariiklik Teaduslik Tehnikaraamatukogu, 1989.

Axelrod, Robert. *The Evolution of Cooperation*. New York: Basic Books, 1984.

Baldersheim, Harald, and Michael Keating (eds). *Small States in the Modern World: Vulnerabilities and Opportunities*. Cheltenham: Edward Elgar, 2015.

Bartel, Fritz. *The Triumph of Broken Promises. The End of the Cold War and the Rise of Neoliberalism*. Cambridge, MA: Harvard University Press, 2022.

Baughn, C. Christopher, and Attila Yaprak. 'Economic Nationalism: Conceptual and Empirical Development'. *Political Psychology* 17, no. 4 (1996): 759–78.

Baysha, Olga. *The Mythologies of Capitalism and the End of the Soviet Project*. Lanham, MD: Lexington Books, 2014.

Beissinger, Mark R. *Nationalist Mobilization and the Collapse of the Soviet State*. Cambridge: Cambridge University Press, 2002.

Berdal, Mats, and Domenik Zaum. *The Political Economy of Statebuilding: Power after Peace*. New York: Routledge, 2013.

Berend, Ivan T. 'Economic Nationalism in Historical Perspective'. In *Handbook of Economic Nationalism*, edited by Andreas Pickel, 2–13. Cheltenham: Edward Elgar, 2022.

Berger, Stefan, and Thomas Fetzer. 'Introduction'. In *Nationalism and the Economy: Explorations into a Neglected Relationship*, edited by Stefan Berger and Thomas Fetzer, 1–20. Budapest: Central European University Press, 2019.

Berghoff, Hartmut, and Uta Andrea Balbier (eds). *The East German Economy, 1945–2010. Falling Behind or Catching Up?* New York: Cambridge University Press, 2013.

Bergman, Annika. 'Adjacent Internationalism: The Concept of Solidarity and Post-Cold War Nordic-Baltic Relations'. *Cooperation and Conflict* 41, no. 1 (2006): 73–97.

Besch, Nadine. 'ArcelorMittal'. In *Lieu de mémoire au Luxembourg II. Jeux d'échelles*, edited by Sonja Kmec and Pit Péporté, 151–6. Luxembourg: Éditions Saint-Paul, 2012.

Biberaj, Elez. *Albania: A Socialist Maverick*. Boulder, CO: Westview Press, 1990.

Billig, Michael. *Banal Nationalism*. Los Angeles: Sage, 1995.

Bischof, Günther, and Peter Ruggenthaler. *Österreich und der Kalte Krieg. Ein Balanceakt zwischen Ost und West*. Graz: Leykam, 2022.

Bishop, Mathew Louis. 'The Political Economy of Small States: Enduring Vulnerability'. *Review of International Political Economy* 19, no. 5 (2012): 942–60.

Bockman, Johanna. *Markets in the Name of Socialism: The Left-Wing Origins of Neoliberalism*. Redwood City: Stanford University Press, 2011.

Bohle, Dorothee, and Béla Greskovits. *Capitalist Diversity on Europe's Periphery*. Ithaca, NY: Cornell University Press, 2012.

Bohle, Dorothee, Vera Šćepanović and Line Rennwald. 'The Return of Economic Nationalism?'. https://www.eui.eu/Documents/MWP/ProgramActivities/2016-2017/MRW/The-Return-of-Economic-Nationalism.pdf (accessed 30 October 2023).

Born, Benjamin, Gernot J. Müller, Moritz Schularick and Petr Sedláček. 'The Cost of Economic Nationalism: Evidence from the Brexit Experiment'. *The Economic Journal*, no. 129 (2019): 2722–44.

Bren, Paulina. 'Mirror, Mirror, on the Wall … Is the West the Fairest of Them All?' In *Imagining the West in Eastern Europe and the Soviet Union*, edited by György Péteri, 172–93. Pittsburgh: Pittsburgh University Press, 2010.

Bretton, Albert. 'The Economics of Nationalism'. *Journal of Political Economy* 4, no. 72 (1964): 376–86.

Brisku, Adrian. 'Dealing with Smallness in Habsburg Bohemia, Ottoman Albania and Tsarist Georgia in the Late-19th and Early-20th Century'. In *The Politics of Smallness in Modern Europe: Size, Identity and International Relations since 1800*, edited by Samuël Kruizinga, 35–54. London: Bloomsbury, 2022.

Brisku, Adrian. *'National Economy-Building' in Albania, Czechoslovakia and Georgia in the 1920s*. London: Routledge, forthcoming.

Brisku, Adrian. 'Renegotiating the Empire, Forging the Nation-State: The Albanian Case through the Political-Economic Thought of Ismail Qemali, Fan Noli and Luigj Gurakuqi'. *Nationalities Papers* 48, no. 1 (2020): 158–74.

Brisku, Adrian. 'Renegotiating the Empire, Forging the Nation-State: The Bohemian/Czechoslovakian Case through the Political-Economic Thought of Thomas G. Masaryk and Karel Kramář'. *Nationalities Papers* 45, no. 4 (2017): 632–50.

Brisku, Adrian. 'Renegotiating the Empire, Forging the Nation-State: The Case of Georgia through the Political Economic Thought of Niko Nikoladze and Noe Zhordania, c. 1870–1920s'. *Nationalities Papers* 44, no. 2 (2016): 299–318.

Bronz, Lawrence, Jeffry Frieden and Stephen Weymouth. 'Populism in Place: The Economic Geography of the Globalization Backlash'. *International Organisation* 75, no. 2 (2021): 1–31.

Brown, Archie. *The Gorbachev Factor*. Oxford: Oxford University Press, 1997.

Brunnbauer, Ulf, and Hannes Grandits (eds). *The Ambiguous Nation: Case Studies from Southeastern Europe in the 20th Century*. Munich: Oldenbourg Verlag, 2013.

Budding, Audrey Helfant. 'Nation/People/Republic: Self-determination in Socialist Yugoslavia'. In *State Collapse in South-Eastern Europe: New Perspectives on Yugoslavia's Disintegration*, edited by Lenard J. Cohen and Jasna Dragović-Soso. 91–130. West Lafayette, IN: Purdue University Press, 2011.

Budziński, Michał. 'Kontakty gospodarcze PRL z Zachodem w dekadzie gierkowskiej. Wybrane zagadnienia z lat 1970–1980'. *The Review of European Affairs* 2, no. 1/3 (2018): 93–106.

Budzowski, Klemens. 'Ewolucja polskiej polityki kursu walutowego'. In *Wybrane aspekty handlu międzynarodowego*, edited by Klemens Budzowski, 83–98. Kraków: Krakowskie Towarzystwo Edukacyjne, 2008.

Bunce, Valerie. 'Peaceful Versus Violent State Dismemberment: A Comparison of the Soviet Union, Yugoslavia, and Czechoslovakia'. *Politics and Society* 27, no. 2 (1999): 217–37.

Burke, Kathleen. 'Witness Seminar on the Origins and Early Development of the Eurobond Market'. *Contemporary European History* 1, no. 1 (1992): 65–87.

Burton, Eric. 'From Convergence to Divergence: Mozambique's Failed Campaign to Join the CMEA and the Reconfiguration of East-South Relations'. *Cold War History*, May 23, 2023, 1–23.

Butschek, Felix. *Vom Staatsvertrag zur EU. Österreichische Wirtschaftsgeschichte von 1955 bis zur Gegenwart*. Vienna: Böhlau, 2004.

Buzássyová, Barbora. 'Socialist Internationalism in Practice: Shifting Patterns of the Czechoslovak Educational Aid Programmes to Sub-Saharan Africa, 1961–1989'. PhD thesis, Slovenská akadémia vied, Historický ústav, 2021.

Calabrese, Matteo. *The Fund Code. A History of Investments Funds in Luxembourg from the Holding Act to the UCITS legislation (1929–1989)*. PhD, University of Luxembourg. Esch-sur-Alzette, 2023.

Calabrese, Matteo, and Benoît Majerus. 'Archaeology of a Treasure Island: Actors and Practices of Holding Companies in Luxembourg (1929–1940)'. *Contemporary European History* (2023): 1–18. doi: 10.1017/S0960777323000437.

Calic, Marie-Janine. 'The Beginning of the End – the 1970s as a Historical Turning Point in Yugoslavia'. In *The Crisis of Socialist Modernity: The Soviet Union and Yugoslavia in the 1970s*, edited by Marie-Janine Calic, Dietmar Nautatz and Julia Obertreis, 66–86. Göttingen: Vandenhoeck & Ruprecht, 2011.

Carney, Richard W. 'Varieties of Hierarchical Capitalism: Family and State Market Economies in East Asia'. *The Pacific Review* 29, no. 2 (2016): 137–63.

Cenckiewicz, Sławomir. 'Geneza Towarzystwa Łączności z Polonią Zagraniczną "Polonia"'. *Pamięć i Sprawiedliwość* 1 (2002): 161–8.

Clift, Ben, and Cornelia Woll. 'Economic Patriotism: Reinventing Control over Open Markets'. In *Economic Patriotism in Open Economies*, edited by Ben Clift and Cornelia Woll, 1–17. London: Routledge, 2013.

Clogg, Richard. 'The Ideology of the 'Revolution of 21 April 1967'. In *Greece under Military Rule*, edited by Richard Clogg and George Yannopoulos, 36–58, London: Secker & Warburg, 1972.

Close, David. *Greece since 1945: Politics, Economy and Society*. New York: Routledge, 2002.

Colantone, Italo, and Piero Stanig. 'The Surge of Economic Nationalism in Western Europe'. *Journal of Economic Perspectives* 33, no. 4 (2019): 128–51.

Colton, Timothy J. *Moscow: Governing the Socialist Metropolis*. Cambridge, MA: Harvard University Press, 1995.

Connor, Walker. 'Eco- or Ethno-Nationalism?' *Ethnic and Racial Studies* 7, no. 3 (1984): 342–59.

Cosovschi, Augustin. 'Between the Nation and Socialism in Yugoslavia. The Debate between Dobrica Ćosić and Dušan Pirjevec in the 1960s'. *Slovanský přehled* 101, no. 2 (2015): 41–63.

Coufoudakis, Van. 'The European Economic Community and the Freezing of the Greek Association, 1967–1974'. *Journal of Common Market Studies* 16, no. 2 (1977): 114–31.

Crane, George T. 'Bringing the Nation Back In'. *Millennium: Journal of International Studies* 27, no. 1 (1998): 55–75.

Crump, Laurien, and Susanna Erlandsson (eds). *Margins for Manoeuvre in Cold War Europe: The Influence of Smaller Powers*. London: Routledge, 2020.

Dallago, Bruno, and Milica Uvalić. 'The Distributive Consequences of Nationalism: The Case of Former Yugoslavia'. *Europe-Asia Studies* 50, no. 1 (1998): 71–90.

D'Costa, Anthony P. 'Geography of Steel Industry'. In *Encyclopedia of Geography* edited by Barney Warf. Thousand Oaks: Sage, 2010.

Decker, Philipp, 'Varieties of Nationalism in the Political Discourses of Habsburg Austria'. *Nations and Nationalism* 29, no. 3 (2023): 888–905.

Dimitris, Papadiamantis A. *Στρατός και Πολιτική Εξουσία. Η Δομή της Εξουσίας στην Μετεμφυλιακή Ελλάδα* (Army and Political Power: The Structure of Power in Post-Civil War Greece). Athens: Exantas Publications, 1985.

Drach, Alexis. 'Removing Obstacles to Integration: The European Way to Deregulation'. In *Financial Deregulation. A Historical Perspective*, edited by Alexis Drach and Youssef Cassis, 76–100. Oxford: Oxford University Press, 2021.

Dragović-Soso, Jasna. 'Yugoslavia's Political Endgame: Serbia and Slovenia in the 1980s'. In *The Routledge Handbook of Balkan and Southeast European History*, edited by John R. Lampe and Ulf Brunnbauer, 481–98. London: Routledge, 2021.

Dyker, David A. *Yugoslavia: Socialism, Development and Debt*. London: Palgrave, 1990.

Edwards, K. C. 'Historical Geography of the Luxembourg Iron & Steel Industry: Presidential Address'. *Transactions and Papers (Institute of British Geographers)* 29 (1961): 1–16.

Eichmann, Erwin. 'Joint Ventures in Hungary: A Model for Socialist States. Law and Policy'. *International Business* 20, no. 2 (1988): 257–94.

Eisler, Jerzy. *'Polskie miesiące' czyli kryzys(y) w PRL*. Warszawa: Instytut Pamięci Narodowej, 2008.

Emizet, Kisangani M., and Vicki L. Hesli. 'The Disposition to Secede: An Analysis of the Soviet Case'. *Comparative Political Studies* 27, no. 4 (1995): 493–536.

Enderle-Burcel, Gertrude, Piotr Franaszek, Dieter Stiefel and Alice Teichova (eds). *Gaps in the Iron Curtain. Economic Relations between Neutral and Socialist Countries in Cold War Europe*. Kraków: Jagiellonian University Press, 2009.

Enderle-Burcel, Gertrude, Dieter Stiefel and Alice Teichova (eds). *'Zarte Bande'. Österreich und die europäischen planwirtschaftlichen Länder – 'Delicate Relationships'. Austria and Europe's Planned Economies*. Innsbruck: Studienverlag, 2006.

Ericson, Richard E. 'Soviet Economic Structure and the National Question'. In *The Post-Soviet Nations: Perspectives on the Demise of the USSR*, edited by Alexander J. Motyl, 240–72. New York: Columbia University Press, 1992.

Estrin, Saul. 'Yugoslavia: The Case of Self-Managing Market Socialism'. *Journal of Economic Perspectives* 5, no. 4 (1991): 187–94.

Feldmann, Magnus. 'The Fast Track from the Soviet Union to the World Economy: External Liberalization in Estonia and Latvia'. *Government and Opposition* 36, no. 4 (2001): 537–58.

Ferguson, Niall. *High Financier. The Lives and Time of Siegmund Warburg*. London: Penguin, 2001.

Ferguson, Niall, Charles S. Maier, Erez Manela and Daniel J. Sargent. *The Shock of the Global: The 1970s in Perspective*. Cambridge, MA: Belknap Press of Harvard University Press, 2010.

Fernández Soriano, V. 'Facing the Greek Junta: The European Community, the Council of Europe and the Rise of Human Rights Politics in Europe'. *European Review of History / Revue européenne d'histoire* 24, no. 3 (2017): 358–76.

Fetzer, Thomas. 'Beyond "Economic Nationalism": Towards a New Research Agenda for the Study of Nationalism in Political Economy'. *Journal of International Relations and Development* 25, no. 1 (2021): 235–59.

Fetzer, Thomas. 'Economic Europeanness'. In *Nationalism and the Economy: Explorations into a Neglected Relationship*, edited by Stefan Berger and Thomas Fetzer, 269–90. Budapest: CEU Press, 2019.

Fetzer, Thomas. 'Nationalism and Economy. State of Field'. *Nationalities Papers* 48, no. 6 (2020): 963–73.

Fetzer, Thomas. 'Nationalism in Political Economy Scholarship'. In *Nationalism and the Economy. Explorations into a Neglected Relationship*, edited by Stefan Berger and Thomas Fetzer, 43–63. Budapest: CEU Press, 2019.

Feygin, Yakov. 'Reforming the Cold War State: Economic Thought, Internationalization, and the Politics of Soviet Reform, 1955–1985'. PhD diss. University of Pennsylvania, 2017.

Foer, Franklin. 'The New Washington Consensus'. *The Atlantic*, 9 May 2023. Available online: https://www.theatlantic.com/ideas/archive/2023/05/biden-economics-industrial-policy-trump-nationalism/673988/ (accessed 11 May 2023).

Fourastié, Jean. *Les Trente Glorieuses, ou la révolution invisible de 1946 à 1975.* Paris: Fayard, 1979.

Franaszek, Piotr. 'Die Handelsbeziehungen zwischen der Volksrepublik Polen und Österreich in der Zeit von 1945–1989'. In *'Zarte Bande.' Österreich und die europäischen planwirtschaftlichen Länder – 'Delicate Relationships.' Austria and Europe's Planned Economies.* Mitteilungen des Österreichischen Staatsarchivs, Sonderband 9, edited by Gertrude Enderle-Burcel, Dieter Stiefel and Alice Teichova, 185–96. Innsbruck: StudienVerlag, 2006.

Franz, Norbert. 'Der Finanzplatz Luxemburg als Ergebnis wirtschaftlichen Bedarfs, politischen Willens und europäischer Integration'. In *Europas Finanzzentren. Geschichte und Bedeutung im 20. Jahrhundert*, edited by Christoph Maria Merki, 149–65. Frankfurt/Main: Campus, 2004.

Frum, David. 'This Is No Time for Protectionism'. *The Atlantic*, 2 March 2022. Available online: https://www.theatlantic.com/ideas/archive/2022/03/biden-economic-nationalism-state-of-the-union/623325/ (accessed 1 July 2023).

Gehler, Michael. *Österreichs Weg in die Europäische Union.* Innsbruck: Studienverlag, 2009.

Gentili, Massimo P. *Jannoni, Sante and Mastrangelo, Mariana. The SICAVs – Luxembourg UCITS and Non-UCITS Investment Companies.* Rome: Bancaria Editrice, 2011.

Georgalas, Georgios H. *Ιδεολογία της Επαναστάσεως: όχι δόγματα, αλλά ιδεώδη* (The Ideology of the Revolution: not Dogmas, but Ideals). Athens: Private Publication, 1968.

Gerner, Kristian, and Stefan Hedlund. *The Baltic States and the End of the Soviet Empire.* London: Routledge, [1993] 2018.

Gilde, Benjamin. *Österreich im KSZE-Prozess 1969–1983. Neutraler Vermittler in humanitärer Mission.* Munich: Oldenbourg, 2013.

Gilpin, Robert. *The Political Economy of International Relations.* Princeton, NJ: Princeton University Press, 1987.

Go, Julian, and Jake Watson. 'Anticolonial Nationalism: From Imagined Communities to Colonial Conflict'. *European Journal of Sociology* 60, no. 1 (2019): 31–68.

Graf, Maximilian. 'Before Strauß: The East German Struggle to Avoid Bankruptcy During the Debt Crisis Revisited'. *The International History Review* 42, no. 4 (2020): 737–54.

Graf, Maximilian. 'Beyond Victims of Communism? Austria and the Human Rights Question in the 1970s'. In *The Human Rights Breakthrough of the 1970s the European Community and International Relations*, edited by Sara Lorenzini, Umberto Tulli and Ilaria Zamburlini, 178–95. London: Bloomsbury, 2021.

Graf, Maximilian. 'Indefinite Coexistence? Austria, the Soviet Union, and Ostpolitik after 1968'. In *The Soviet Union and Cold War Neutrality and Nonalignment in Europe*, edited by Mark Kramer, Aryo Makko and Peter Ruggenthaler, 233–59. Lanham, MD: Lexington Books, 2021.

Graf, Maximilian. 'Kreisky und Polen. Schlaglichter auf einen vernachlässigten Aspekt der österreichischen "Ostpolitik"'. In *Bananen, Cola, Zeitgeschichte: Oliver Rathkolb und das lange 20. Jahrhundert*, 2nd edn, edited by Lucile Dreidemy, Richard Hufschmied, Agnes Meisinger, Berthold Molden, Eugen Pfister, Katharina Prager, Elisabeth Röhrlich, Florian Wenninger and Maria Wirth, 692–706. Vienna: Böhlau, 2015.

Graf, Maximilian. *Österreich und die DDR 1949–1990. Politik und Wirtschaft im Schatten der deutschen Teilung*. Vienna: ÖAW, 2016.

Graf, Maximilian. 'Österreich und die "polnische Krise" im Kontext 1980–1983'. In *Österreich – Polen. Stationen gemeinsamer Geschichte im 20. Jahrhundert*, edited by Peter Ruggenthaler and Wanda Jarząbek, 201–21. Graz: Leykam, 2021.

Graf, Maximilian. 'The Accession of the Neutrals: (Re)assessing the First Post-Cold War Enlargement of the EU'. In *European Integration and the Global Financial Crisis. Looking Back on the Maastricht Years, 1980s–1990s*, edited by Michele Di Donato and Silvio Pons, 91–111. Cham: Palgrave Macmillan, 2023.

Graf, Maximilian, and Agnes Meisinger (eds). *Österreich im Kalten Krieg. Neue Forschungen im internationalen Kontext*. Göttingen: Vandenhoeck & Ruprecht, 2016.

Graf, Maximilian, and Peter Ruggenthaler, 'Entspannung trotz Krisen? Zu den Beziehungen zwischen Österreich und Polen vom Staatsvertrag bis zum Ende des Kalten Kriegs 1955–1990'. In *Österreich – Polen. Stationen gemeinsamer Geschichte im 20. Jahrhundert*, edited by Peter Ruggenthaler and Wanda Jarząbek, 173–200. Graz: Leykam, 2021.

Grala, Dariusz T. 'Przedsiębiorstwa z kapitałem zagranicznym pochodzenia polonijnego jako enklawa kapitalizmu w PRL i "inkubator przedsiębiorczości" liderów biznesu w III RP'. *UR Journal of Humanities and Social Sciences* 12, no. 3 (2019): 75–100.

Grala, Dariusz T. *Reformy gospodarcze w PRL (1982–1989). Próba ratowania socjalizmu*. Warszawa: Wydawnictwo TRIO, 2005.

Gray, William G. *Germany's Cold War: The Global Campaign to Isolate East Germany, 1949–1969*. Chapel Hill: University of North Carolina Press, 2003.

Griffiths, Ryan D. *Age of Secession: The International and Domestic Determinants of State Birth*. Cambridge: Cambridge University Press, 2016.

Grigoriadis, Solon N. Ιστορία της Σύγχρονης Ελλάδας 1941–1974: Δικτατορία 1967–1974 (History of Modern Greece 1941–1974: Dictatorship 1967–1974), vol. III. Athens: Polaris Publications, 2011.

Hall, Derek. 'Japanese Spirit, Western Economics: The Continuing Salience of Economic Nationalism in Japan'. *New Political Economy* 9, no. 1 (2004): 79–99.

Hall, Peter A., and David Soskice. 'An Introduction to Varieties of Capitalism'. In *Varieties of Capitalism: The Institutional Foundations of Comparative Advantage*,

edited by Peter A. Hall and David Soskice, 1–70. Oxford: Oxford University Press, 2001.
Hall, Peter A., and David Soskice (eds). *Varieties of Capitalism: Institutional Foundations of Comparative Advantage*. Oxford: Oxford University Press, 2001.
Harisch, Immanuel R. '10 East German Friendship Brigades and Specialists in Angola: A Socialist Globalization Project in the Global Cold War'. In *Transregional Connections in the History of East-Central Europe*, edited by Katja Castryck-Naumann, 291–324. Oldenbourg: De Gruyter, 2021.
Hatzky, Christine. 'Os Bons Colonizadores: Cuba's Educational Mission in Angola, 1976–1991'. *Safundi* 9, no. 1 (January 2008): 53–68.
Haug, Hilde Katrine. *Creating a Socialist Yugoslavia. Tito, Communist Leadership and the National Question*. New York: I.B. Tauris, 2012.
Heilperin, Michael A. *Studies in Economic Nationalism*. Geneva: Publications de l'Institute Universitaire de Hautes Études Internationales, no. 35, 1960.
Helleiner, Eric. 'Conclusion: The Meaning and Contemporary Significance of Economic Nationalism'. In *Economic Nationalism in a Globalizing World*, edited by Eric Helleiner and Andreas Pickel, 220–34. Ithaca, NY: Cornell University Press, 2005.
Helleiner, Eric. 'Economic Nationalism as a Challenge to Economic Liberalism? Lessons from the 19th Century'. *International Studies Quarterly* 46, no. 3 (2002): 307–29.
Helleiner, Eric. 'The Diversity of Economic Nationalism'. *New Political Economy*, 26, no. 2 (2021): 229–38. https://doi.org/10.1080/13563467.2020.1841137.
Helleiner, Eric. *The Neomercantilists: A Global Intellectual History*. Ithaca, NY: Cornell University Press, 2021.
Helleiner, Eric, and Andreas Pickel (eds). *Economic Nationalism in a Globalizing World*. Ithaca, NY: Cornell University Press, 2005.
Hemstad, Ruth. 'Promoting Norden and Nordic Cooperation in the 1930s: Social Democratic Visions and Transmedial Manifestations'. In *Nordic Media Histories of Propaganda and Persuasion*, edited by Fredrik Norén, Emily Stjernholm and C. Claire Thompson, 31–54. London: Palgrave Macmillan, 2023.
Herrera, Yoshiko M. *Imagined Economies: The Sources of Russian Regionalism*. Cambridge: Cambridge University Press, 2005.
Heuser, Beatrice. *Western 'Containment' Policies in the Cold War: The Yugoslav Case, 1948–1953*. London: Routledge, 1989.
Hieronimy, Otto (ed.). *The New Economic Nationalism*. London: Macmillan Press, 1980.
Hirsch, Mario. 'The Luxembourg Model Has Reached Its Limits. Social Partnership and Tripartite Arrangements Work Only under Fair Weather Conditions'. Paper presented at the Politicologenetmaal, Leuven, 2010. https://soc.kuleuven.be/web/files/11/72/W1B-122.pdf (accessed 12 May 2023).
Hoffmann, Dierk (ed.). *Die zentrale Wirtschaftsverwaltung in der SBZ/DDR. Akteure, Strukturen, Verwaltungspraxis*. Berlin: De Gruyter, 2016.
Hogan, William W. 'Economic Reforms in the Sovereign States of the Soviet Union'. *Brookings Papers on Economic Activity* 22, no. 2 (1991): 303–20.

Höll, Otmar. 'The Foreign Policy of the Kreisky Era'. In *The Kreisky Era in Austria*, edited by Günter Bischof and Anton Pelinka, 32–77. New Brunswick, NJ: Taylor & Francis Inc, 1994.

Holmén, Janne. *Den politiska läroboken – Bilden av USA och Sovjetunionen i norska, svenska och finländska läroböcker under Kalla Kriget*. Uppsala: Uppsala universitet, 2006.

Hroch, Miroslav. *European Nations: Explaining Their Formation*. London: Verso Book, 2015.

Huberty, Martine. 'Luxembourg. Comfortably Cohesive'. In *Keeping Europeans Together: Assessing the State of EU Cohesion*, edited by Josef Janning, 91–4. London: European Council on Foreign Relations, 2016.

Ilves, Toomas Hendrik. 'Iseseisev Eesti riik maailmas'. In *Metsaülikool 1983–2005*, edited by Tiina Kirss, 336–41. N.p.: Kotkajärve Metsaülikool, 2012.

Iordanoglou, Chrysafis I. *Η Ελληνική Οικονομία μετά το 1950* (The Greek Economy after 1950). Athens: Bank of Greece, 2020.

IPSE (Identités, Politiques, Sociétés, Espaces) (ed.). *Doing Identity in Luxembourg. Subjective Appropriations – Institutional Attributions – Socio-Cultural Milieus*. Bielefeld: transcript, 2011.

Ironside, Kirsty. '"Because of Him, We Have Pizza Hut!" Joint Ventures and the Opening Up of the Soviet Economy under Gorbachev'. *Russian History* 4 (2022): 238–63.

Ivešić, Tomaž. 'The Yugoslav National Idea under Socialism: What Happens When a Soft Nation-Building Project Is Abandoned?' *Nationalities Papers* 49, no. 1 (2021): 142–61.

Jakir, Aleksandar. 'The Economic Trigger – The Status of "Nationality" in a "Self-Managed" Economy During the 1960s and 1970s in Socialist Yugoslavia'. In *The Crisis of Socialist Modernity. The Soviet Union and Yugoslavia in the 1970s*, edited by Marie-Janine Calic, Dietmar Neutatz and Julia Obertreis, 134–55. Göttingen: Vandenhoeck & Ruprecht, 2011.

Jakovina, Tvrtko. *Treća Strana Hladnog Rata*. Zaprešić: Fraktura, 2011.

Jarząbek, Wanda. 'Polish Economic Policy at the Time of Détente'. *European Review of History/Revue européenne d'histoire* 21, no. 2 (2014): 293–309.

Jensen-Eriksen, Niklas. 'Business, Economic Nationalism and Finnish Foreign Trade during the 19th and 20th Centuries'. *Revue française d'histoire économique* 1, no. 3 (2015): 40–57.

Jesse, N. G., and J. R. Dreyer. *Small States in the International System: At Peace and at War*. Lanham, MD: Lexington Books, 2016.

Johnson, Harry. 'Economic Nationalism in New States'. In *Nationalism*, edited by John Hutchinson and Anthony D. Smith, 236–40. Oxford: Oxford University Press, 1994.

Jović, Dejan. *Yugoslavia: A State That Withered Away*. West Lafayette, IN: Purdue University Press, 2009.

Judt, Matthias. *Der Bereich Kommerzielle Koordinierung. Das DDR-Wirtschaftsimperium des Alexander Schalck-Golodkowski – Mythos und Realität*. Berlin: Ch. Links, 2013.

Judt, Matthias. 'Kompensationsgeschäfte der DDR – Instrumente einer europäischen Ost-West-Wirtschaftsintegration?'. *Jahrbuch für Wirtschaftsgeschichte* 49, no. 2 (2008): 117–38.

Judt, Tony. *Poválečná Evropa: historie po roce 1945*. Praha: Slovart, 2008.

Juurak, Raivo. 'Nii nagu see oli'. In *Jäljed: Meenutusi täiskasvanuhariduse lähiajaloost Eestis*, edited by Marika Seppius, 15–41. Tallinn: SE & JS, 2000.

Kaiser, Wolfram. 'Transnational Practices Governing European Integration: Executive Autonomy and Neo-Corporatist Concertation in the Steel Sector'. *Contemporary European History* 27 (2018): 238–57.

Kakridis, Andreas. 'Economic Policy under the Greek Dictatorship'. In *The Greek Military Dictatorship: Revisiting a Troubled Past, 1967–1974*, edited by Othon Anastasakis and Katerina Lagos, 73–102. New York: Berghahn Books, 2021.

Kallas, Siim, and Mart Sõrg. 'Currency Reform'. In *Transforming the Estonian Economy*, edited by Olev Lugus, 54–70. Tallinn: International Center for Economic Growth, 1995.

Kallivretakis, Leonidas. *Δικτατορία και Μεταπολίτευση* (Dictatorship and Metapolitefsi). Athens: Themelio Publications, 2021.

Kansikas, Suvi. *Socialist Countries Face the European Community: Soviet-Bloc Controversies over East-West Trade*. Brussels: Peter Lang, 2014.

Karamouzi, Eirini. 'Taking a Stance, the European Community and the Greek Junta'. In *The Greek Junta and the International System a Case Study of Southern European Dictatorships, 1967–74*, edited by Antonis Klapsis, Constantine Arvanitopoulos, Evanthis Hatzivassiliou and Effie G. H. Pedaliu, 110–23. New York: Taylor & Francis, 2020.

Karner, Stefan, and Peter Ruggenthaler. 'Austria and the End of the Prague Spring: Neutrality in the Crucible?'. In *The Prague Spring and the Warsaw Pact Invasion of Czechoslovakia in 1968. Harvard Cold War Studies Book Series*, edited by Günter Bischof, Stefan Karner and Peter Ruggenthaler, 419–39. Lanham, MD: Lexington Books, 2010.

Kasekamp, Andres. *A History of the Baltic States*. 2nd edn. London: Palgrave, 2018.

Kastil, Ines. 'Von der Verstaatlichung zur Privatisierung – Untersuchung eines wirtschaftstheoretischen und wirtschaftspolitischen Paradigmenwechsels am Beispiel Österreich'. PhD diss., University of Vienna, 2006.

Katzenstein, Peter J. *Small States in World Markets: Industrial Policy in Europe*. Ithaca, NY: Cornell University Press, 1985.

Katzenstein, Peter J. 'Small States and Small States Revisited'. *New Political Economy* 8, no. 1 (2003): 9–30.

Kazakos, Panagiotis. *Ανάμεσα σε Κράτος και Αγορά. Οικονομία και Οικονομική Πολιτική στη Μεταπολεμική Ελλάδα, 1944 – 2000* (Between State and Market: Economy and Economic Policy in Post-War Greece, 1944–2000). Athens: Patakis Publications, 2001.

Kazakos, Panagiotis. 'Πολιτικοί Θεσμοί και Οικονομική Ανάπτυξη: Η Εμπειρία της Δικτατορίας (Political Institutions and Economic Development: The Dictatorship Experience)'. In *Η Δικτατορία των Συνταγματαρχών και η Αποκατάσταση της Δημοκρατίας* (The Dictatorship of the Colonels & the Restoration of Democracy), edited by P. Sourlas, 136–67, Athens: Foundation of the Greek Parliament Publications, 2016.

Keating, Michael. 'Preface: Outline of the Issues. Small States in the Global Era'. In *Small States in the Modern World: Vulnerabilities and Opportunities*, edited by Harald Baldersheim and Michael Keating, xi–xv. Cheltenham: Edward Elgar, 2015.

Keating, Michael. 'The Political Economy of Small States in Europe'. In *Small States in the Modern World: Vulnerabilities and Opportunities*, edited by Harald Baldersheim and Michael Keating, 3–22. Cheltenham: Edward Elgar, 2015.

Keynes, John M. 'National Self-Sufficiency'. *The Yale Review* 22, no. 4 (1933): 1–7.

Kilian, W. *Die Hallstein-Doktrin: der diplomatische Krieg zwischen der BRD und der DDR 1955–1973. Aus den Akten der beiden deutschen Außenministerien.* Berlin: Duncker & Humblot, 2001.

Kiran, Jyjan. 'Expanding the Framework of the Varieties of Capitalism: Turkey as a Hierarchical Market Economy'. *Journal of Eurasian Studies* 9 (2018): 42–51.

Kjærsgaard, Kristine. 'Confronting the Greek Military Junta: Scandinavian Joint Action under the European Commission on Human Rights, 1967–70'. In *The 'Long 1970s': Human Rights, East-West Détente and Transnational Relations*, edited by Poul Villaume, Rasmus Mariager and Helle Porsdam, East-West Détente and Transnational Relations, 51–69. London: Routledge, 2016.

Klabjan, Borut. '"Transnacionalne politike, nacionalna diplomacija?" Slovenci in delovna skupnost Alpe-Jadran, 1978–1991'. *Acta Histriae* 21, no. 3 (2013): 409–26.

Kmec, Sonja. 'Batty Weber und das Konzept der "Mischkultur": ein Vorgriff auf die heutige Interkulturalitätsdebatte'. In *Komponistinnen in Luxembourg – Helen Buchholtz und Lou Koster*, edited by Danielle Roster and Melanie Unseld, 39–58. Vienna: Böhlau, 2014.

Knöbl, Adalbert, Andres Sutt and Basil Zavoico. 'The Estonian Currency Board: Its Introduction and Role in the Early Success of Estonia's Transition to a Market Economy'. IMF Working Paper, 2002.

Koch, Natalie. 'The Political Geography of Economic Nationalism'. In *Handbook of Economic Nationalism*, edited by Andreas Pickel, 14–28. Northampton: Edward Elgar Publishing, 2022.

Kochanowski, Jerzy. *Rewolucja Międzypaździernikowa. Polska 1965–1957.* Kraków: Znak, 2017.

Kofman, Jan. *Economic Nationalism and Development: Central and Eastern Europe between the Two World Wars.* London: Routledge, 1992.

Kõll, Anu Mai. 'Economy and Ethnicity in the Hands of the State: Economic Change and the National Question in Twentieth-Century Estonia'. In *Economic Change and the National Question in Twentieth-Century Europe*, edited by Alice Teichova, Herbert Matis and Jaroslav Pátek, 357–81. Cambridge: Cambridge University Press, 2000.

Kolnberger, Thomas. ‘Forever Small? A Longue Durée Perspective on Luxembourg’s Extantism, Governance and Security’. In *Agency, Security and Governance of Small States: A Global Perspective*, edited by Thomas Kolnberger and Harlan Koff, 65–84. London: Routledge, forthcoming.

Kolnberger, Thomas. ‘Geldpolitik ohne eigene Währung? Luxemburg im Halbschatten von Lateinischer Münzunion (1865–1914/1926) und Deutschem Zollverein (1842–1919)’. *VWSG – Vierteljahresschrift für Sozial- und Wirtschaftsgeschichte* 110, no. 3 (2023): 336–69.

Kolnberger, Thomas, and Harlan Koff (ed.). *Agency, Security and Governance of Small States: A Global Perspective*. London: Routledge, forthcoming.

Komornicka, Aleksandra. ‘From “Economic Miracle” to the “Sick Man of the Socialist Camp”. Poland and the West in the 1970s’. In *European Socialist Regimes’ Fateful Engagement with the West: National Strategies in the Long 1970s*, edited by Angela Romano and Federico Romero, 78–106. London: Routledge, 2021.

Konstas, Dimitris H. *Ελληνική Υπόθεση Στο Συμβούλιο Της Ευρώπης 1967–1969: Θεωρία και Πρακτική Πολιτικής Πιέσεως από Διεθνείς Οργανισμούς* (The Greek Case in the Council of Europe 1967–1969: Theory and Practice of Political Pressure from International Organizations). Athens: Papazisis Publications, 1976.

Koselleck, Reinhart. *Futures Past: On the Semantics of Historical Time*. New York: Columbia University Press, 2004.

Kotkin, Stephen. *Uncivil Society: 1989 and the Implosion of the Communist Establishment*. New York: Modern Library, 2009.

Kreutzmüller, Christoph. ‘Introduction’. In *National Economies: Volks-Wirtschaft, Racism and Economy in Europe between the Wars (1918–1939/45)*, edited by Christoph Kreutzmüller, Michael Wildt and Moshe Zimmerman, 1–17. Newcastle upon Tyne: Cambridge Scholars, 2015.

Kriechbaumer, Robert. *Die Ära Kreisky. Österreich 1970–1983 in der historischen Analyse, im Urteil der politischen Kontrahenten und in Karikaturen von Ironimus*. Vienna: Böhlau, 2004.

Krieps, Robert and Alexandre Krieps. ‘La crise sidérurgique et le “modèle luxembourgeois” Lorsque le droit est dépassé’. In *Droit des entreprises en difficulté, Institut international de droit d’expression française (IDEF)*, edited by Eugène Schaeffer, 410–24. Bruxelles: Bruylant, 1991.

Krikmann, Arvo. ‘Jokes in Soviet Estonia’. *Folklore: Electronic Journal of Folklore* 43 (2009): 43–66.

Kruizinga, Samuël. ‘Introduction’. In *The Politics of Smallness in Modern Europe Size, Identity and International Relations since 1800*, edited by Samuël Kruizinga, 1–14. London: Bloomsbury Academic, 2022.

Kruizinga, Samuël (ed.). *The Politics of Smallness Modern Europe: Size, Identity and International Relations since 1800s*. London: Bloomsbury Academic, 2022.
Kruizinga, Samuël, and Karen Gram-Skjoldager. 'Conclusion'. In *The Politics of Smallness in Modern Europe: Size, Identity and International Relations since 1800*, edited by Samuël Kruizinga, 205–13. London: Bloomsbury Academic, 2022.
Kukk, Kalev. *Eesti majanduse 100 aastat*. Tallinn: Post Factum, 2019.
Küng, Andres. *Estland vaknar*. 2nd edn. Stockholm: Sellin & Blomquist Förlag, 1990.
Kuppe, Johannes. 'Die Beziehungen zwischen der DDR und Griechenland'. In *Die Westpolitik der DDR. Beziehungen der DDR zu ausgewählten westlichen Industriestaaten in den 70er und 80er Jahren*, edited by Hans J. Veen and Peter R. Weilemann, 237–64. Melle: Ernst Knoth, 1989.
Lacina, Vlastislav. *Formování československé ekonomiky 1918–1923*. Praha: Academia, 1990.
Lainela, Seija, and Pekka Sutela. *The Baltic Economies in Transition*. Helsinki: Bank of Finland, 1994.
Lampe, John R. *Yugoslavia as History: Twice There Was a Country*. Cambridge: Cambridge University Press, 2000.
Lan, Xiaohan, and Ben G. Li. 'The Economics of Nationalism'. *American Economic Journal: Economic Policy* 7, no. 2 (2015): 294–325.
Lassiter, Jessica, Timothy O. Bisping and Joseph Horton. 'Central Banking in Transition Economies: Estonia and Belarus'. *International Journal of Commerce and Management* 20, no. 4 (2010): 331–8.
Lauk, Epp. 'Restoring Democratic Discourse in the Estonian Press (1987–1990)'. In *The Challenge of the Baltic Sea Region. Culture, Ecosystems, Democracy*, edited by Göran Bolin, Monica Hammer, Frank-Michael Kirsch and Wojciech Szrubka, 307–21. Stockholm: Södertörn University College, 2005.
Lauristin, Marju, and Peeter Vihalemm. 'Estonian Mass Media: Past, Present and Future'. *European Journal of Communication* 5, no. 4 (1990): 489–500.
Lazarević, Žarko. 'Disparities and Economic Nationhood in Yugoslavia'. In *Nationalism and the Economy: Explorations into a Neglected Relationship*, edited by Stefan Berger and Thomas Fetzer, 115–38. Budapest: Central European University Press, 2018.
Lazarević, Žarko. 'Economy and Nationalism in Yugoslavia'. In *History and Culture of Economic Nationalism in East Central Europe*, edited by Helga Schultz and Eduard Kubů, 265–77. Berlin: Berliner Wissenschafts-Verlag, 2006.
Lees, Lorraine M. *Keeping Tito Afloat: The United States, Yugoslavia and the Cold War*. University Park, PA: Penn State University Press, 1997.
Leff, Carol Skalnik. 'Democratization and Disintegration in Multinational States: The Breakup of the Communist Federations'. *World Politics* 51 (1999): 205–35.
Lesiakowski, Krzysztof. 'Kierunki działalności kontrolnej NIK wobec przedsiębiorstw polonijno-zagranicznych w latach osiemdziesiątych XX wieku'. *Komunizm. System/Ludzie/Dokumentacja* 8 (2019): 51–72.

Levi-Faur, David. 'Economic Nationalism: from Friedrich List to Robert Reich'. *Review of International Studies* 23, no. 3 (1997): 359–70.

Lieven, Dominic. 'Russian Empires'. In *Sovereignty after Empire: Comparing the Middle East and Central Asia*, edited by Sally Cummings and Raymond Hinnebusch, 25–43. Edinburgh: Edinburgh University Press, 2011.

Liivik, Olev. 'Glasnost Policy Reaching Estonia: Fear and Hope in the Protest Letters of Estonian Residents during the Campaign against the Phosphorite Mines in 1987'. In *The Baltic States and the End of the Cold War*, edited by Kaarel Piirimäe and Olaf Mertelsmann, 123–51. Berlin: Peter Lang, 2018.

Linden, André. '"Un beau petit pays"?: Bilder und Diskurse um das Luxemburg der fünfziger Jahre'. In *Le Luxembourg des années 50: une société de petite dimension entre tradition et modernité = Luxemburg in den 50er Jahren: eine kleine Gesellschaft im Spannungsfeld von Tradition und Modernität*, edited by Musée d'histoire de la Ville de Luxembourg (Publications scientifiques du MHV 3), 197–243. Luxembourg: MHV.

List, Friedrich. *National System of Political Economy. vol. 2*. New York: Cosimo Classics, 2006.

List, Friedrich. *The National System of Political Economy (translation of the German original of 1841)*. London: Longmans, Green, 1909.

Lorenzini, Sara. 'The Socialist Camp and the Challenge of Economic Modernization in the Third World'. In *The Cambridge History of Communism*, edited by Norman Naimark, Silvio Pons and Sophie Quinn-Judge, 341–63. Cambridge: Cambridge University Press, 2017.

Lynn, Mathew. 'Labor's Disastrous Switch to Economic Nationalism'. The Spectator, 5 July 2021. Available online: https://www.spectator.co.uk/article/labour-s-disastrous-switch-to-economic-nationalism/ (accessed 30 June 2023).

Maass, Matthias. 'The Elusive Definition of the Small State'. *International Politics* 46, no. 1 (2009): 65–83.

Maddison, Angus. *The World Economy. Volume 1. A Millennial Perspective*. Paris: OECD, 2006.

Made, Tiit. *Eesti ärkab*. Stockholm: Kirjastus Välis-Eesti ja EMP, 1988.

Maes, Ivo, and Ilaria Pasotti. 'The European Payments Union and the Origins of Triffin's Regional Approach towards International Monetary Integration'. NBB Working Paper, no. 301, Brussels: National Bank of Belgium, 2016.

Majerus, Benoît. 'Écrire l'histoire de la place financière d/au Luxembourg'. In *Surveillance, indépendance et intégrité. 75e anniversaire du contrôle prudentiel et de la surveillance de la place financière au Luxembourg*, edited by Claude Marx, Marc Limpach and Benoît Majerus, 119–28. Luxembourg: CSSF, 2020.

Makrydimitris, Antonis. *Οι Υπουργοί των Εξωτερικών της Ελλάδας 1829–2000* (The Foreign Ministers of Greece 1829–2000). Athens: Kastaniotis Publications, 2000.

Malycha, Andreas. *Die SED in der Ära Honecker. Machtstrukturen, Entscheidungsmechanismen und Konfliktfelder in der Staatspartei 1971–1989*. Munich: Oldenbourg, 2014.

Maragkou, Konstantina. *Britain, Greece and the Colonels, 1967–74: Between Pragmatism and Human Rights*. London: Hurst, 2019.

Mark, James, Artemy M. Kalinovsky and Steffi Marung (eds). *Alternative Globalizations: Eastern Europe and the Postcolonial World*. Bloomington, IN: Indiana University Press, 2020.

Mark, James, Bogdan C. Iacob, Tobias Rupprecht and Ljubica Spaskovska, '1989'. In *1989: A Global History of Eastern Europe (New Approaches to European History, p. I)*, edited by T. C. W. Blanning and Brendan Simms. Cambridge: Cambridge University Press, 2019.

Marknadsguide Sovjetunionen. Stockholm: Exportrådet, 1989.

Martell, Luke. 'The Third Wave in Globalisation Theory'. *International Studies Review* 9 (2007): 173–96.

Matala, Saara. *A History of Cold War Industrialization. Finnish Ship Building between East and West*. London: Routledge, 2021.

Mayrhofer, Ralph. *Steyr-Daimler-Puch AG Die Krise des traditionellen Industriekonzernes und ihre Auswirkungen auf die Region Steyr*. Steyr: W. Ennsthaler, 1989.

Mazower, Mark (ed.). *After the War was over: Reconstructing the Family, Nation, and State in Greece, 1943–1960*. Princeton, NJ: Princeton University Press, 2000.

Meisinger, Agnes. 'Die österreichische Haltung zum Boykott der Olympischen Sommerspiel in Moskau 1980 unter besonderer Berücksichtigung der Rolle Bruno Kreiskys'. MA-thesis, University of Vienna, 2012.

Meletopoulos, Meletes. *Η Δικτατορία των Συνταγματαρχών: Κοινωνία, Ιδεολογία, Οικονομία* (The Dictatorship of the Colonels, Society, Ideology, Economy). Athens: Papazisis Publications, 1996.

Menclová, Barbora. 'Czechoslovak Forest Experts in Cold War Angola'. *Prague Papers on the History of International Relations* 1–2 (2021): 79–92.

Menclová, Barbora. 'Mezi globálními ambicemi a ekonomickým pragmatismem: Českoslovenští experti v Angole a Mosambiku za studené války'. PhD diss., Univerzita Karlova, Fakulta sociálních věd: 2023.

Mény, Yves, and Vincent Wright. 'State and Steel in Western Europe'. In *The Politics of Steel: Western Europe and the Steel Industry in the Crisis Years (1974–1984)*, edited by Yves Meny, Martin Rhodes and Vincent Wright, 1–110. Berlin: De Gruyter, 1987.

Mikecz, Robert. 'The Cornerstone of Economic Nationalism: National Self-Image'. *Fudan Journal of the Humanities and Social Sciences* 12, no. 4 (2019): 587–608.

Miljan, Toivo. 'The Proposal to Establish Economic Autonomy in Estonia'. *Journal of Baltic Studies* 20, no. 2 (1989): 149–64.

Miller, Chris. *The Struggle to Save the Soviet Economy: Mikhail Gorbachev and the collapse of the USSR*. Chapel Hill: UNC Press, 2016.

Minotou, Marietta D. *Η Ελλάδα στο Σταυροδρόμι των Ευρωπαϊκών Επιλογών 1957–1959, Η Απόφαση της Κυβέρνηση Κωνσταντίνου Καραμανλή για τη σύνδεση με την ΕΟΚ* (Greece at the Crossroads of European Choices 1957–1959, The Decision of the Government of Costantinos Karamanlis to join the EEC). Athens: Papazisis Publications, 2019.

Misiunas, Romuald J., and Rein Taagepera. *The Baltic States: Years of Dependence, 1940–1990*. Exp. and upd. edn. Berkeley: University of California Press, 1993.

Moyse, Laurent, Claude Meiers and Michel Maquil. *The Architects of Luxembourg's Financial Industry: Personal Accounts of the Origin and Growth of the International Financial Centre*. Luxembourg: Éditions Saint Paul, 2014.

Mueller, Wolfgang. *A Good Example of Peaceful Coexistence? The Soviet Union, Austria, and Neutrality, 1955–1991*. Vienna: ÖAW, 2011.

Mueller, Wolfgang. 'Recognition in Return for Détente. Brezhnev, the EEC, and the Moscow Treaty with West Germany, 1970–1973'. *Journal of Cold War Studies* 13, no. 4 (2011): 79–100.

Müller, Stefan A., Daniel Schiffl and Adamentios T. Skordos. *Heimliche Freunde: Die Beziehungen Österreichs zu den Diktaturen Südeuropas nach 1945: Spanien, Portugal, Griechenland*. Cologne: Böhlau, 2016.

Mylonas, Harris. 'Nation-Building'. In *Oxford Bibliographies in International Relations*, edited by Patrick James. New York: Oxford University Press, 2017.

Mylonas, Harris, and Maya Tudor (eds). *Varieties of Nationalism: Communities, Narratives, Identities*. Cambridge: Cambridge University Press, 2023.

Nafpliotis, Alexandros. *Britain and the Greek Colonels: Accommodating the Junta in the Cold War*. London: I.B. Tauris, 2013.

Nagle, Angela. 'The Washington Consensus Is Dead'. *The New Statesman*, 18 March 2023. Available online: https://www.newstatesman.com/the-weekend-essay/2023/03/washington-consensus-dead (accessed 13 May 2023).

Nakano, Takeshi. 'Theorizing Economic Nationalism'. *Nation and Nationalism* 10, no. 3 (2004): 211–29.

Nielsen-Stokkeby, Bernd. *Baltische Erinnerungen: Estland, Lettland, Litauen zwischen Unterdrückung und Freiheit*. Exp. and upd. edn. Bergisch-Gladbach: Gustav Lübbe Verlag, 1991.

Nitschke, Bernadetta. 'Działalność Towarzystwa Łączności z Polonią Zagraniczną "Polonia" wobec polskiej emigracji w latach 1955–1970'. *Annales Universitatis Mariae Curie-Skłodowska* 19, no. 1 (2012): 159–85.

Nitschke, Bernadetta. 'Walka o "dusze" Polonii. Formy pozyskiwania polskich środowisk emigracyjnych w okresie lat 60'. *Atheneum. Polskie Studia Politologiczne* 33 (2012): 65–79.

Nitschke-Szram, Bernadetta. 'Ekonomiczny wymiar współpracy Polskiej Rzeczpospolitej Ludowej z Polonią na przykładzie działalności przedsiębiorstw polonijno-zagranicznych'. *Studia Zachodnie* 19 (2017): 209–28.

Nölke, Andreas, and Arjan Vliegenthart. 'Enlarging the Varieties of Capitalism: The Emergence of Dependent Market Economies in East Central Europe'. *World Politics* 61, no. 4 (2009): 670–702.

Norkus, Zenonas. 'Võrdlev pilguheit Eesti, Läti ja Leedu postkommunistlikule arengule'. In *Eesti inimarengu aruanne 2010/2011. Inimarengu Balti rajad: muutuste kaks aastakümmet*, 22–31. Tallinn: Eesti Koostöö Kogu, 2011.

Nove, Alec. *An Economic History of the USSR 1917–1991*. 3rd edn. Harmondsworth: Penguin Books, 1992.

Nurmi, Raimo, and Raoul Üksvärav. 'How Estonian Managers Experienced the Transformation to Independence and Market Economy in 1990–1991'. *Management International Review* 33, no. 2 (1993): 171–81.

Nyíri, Pál. 'From Class Enemies to Patriots: Overseas Chinese and Emigration Policy and Discourse in the People's Republic of China'. In *Globalizing Chinese Migration. Trends in Europe and Asia*, edited by Pál Nyíri and Igor Saveliev, 208–41. Aldershot: Ashgate 2005.

Obadić, Ivan. 'A Troubled Relationship: Yugoslavia and the European Economic Community in Détente'. *European Review of History / Revue européenne d'histoire* 21, no. 2 (2014): 329–48.

Osman, Tarek. *Egypt on the Brink: From Nasser to the Muslim Brotherhood*. New Haven, CT: Yale University Press, 2013.

Overbeck, Michael. 'Montanarchäologie in Luxemburg – Eisenverhüttung am Vorabend des Hochofenzeitalters'. In *Terres Rouges – Mutations. Mémoires et perspectives du Bassin Minier 1 (Approche internationale et transnationale)*, edited by Michel Pauly, 21–31. Luxembourg: Fondation Bassin Minier, 2010.

Palm, Thomas. 'The Suurupi Program: Estonian Economic Policy for the Transition'. *Journal of Baltic Studies* 23, no. 3 (1992): 283–98.

Panoutsopoulos, Anastasios. 'Η Αφρικανική διάσταση της εξωτερικής πολιτικής των συνταγματαρχών: Λιβύη, Κονγκό, Κεντροαφρικανική, 1967–1974 (The African dimension of the foreign policy of the Colonels: Libya, Congo, Central Africa, 1967–1974)'. In *Η Δικτατορία των Συνταγματαρχών: Ανατομία μιας Επταετίας* (The Dictatorship of the Colonels: Anatomy of a Seven-year Period), edited by S. Vlachopoulos, D. Kairidis and A. Klapsis, 408–30. Athens: Patakis Publications, 2019.

Paquin, Stéphane. *La revanche des petites nations: Le Québec, l'Ecosse et la Catalogne face à la mondalisation*. Montreal: VLB éditeur, 2001.

Paslovsky, Leo. *Economic Nationalism of the Danubian States*. London: Macmillan, 1928.

Pauly, Michel. *Geschichte Luxemburgs*. München: C.H. Beck, 2011.

Pavlowitch, Stevan K. 'Yugoslavia: Internal Problems and International Role'. In *The Making of Détente: Eastern and Western Europe in the Cold War*, edited by Wilfried Loth and Georges-Henri Soutou, 77–88. New York: Routledge, 2008.

Pechlivanis, Paschalis. 'An Uneasy Triangle: Nicolae Ceauşescu, the Greek Colonels and the Greek Communists (1967–1974)'. *The International History Review*, 43, no. 3 (2021): 598–613.

Pelt, Mogens. 'West Germany's Policy toward Greece during the Junta Period in the Context of "Burden-Sharing"'. In *The Greek Military Dictatorship: Revisiting a Troubled Past, 1967–1974*, edited by Othon Anastasakis and Katerina Lagos, 295–319. New York: Berghahn Books, 2021.

Péporté, Pit, Sonja Kmec, Benoît Majerus and Michel Margue. *Inventing Luxembourg. Representations of the Past, Space and Language from the Nineteenth to the Twenty-First Century*. Leiden: Brill, 2010.

Peters, Florian. '"Rette sich, wer kann!" Die wirtschaftlichen Reformanläufe der polnischen Kommunisten in den 1980er-Jahren'. *Jahrbuch für historische Kommunismusforschung*, 105–19. Berlin: Metropol Verlag, 2020.

Petritsch, Wolfgang. *Bruno Kreisky. Die Biografie*. Sankt Pölten: Residenz Verlag, 2010.

Pfoertner André. 'Die Steyr-Daimler-Puch AG (SDPAG)'. In *Unternehmer, Firmen, Produkte Memoria Austriae*, edited by Emil Brix, Ernst Bruckmüller and Hannes Stekl, 311–35. Vienna: Oldenbourg Wissenschaftsverlag, 2005.

Pfundner, Martin. *Die Auto-Österreicher. Wegbereiter der Mobilität*. Klosterneuburg, 2006.

Pickel, Andreas. 'Explaining, and Explaining with, Economic Nationalism'. *Nations and Nationalism* 9, no. 1 (2003): 105–27.

Pickel, Andreas. 'Introduction: False Oppositions, Recontextualizing Economic Nationalism in a Globalizing World'. In *Economic Nationalism in a Globalizing World*, edited by Eric Helleiner and Andreas Pickel, 1–20. Ithaca, NY: Cornell University Press, 2005.

Pickel, Andreas. 'Introduction to the Handbook of Economic Nationalism'. In *Handbook of Economic Nationalism*, edited by Andreas Pickel, xi–xxxi. Cheltenham: Edward Edgar, 2022.

Pihlamägi, Maie. 'Administrative Shakeup in Industry and Construction: The 1957–1965 "Sovnarkhoz" Reform in the Estonian SSR'. *Nordost-Archiv: Zeitschrift für Regionalgeschichte* 22 (2013): 237–61.

Piirimäe, Kaarel. 'Estonia "Has No Time": Existential Politics at the End of Empire'. *Connexe: les espaces postcommunistes en question(s)* 6 (2020): 21–50.

Piirimäe, Kaarel. 'Gorbachev's New Thinking and how its Interaction with Perestroika in the Republics Catalysed the Soviet Collapse'. *Scandinavian Journal of History* 47, no. 3 (2020): 1–25.

Piketty, Thomas. *Capital and Ideology*, translated by Arthur Goldhammer. Cambridge, MA: Belknap Press of Harvard University Press, 2020.

Pillarisetti, Ram J., Roger Lawrey, Shamim Siddiqui and Jessica Lai Teck Choo. 'Small Economies in a Globalizing World: Economic Development, Human-Wellbeing and Sustainability'. In *Small Economies and Global Economics*, edited by Ram J.

Pillarisetti, Roger Lawrey, Joyce Teo Siew Yean, Shamim A. Siddiqui and Azman Ahmad, 1–20. New York: Nova Science, 2008.

Porter-Szűcs, Brian. 'From Homo Sovieticus to Homo Economicus: The Transformation of the Human Subject in Polish Socialist Economic Thought'. *East European Politics and Societies and Cultures* 34, no. 3 (2020): 546–70.

Průcha, Václav et al. *Hospodářské a sociální dějiny Československa 1918–1992. 1: Období 1918–1945*. Brno: Doplnek, 2004.

Pryke, Sam. 'Economic Nationalism: Theory, History and Prospects'. *Global Policy* 3, no. 3 (2012): 257–396.

Pula, Besnik. *Globalization under and after Socialism: The Evolution of Transnational Capital in Central and Eastern Europe*. Stanford, CA: Stanford University Press, 2018.

Quasten, Heinz. *Die Wirtschaftsformation der Schwerindustrie im Luxemburger Minett*. Saarbrücken: Universität des Saarlandes, 1970.

Radde, Jürgen. *Der Diplomatische Dienst der DDR: Namen und Daten*. Cologne: Verlag Wissenschaft und Politik, 1977.

Raig, Ivar. 'Saaremaa eksperiment, IME agraarprogramm ja Rahvarinde maaelu edendamise töörühm'. In *Eesti Rahvarinne 30: Artiklite kogumik I Rahvarinde ajaloo I konverentsiks 30. septembril 2018 Rahvusraamatukogus*, edited by Ester Šank, 158–66. Tallinn: Rahvarinde Muuseum and MTÜ Rahvarinde Pärimusselts, 2018.

Ramet, Sabrina. *The Three Yugoslavias: State-Building and Legitimation, 1918–2005*. Washington, DC: Woodrow Wilson Center Press, 2006.

Ramšak, Jure. '"Socialistična" gospodarska diplomacija: Dejavnost socialistične republike Slovenije na področju mednarodnih ekonomskih odnosov 1974–1980'. *Annales: Series Historia et Sociologia* 24, no. 4 (2014): 733–48.

Rathkolb, Oliver. *Internationalisierung Österreichs seit 1945*. Innsbruck: StudienVerlag, 2006.

Rathkolb, Oliver. 'The Kreisky Era, 1970–1983'. In *Austria in the Twentieth Century*, edited by Rolf Steininger, Günter Bischof and Michael Gehler, 263–93. New Brunswick, NJ: Transaction, 2009.

Reeves, Rachel. 'Labour's Plan for a Stronger, More Secure Economy'. Labour.org.uk, 12 June 2022. Available online: https://labour.org.uk/press/labours-plan-for-a-stronger-more-secure-economy/ (accessed 30 June 2023).

Reicher, Dieter. 'Wettbewerb und Nation – Überlegungen zum Problem des Begriffs "Wirtschaftsnationalismus"'. In *Ökonomischer Nationalismus. Soziologische Analysen wirtschaftlicher Ordnungen*, edited by Klaus Kraemer and Sascha Münnich, 39–72. Frankfurt/Main: Campus, 2021.

Reinikainen, Veikko, and Urpo Kivikari. 'On the Theory of East-West Economic Relations'. In *Finnish-Soviet Economic Relations*, edited by Oleg Bykov, Igor Korolev and Kari Möttölä, 3–20. London: Macmillan Press, 1983.

Resch, Andreas. 'Der österreichische Osthandel im Spannungsfeld der Blöcke'. In *Zwischen den Blöcken. NATO, Warschauer Pakt und Österreich*, edited by Manfried Rauchensteiner, 497–556. Vienna: Böhlau, 2010.

Rioux, X. Hubert. *Small Nations, High Ambitions: Economic Nationalism and Venture Capital in Quebec and Scotland.* Toronto: University of Toronto Press, 2020.

Röhrlich, Elisabeth. *Kreiskys Außenpolitik. Zwischen österreichischer Identität und internationalem Programm. Zeitgeschichte im Kontext 2.* Göttingen: V&R unipress, 2009.

Romano, Angela. 'Untying Cold War Knots: The European Community and Eastern Europe in the Long 1970s'. *Cold War History* 14, no. 2 (2014): 153–73.

Romano, Angela, and Federico Romero (eds). *European Socialist Regimes. Fateful Engagement with the West: National Strategies in the Long 1970s.* London: Routledge/ Taylor & Francis Group, 2021.

Romero, Federico. 'Socialism between Détente and Globalisation'. In *European Socialist Regimes' Fateful Engagement with the West: National Strategies in the Long 1970s*, edited by Angela Romano and Federico Romero, 11–30. London: Routledge 2021.

Rosas, Fernando. *História a História. África.* Lisbon: Tinta-da-China, 2018.

Roshwald, Aviel. *Ethnic Nationalism and the Fall of Empires: Central Europe, Russia and the Middle East 1914–1923.* London: Routledge, 2001.

Ruutsoo, Rein. 'The Emergence of Civil Society in Estonia'. In *Between Plan and Market: Social Change in the Baltic States and Russia*, edited by Blom Raimo, 97–122. Berlin: De Gruyter, 1996.

Ruzicic-Kessler, Karlo. 'Italy and Yugoslavia: From Distrust to Friendship in Cold War Europe'. *Journal of Modern Italian Studies* 19, no. 5 (2014): 641–64.

Ruzicic-Kessler, Karlo. 'The Path to Interregional Cooperation in Cold War Europe: The Alps-Adriatic Region'. In *Breaking Down Bipolarity: Yugoslavia's Foreign Relations during the Cold War*, edited by Martin Previšić, 189–210. Berlin: De Gruyter, 2021.

Saharov, Juhan. 'An Economic Innovation as an Icebreaker: The Contractual Work Experiment in Soviet Estonia in 1985'. In *The Baltic States and the End of the Cold War*, edited by Kaarel Piirimäe and Olaf Mertelsmann, 65–84. Berlin: Peter Lang, 2018.

Saharov, Juhan. 'From an Economic Term to a Political Concept: The Conceptual Innovation of "Self-Management" in Soviet Estonia'. *Contributions to the History of Concepts* 16, no. 1 (2021): 116–40.

Saharov, Juhan. 'From Future Scenarios to Sovereignty Declarations: Estonian Cyberspeak and the Breakup of the Soviet Union'. *Europe-Asia Studies* 74, no. 5 (2022): 809–31.

Salam, Reihan. 'Trump Can't Have It Both Ways'. *The Atlantic*, 2 March 2018. Available online: https://www.theatlantic.com/politics/archive/2018/03/trumps-economic-nationalism/554732/ (accessed 30 June 2023).

Savisaar, Edgar. *Peaminister: Eesti lähiajalugu 1990–1992.* Tartu, Estonia: Kleio, 2004.

Šćepanović, Vera. 'National Interests and Foreign Direct Investment in East-Central Europe after 1989'. In *Nationalism and the Economy. Explorations into a Neglected Relationship*, edited by Stefan Berger and Thomas Fetzer, 209–38. Budapest: Central European University Press, 2019.

Scheiber, Noam. 'The Biden Team Wants to Transform the Economy. Really'. *The New York Times Magazine*, 11 February 2021. Available online: https://www.nytimes.com/2021/02/11/magazine/biden-economy.html (accessed 30 June 2023).

Schneider, Ben Ross. 'Hierarchical Market Economies and Varieties of Capitalism in Latin America'. *Journal of Latin American Studies* 41, no. 3 (2009): 553–75.

Schultz, Helga. 'Introduction: The Double Edged Sword of Economic Nationalism'. In *History and Culture of Economic Nationalism in East Central Europe*, edited by Helga Schultz and Eduard Kubů, 9–25. Berlin: Berliner Wissenschafts-Verlag, 2006.

Schulze, Max-Stephan, and Nikolaus Wolff. 'Economic Nationalism and Economic Integration: The Austro-Hungarian Empire in the Late Nineteenth Century'. CESifo Working Paper no. 2813. Munich: Centre for Economic Studies and ifo Institute, 2009.

Seidel, Hans. *Wirtschaft und Wirtschaftspolitik in der Kreisky-Ära*. Vienna: Böhlau, 2017.

Sepp, Urmas. 'Estonia's Transition to a Market Economy'. *Review of Economics in Transition*, no. 5. Helsinki: Bank of Finland, 1995.

Sherlock, Thomas. *Historical Narratives in the Soviet Union and Post-Soviet Russia: Destroying the Settled Pact, Creating an Uncertain Future*. Basingstoke: Palgrave Macmillan, 2007.

Shulman, Stephen. 'Nationalist Sources of International Economic Integration'. *International Studies Quarterly* 44, no. 3 (2000): 365–90.

Sikora, Mirosław. 'Koncesjonowany kapitalizm. Służba Bezpieczeństwa MSW a "spółki polonijne" w PRL (1976–1989)'. *Dzieje Najnowsze* 45, no. 3 (2014): 125–46.

Simpson, Archie W. *A Theory of Disfunctionality [sic]: The European Micro-states as Disfunctional [sic] States in the International System*. Wilmington: Vernon Press, 2021.

Skidelsky, Robert. *Money and Government: A Challenge to Mainstream Economics*. UK: Allen Lane, an Imprint of Penguin Books, 2018.

Škorianec, Viljenka. *Osimska pogajanja*. Koper: Založba Annales, 2007.

Slobodian, Quinn. *Crack-Up Capitalism*. New York: Metropolitan Books, 2023.

Slobodian, Quinn. *Globalists: The End of Empire and the Birth of Neoliberalism*. Cambridge, MA: Harvard University Press, 2018.

Smith, Adam. *An Inquiry into the Nature and Causes of the Wealth of Nations*. Chichester: Capstone, 2010.

Smith, Graham. 'The Resurgence of Nationalism'. In *The Baltic States: The National Self-Determination of Estonia, Latvia and Lithuania*, edited by Graham Smith, 121–43. New York: St. Martin's Press, 1994.

Smith, Tony. 'New Bottles for New Wine: A Pericentric Framework for the Study of the Cold War'. *Diplomatic History* 24, no. 4 (2000): 567–91.

Spechler, Martin C. 'The Economic Advantages of Being Peripheral: Subordinate Nations in Multinational Empires'. *East European Politics and Societies* 4, no. 3 (1989): 448–64.

Steiner, André. *The Plans that Failed. An Economic History of the GDR*. New York: Berghahn, 2010.

Steiner, Ludwig. *Der Botschafter: Ein Leben für Österreich*. Bozen: Athesia, 2015.

Steiner, Ludwig. *Diplomatie – Politik: ein Leben für die Einheit Tirols – ein Leben für Österreich 1972 – 2007*. Bozen: Tyrolia, 2008.

Stergiou, Andreas. 'Ελληνική Χούντα και Ανατολική Γερμανία: Μια θερμή ιστορία του Ψυχρού Πολέμου (Greek Junta and East-Germany: A fervent story of the Cold War)'. *Κλειώ*, I (2004): 123–44.

Stergiou, Andreas. *Greece's Ostpolitik Dealing with the 'Devil'*. Cham: Springer International Publishing, 2021.

Stergiou, Andreas. *Im Spagat zwischen Solidarität und Realpolitik: Die Beziehungen zwischen der DDR und Griechenland und das Verhältnis der SED zur KKE*. Möhnesee: Bibliopolis, 2001.

Stiefel, Dieter. *Verstaatlichung und Privatisierung in Österreich. Illusion und Wirklichkeit*. Vienna: Böhlau, 2011.

Stöcker, Lars Fredrik. 'In the Spirit of Perestroika? Swedish Involvement in the Soviet Baltic Economies, 1988–1991'. *Zeitschrift für Ostmitteleuropa-Forschung* 68, no. 4 (2019): 577–602.

Stöger, Robert. 'Die verstaatlichte Industrie in der Zweiten Republik'. In *Karl Waldbrunner. Pragmatischer Visionär für das neue Österreich*, edited by Hannes Androsch, Anton Pelinka and Manfred Zollinger, 237–58. Vienna: Carl Gerold's Sohn Verlagsbuchandlung, 2006.

Stola, Dariusz. *Kraj bez wyjścia? Migracje z Polski 1949–1989*. Warszawa: PAN ISP, 2010.

Stourzh, Gerald, and Wolfgang Mueller. *A Cold War over Austria: The Struggle for the State Treaty, Neutrality, and the End of East-West Occupation, 1945–1955*. Lanham, MD: Lexington Books, 2018.

Stråth, Bo. *The Brandt Commission and the Multinationals: Planetary Perspectives*. London: Routledge, 2023.

Suesse, Marvin. *The Nationalist Dilemma. A Global History of Economic Nationalism, 1776- Present*. Cambridge: Cambridge University Press, 2023.

Summer, Franz. *Das VOEST-Debakel*. Vienna: Orac, 1987.

Suppan, Arnold, Gerald Stourzh and Wolfgang Mueller (eds). *Der österreichische Staatsvertrag 1955. Internationale Strategie, rechtliche Relevanz, nationale Identität. The Austrian State Treaty. International Strategy, Legal Relevance, National Identity*. Vienna: ÖAW, 2005.

Suppan, Arnold, and Wolfgang Mueller (eds). *Peaceful Coexistence or Iron Curtain? Austria, Neutrality, and Eastern Europe in the Cold War and Détente, 1955–1989.* Vienna: Lit, 2009.

Suyarkulova, Mohira. 'Reluctant Sovereigns? Central Asian States' Path to Independence'. In *Sovereignty after Empire: Comparing the Middle East and Central Asia*, edited by Sally Cummings and Raymond Hinnebusch, 127–53. Edinburgh: Edinburgh University Press, 2011.

Sveriges handel med Östeuropa och Sovjetunionen – i ett svenskt och internationellt perspektiv. Stockholm: Statens Industriverk, 1990.

Szlajfer, Henryk (ed.). *Economic Nationalism in East Central Europe and South America, 1919–1939*. Geneva: Librarie Droz, 1990.

Szobi, Pavel. 'Czechoslovak Economic Interests in Angola in the 1970s and 1980s'. In *Between East and South*, edited by Anna Calori, Anne-Kristin Hartmetz, Bence Kocsev, James Mark and Jan Zofka, 165–96. Berlin: De Gruyter, 2019.

Szporluk, Roman. *Communism and Nationalism: Karl Marx versus Friedrich List.* Oxford: Oxford University Press, 1988.

Taagepera, Rein. *Estonia: Return to Independence*. New York: Routledge, 2018.

Taagepera, Rein. 'Estonia's Road to Independence'. *Problems of Communism* 6 (1989): 11–26.

Terk, Erik, and Liina Tõnisson. 'IME programm ja Ravarinne: vastastikune võimendus'. In *Eesti Rahvarinne 30: Artiklite kogumik I Rahvarinde ajaloo I konverentsiks 30. septembril 2018 Rahvusraamatukogus*, edited by Ester Šank, 132–57. Tallinn: Rahvarinde Muuseum and MTÜ Rahvarinde Pärimusselts, 2018.

Thanos, Veremis. *Ο Στρατός στην Ελληνική Πολιτική* (Military in Greek Politics). Athens: Kourier Publications, 2020.

Ther, Philipp. *Europe since 1989: A History*. Princeton, NJ: Princeton University Press, 2018.

Thewes, Guy. 'La silhoutte de la ville'. In *Lieu de mémoire au Luxembourg – Erinnerungsorte in Luxemburg*, edited by Sonja Kmec and Pit Péporté, 253–8. Luxembourg: Éditions Saint-Paul, 20072.

The White House. 'President Joe Biden Investing in America'. Whitehouse.gov. Available online: https://www.whitehouse.gov/invest/ (accessed 30 June 2023).

The White House. 'Remarks by National Security Advisor Jake Sullivan on Renewing American Leadership at the Brookings Institutions'. Whitehouse.gov, 27 April 2023. Available online: https://www.whitehouse.gov/briefing-room/speeches-remarks/2023/04/27/remarks-by-national-security-advisor-jake-sullivan-on-renewing-american-economic-leadership-at-the-brookings-institution/ (accessed 11 May 2023).

Thorhallsson, Baldur. 'Studying Small States: A Review'. *Small States & Territories* 1, no. 1 (2018): 17–34.

Todorovic, Ilija Ika. 'Regional Economic Nationalism in the Former Yugoslavia'. In *The South Slav Conflict: History, Religion, Ethnicity, and Nationalism*, edited by Raju G.C. Thomas and H. Richard Friman, 159–89. New York: Routledge, 1996.
Tooze, Adam. 'Imagining National Economies: National and International Economic Statistics, 1900–1950'. In *Imagining Nations*, edited by Geoffrey Cubitt, 212–28. Manchester: Manchester University Press, 1998.
Tracy, Michael (ed.). *Farmers and Politics in France*. Enstone, UK: The Arkleton Trust, 1991.
Trausch, Gilbert. *L'ARBED dans la sociéte luxembourgeoise*. Luxembourg: Victor Buck/ ARBED S.A., 2000.
Trecker, Max. *Red Money for the Global South. East-South Economic Relations in the Cold War*. London: Routledge, 2021.
Tribe, Keith. *Constructing Economic Science: The Invention of a Discipline 1850–1950*. New York: Oxford University Press, 2022.
Tribe, Keith. 'Preface'. In *Max Weber, Economy and Society*, edited and translated by Keith Tribe, vii–xi. Cambridge: Harvard University Press, 2019.
Tsakas, Christos. *Post-war Greco-German Relations, 1953–1981: Economic Development, Business Interests and European Integration*. Cham: Palgrave Macmillan, 2022.
Tschacher, Werner. 'Landschaftsnamen als Textur und Identitätskonstrukt: die Benennungen des Minetts'. *Hémecht, Revue d'Histoire luxembourgeoise – transnationale, locale, interdisciplinaire* 75, no. 3 (2023): 286–312.
Tsygankov, Andrei P. *Pathways after Empire: National Identity and Foreign Economic Policy in the Post-Soviet World*. Lanham, MD: Rowman and Littlefield, 2001.
Udovič, Boštjan, and Danijela Jačimović. 'Osamosvojitev držav in »pozaba« zgodovinskih dosežkov: Primer ne-nadaljevanja gospodarske diplomacije jugoslavije v Sloveniji in Črni Gori po njuni osamosvojitvi'. *Annales. Series Historia et Sociologia* 29, no. 1 (2019): 55–68.
Unkovski-Korica, Vladimir. *The Economic Struggle for Power in Tito's Yugoslavia, From World War II to Non-Alignment*. London: I.B. Tauris, 2019.
Vaïsse, Maurice. 'France and the Greek Colonels'. In *The Greek Junta and the International System a Case Study of Southern European Dictatorships, 1967–74*, edited by Antonis Klapsis, Constantine Arvanitopoulos, Evanthis Hatzivassiliou and Effie G. H. Pedaliu, 39–47. New York: Taylor & Francis, 2020.
Van de Kerkhof, Stefanie. 'Die Industrialisierung der lothringisch-luxemburgischen Minett-Region'. In *Die Industrialisierung europäischer Montanregionen im 19. Jahrhundert*, edited by Toni Pierkemper. Stuttgart: Franz Steiner Verlag, 2002.
Vasilakis, Manolis (ed.). *Από τον Ανένδοτο στη Δικτατορία* (From the Unrelentless Struggle to Dictatorship). Athens: Papazisis Publications, 2009.
Venesaar, Urve, and Endel Vitsur. 'Development of Entrepreneurship in Estonia'. Working Paper no. 1. Tallinn: Estonian Academy of Sciences, Institute of Economics, 1993.

Vetterle, Tobias. Die Teilhabe am Politischen. Eine Diskursgeschichte der 'politischen Partizipation' in Luxemburg, 1960–90. PhD diss., University of Luxembourg.

Vihalemm, Peeter. *Baltic Media in Transition*. Tartu: Tartu University Press, 2002.

Wagner, Johann-Philipp. *Thomasmehl. Ernteerträge und Nahrungsmittel-Versorgung im Großherzogtum Luxemburg unter dem Kriegseinfluß*. Luxemburg: Jos. Beffort, 1917.

Walden, Sauteris. *Παράταιροι εταίροι. Ελληνική δικτατορία, κομμουνιστικά καθεστώτα και Βαλκάνια, 1967–1974* (Unseemly Partners: Greek Dictatorship, Communist Regimes and the Balkans, 1967–1974). Athens: Polis Publications, 2009.

Walther, Olivier, Christian Schulz and Sabine Dörry. 'Specialised International Financial Centres and Their Crisis Resiliences: The Case of Luxembourg'. *Geographische Zeitschrift* 99, nos. 2–3 (2011): 123–42.

Wasilewski, Jacek. 'Społeczeństwo Polskie, Społeczeństwo Chłopskie'. *Studia Socjologiczne* 200, no. 1 (2011): 353–68.

Weisbrode, Kenneth. 'The New Diplomatic History. An Open Letter to the Membership of SHAFR Passport' (2008). Available online: https://newdiplomatichistory.org/wp-content/uploads/2019/05/The-New-Diplomatic-History.pdf (accessed 14 March 2023).

Wirsching, Andreas. '"Kaiser ohne Kleider?" Der Nationalstaat und die Globalisierung'. *Vierteljahreshefte für Zeitgeschichte* 68, no. 4 (2020): 659–85.

Wolf, Martin. *The Crisis of Democratic Capitalism*. UK, USA: Allen Lane an Imprint of Penguin Books, 2023.

Xydis, Stephen G. 'Coups and Countercoups in Greece, 1967–1973'. *Political Science Quarterly* 89, no. 3 (1974): 507–38.

Yannopoulos, George (ed.). *Greece and the EEC Integration and Convergence*. New York: Macmillan, 1986.

Zaccaria, Benedetto. 'Debito e condizionalità? L'amministrazione Reagan e l'ammissione della Polonia al FMI (1981–1986)'. *Rivista italiana di Storia internazionale* 3, no. 2 (2020): 295–316.

Zaccaria, Benedetto. 'From Liberalism to Under-Development: The Yugoslav Elites Facing Western European Economic Integration in the "Long 1970s"'. In *European Socialist Regimes' Fateful Engagement with the West: National Strategies in the Long 1970s*, edited by Angela Romano and Federico Romero, 221–48. London: Routledge, 2020.

Zaccaria, Benedetto. *La strada per Osimo. Italia e Jugoslavia allo specchio (1965–1975)*. Milano: Franco Angeli, 2018.

Zaccaria, Benedetto. *The EEC's Yugoslav Policy in Cold War Europe, 1968–1980*. London: Palgrave Macmillan, 2016.

Zaccaria, Benedetto. 'Yugoslavia, Italy, and European Integration: Was Osimo 1975 a Pyrrhic Victory?' *Cold War History* 20, no. 4 (2020): 503–20.

Zahlen, Paul. *'L'évolution économique globale du Luxembourg sur la longue durée' (Le Luxembourg 1960–2010)*. Luxembourg: STATEC (Institute national de la statistique et des études économiques), 2012.

Zahlen, Paul (ed.). *The Luxembourg Economy in 2003–2004. A Kaleidoscope*. Luxembourg: STATEC (Institute national de la statistique et des études économiques), 2005.
Zahra, Tara. *Against the World: Anti-Globalism and Mass Politics between the World Wars*. New York: W. W. Norton, 2023.
Zatlin, Jonathan R. *The Currency of Socialism. Money and Political Culture in East Germany*. Cambridge: Cambridge University Press, 2007.
Zisserman-Brodsky, Dina. *Constructing Ethnopolitics in the Soviet Union: Samizdat, Deprivation and the Rise of Ethnic Nationalism*. New York: Palgrave Macmillan, 2003.
Zubok, Vladislav M. *Collapse: The Fall of the Soviet Union*. New Haven, CT: Yale University Press, 2021.

Index

Note: Endnotes are indicated by the page number followed by 'n' and the endnote number, e.g., 20 n.1 refers to endnote 1 on page 20.

www.ingramcontent.com/pod-product-compliance
Ingram Content Group UK Ltd.
Pitfield, Milton Keynes, MK11 3LW, UK
UKHW020738190926
475689UK00003B/152

9 781350 428638